THE THEOLOGY AND PHILOSOPHY OF ELIADE

The Theology and Philosophy of Eliade

A Search for the Centre

Carl Olson
Associate Professor of Religious Studies
Allegheny College, Meadville, Pennsylvania

ST. JOSEPH'S UNIVERSITY

3 9353 00277 2398

BL
43
.E4
O47
1992

St. Martin's Press   New York

© Carl Olson 1992

All rights reserved. For information, write:
Scholarly and Reference Division,
St. Martin's Press, Inc., 175 Fifth Avenue,
New York, N.Y. 10010

First published in the United States of America in 1992

Printed in Hong Kong

ISBN 0–312–07906–0

Library of Congress Cataloging-in-Publication Data
The theology and philosphy of Eliade : a search for the centre /
Carl Olson.
        p.   cm.
Includes bibliographical references and index.
ISBN 0–312–07906–0
1. Eliade, Mircea, 1907–   .   I. Title.
BL43.E4047   1992
291'.092—dc20   92-4275
                                                          CIP

This work is dedicated to the memory of Hy and his wonderful sense of humour and to Lucy for introducing me to books.

2772398

Contents

Preface

Previously-published books on the contributions of Mircea Eliade to the history of religions have tended to emphasize his methodology. Although the present work shares this methodological concern, its focus is much wider and tries to indicate the many facets and implications of Eliade's scholarship as a historian of religions. In other words, the intention is to view Eliade from a variety of perspectives. The overall purpose of this study is to look at his work as a historian of religions, a theologian, a philosopher, a novelist, and as someone engaged in cross-cultural dialogue. In a few of the chapters, we will place Eliade within his historical context with relation to the possibility of a science of religion and his theory of myth. Those unfamiliar with the works of Eliade might find the subtitle of this manuscript a little odd. It is my contention that one cannot separate the scholarly work of Eliade from his own personal quest for meaning in life. Not only does the symbolism of the centre play an important role in his scholarly studies, it also assumes a personal existential importance for his own quest for a centre of existence. Thus Eliade's scholarship can be interpreted as both an attempt to understand religious phenomena and as a personal pilgrimage to the meaningful centre of existence, a theme that runs throughout his works and one that concludes this book.

After a brief review of Eliade's life and examples of the types of criticism levelled against him, he is set within the context of the development of *Religionswissenschaft* in order to clarify the distinction between *Geisteswissenschaft* from *Naturwissenschaft* and to reexamine the possibility of a science of religion in Eliade's works and in the scholarly study of religion in general. Besides briefly reviewing some criticism of Eliade's method for its alleged lack of scientific rigour, the second chapter will show that Eliade's critics embrace a positivistic model of science that is fallacious when compared to some contemporary philosophers of science and what they perceive to be the actual way the scientific method is practised. By reviewing Eliade's own comprehension of science and its relationship to his scholarly discipline, we will discover that he comprehends his discipline as *Geisteswissenschaft* and not *Naturwissenschaft* and that religious phenomena themselves demand an imaginative and intuitive approach.

Since the problem of hermeneutics is central to Eliade's work, most critics have focused their attention on the shortcomings of his approach, but few have considered the fore-structure of his hermeneutics. Rather than systematically explaining his hermeneutics, the third chapter will take a cue from Gadamer and look at the presuppositions, pre-understanding, and anticipations that Eliade brings with him to his interpretative task. We will discuss sacred language, the unity of his method, situation and horizon and his call for a total hermeneutics. With its methodological unity grounded in human consciousness, the historian of religions is not limited by his/her historicity. Not only are past religious phenomena and events potentially contemporary for the interpreter, one can also become aware of other situations through the myths, symbols and rites of another religious culture that disclose the boundary situations of *homo religiosus*. Eliade conceives of total hermeneutics as reaching beyond simply interpreting and understanding religious facts to thinking about them. Thus total hermeneutics stimulates philosophical thought, and presupposes that this will lead to a change in human beings and be a source for new cultural values. While considering his hermeneutics, we will also compare aspects of his position with that of Jacques Derrida, the postmodernist deconstructionist.

If Chapters 2 and 3 are more concerned with the work of Eliade as a historian of religions, Chapter 4 will examine the theological aspects of his work. After an examination of the fallenness of the human situation and his understanding of God, we will discover that the key to understanding Eliade's theological reflections is the role of nostalgia. This will necessitate a discussion of what Eliade calls cosmic Christianity, a natural religion sanctified by the presence of Jesus that is in tune with cosmic rhythms and bereft of dogmatic teachings and history. Cosmic Christianity is pervaded by an aura of nostalgia, which Eliade conceives as a vision of rebirth, resacralization and remythologization of contemporary culture. Throughout the discussion of his theology, we will compare Eliade's position with that of Mark C. Taylor, a deconstructionist of Christian theology, and the latter's development of a postmodern a/theology.

From the theological aspects of Eliade's work, we move to his participation in and contribution to cross-cultural dialogue. This chapter tends to overlap with that on the fore-structure of his hermeneutics. According to Eliade, the history of religions paves the way for religious ecumenism between religions that are still alive and those long dead because it embodies an ecumenical and dialogical spirit. For members of Western culture, intercultural dialogue possesses certain benefits: it avoids sterile provincialism; enhances self-understanding; enriches one's consciousness; obliges one to delve into the history of the human spirit; and stimulates philosophic thinking. For Eliade, hermeneutics is the means by which to begin dialogue. We will compare Eliade's conception of dialogue with that of Julia Kristeva, a postmodernist with a psycho-linguistic philosophical approach, and the later two-volume work of Jürgen Habermas on communication.

The sixth chapter, on Eliade's theory of myth, will complement the chapters on hermeneutics and his theology. By considering the soteriological nature of myth, it will be possible to understand in what ways it saves modern beings by overcoming doubts, stimulating human initiative and creativity, modifying and liberating beings from desacralization and demystification. This chapter will serve as a complement to Chapter 3 on the fore-structure of his hermeneutics. We will also compare Eliade's position to that of Derrida, Kristeva, and Eric Gould, a deconstructive literary critic, with respect to sign, symbol and myth.

Since myths and symbols reveal Being, it is necessary to consider Eliade's theory of archaic ontology. Like the heroic Parsifal of the Holy Grail legend, contemporary beings must ask the ontological question, an inquiry that is interconnected with the cosmos and meaning. Before one can find one's way to one's spiritual destiny, one must ask the pertinent ontological question, because there is nothing prior to this profound question and ontology is equivalent to religion. Eliade conceives this aspect of his work as philosophical in nature. By trying to grasp Eliade's answer to the ontological question, we will try to determine his response to several questions. What are the two basic modes of being? What is the ontology of religious language? What is the place of ontology in rites of initiation? What is the relationship between being and non-being? What are the implications of Eliade's archaic ontology? Is he imposing his own ontology upon his material or is it derived from the religious phenomena that he investigates? Within certain limits, we will apply a kind of validity test to his theory of archaic ontology by comparing his theory to the world-views of some Native American Indians and African tribes. We will also compare Eliade's archaic ontology with the ontological stance of Derrida.

After a discussion of his theory of archaic ontology, we will consider the concept of power in Eliade's works by comparing his theory with that offered by Gerardus van der Leeuw, the Dutch historian of religion, and Michel Foucault, a postmodern historian, by considering the following: the nature of power; power, space and time; power, symbol and myth; and possessors of power. We will demonstrate that the concept of power is the central organizing principle for van der Leeuw and Foucault, whereas the distinction between the sacred and profane is the organizing principle for Eliade. We will conclude by offering some personal reflections on power.

In the ninth chapter, we will examine Eliade's views on time from the perspectives of his roles as both a historian of religions and a literary figure.

We will compare Eliade's view of time with those of Augustine, Hegel and Foucault in order to highlight the peculiarities of Eliade's position. After reviewing Eliade's comprehension of two kinds of time and its implications for *homo religiosus* of archaic cultures and modern beings, we will discuss what he means by the terror of history, the response to the terror of history in the form of an abolition of time by means of an eternal return to a primordial history embodied in myth, and the relationship between time and nostalgia. By considering this final element of his theory of time, we will be able to complement Eliade's views on cosmic Christianity in Chapter 4.

I want to thank my colleague Jim Sheridan for his critical comments and suggestions for revisions. Conversations with my other colleagues have stimulated me, and their friendship nurtured this work. I also want to thank Provost Andy Ford and President Daniel Sullivan of Allegheny College for encouraging an environment of intellectual inquiry.

Acknowledgements

I want to thank the editors of *Numen* for permission to reprint an article entitled 'Theology of Nostalgia: Reflections on the Theological Aspects of Eliade's Work,' Vol. XXVI, Fasc. 1 that appears in this book in an expanded form as Chapter 4. And appreciation also goes to the editors of *Studia Theologica* for permission to reprint an article entitled 'The Concept of Power in the Works of Eliade and van der Leeuw' that appeared in Volume 42 in 1988 and is expanded in the present text as Chapter 8.

1 Introduction

Among the many sub-disciplines under the broad umbrella of Religious Studies is the history of religions. This relatively recent sub-discipline is commonly associated with such religious theorists as C. J. Bleeker, W. Brede Kristensen, Raffaele Pettazzoni, Gerardus van der Leeuw, Geo Widengren and Mircea Eliade. Although a particular historian of religions may be an expert in a single religious tradition, his/her scope is usually much wider and comparative in nature. The most recent grand theorist within the history of religions is Eliade. Because Eliade envisions a very broad scope for the history of religions that includes philosophical and theological implications, his basic methodology and goals raise a series of questions. Does he understand his discipline as a science? How does he interpret religious phenomena? Even more fundamentally, what kinds of presuppositions does he bring to the hermeneutical task? What type of theology emerges from his work? What are some of the philosophical biases and implications of his contributions? If his method possesses a major comparative component, does this render feasible a dialogue between different religious traditions? In order to respond to these questions and others, it is necessary to view Eliade more than simply as a historian of religions. We must view him also as a theologian, philosopher and novelist in order to obtain a more complete view of his contributions to the study of religion. This study intends to be more multi-dimensional than other works on Eliade, and to take into consideration the more personal aspect of Eliade's work in the form of an interior pilgrimage to find the centre of human existence. In other words, Eliade's various works need to be viewed as his own personal quest for meaning. Thus his many contributions to the study of religion are more than dry, objective, descriptive and interpretative analysis of the religious phenomena that he encounters in his works. In order to comprehend the personal aspect of his work and quest, we need first to review his life; his search for a centre of existence is discussed in a final chapter.

REVIEW OF ELIADE'S LIFE

The life of Mircea Eliade resembles in many ways an odyssey through a labyrinth. He was born in Bucharest on 9 March 1907, the second of three children. His father was an army officer and never rose above the rank of

1

captain. The young Eliade thought that he was different from his class-mates, that he was predestined to be on the edge of society and that he would have to discover a new path for himself.[1] As a young student, he studied various scientific subjects and was an active writer, using his attic bedroom as his base of literary activity and place of solitude. He relates in his autobiography the celebration of the appearance of his one-hundredth article in 1925 with some friends.[2] He admits that he could not be integrated into his culture and moulded by prevailing patterns. Through his mentor Nae Ionescu, Eliade became a salaried writer for the newspaper *Cuvântul* (The Word) in 1926 for which he wrote essays of opinion, book reviews and informative articles on various topics and people. Eliade claims that as his cultural horizon grew he became open to foreign adventures.[3]

After completing his philosophy degree with a thesis on Pico della Mirandola, Campanella and Giordano Bruno, Eliade set out on an adventure to India in 1928 to study with Surendranath Dasgupta, a renowned scholar of Indian philosophy, at the University of Calcutta supported by a scholarship from the Maharajah Manindra Chandra Nandy of Kassimbazar. Although it had its roots in his philosophical studies in Rome, Eliade's work in India was an attempt to satisfy his 'passion for transcendence, mysticism, and Oriental spiritualism'.[4] After a romantic interlude with a member of Dasgupta's household and ejection from the home by his mentor, Eliade took up residence in an *ashram* at Rishikesh and practised yoga for six months with Swami Shivananda. After completing his doctoral thesis on yogic techniques, he returned to Rumania to serve in the military in order to satisfy his mandatory one-year commitment. In 1933, he gained critical and popular success with the publication of *Maitreyi*, a literary reworking of his romantic involvement in India for which he won the Tekirghiol-Eforia prize sponsored by the state publishing house, Cultura Nationala, for the best novel by a young writer.

During the 1930s, Eliade also published other works of fiction. His first published novel was *Isabel si apele diavolului* (Isabel and the Devil's Waters, 1930). Using the Joycean stream-of-consciousness technique, Eliade wrote *Lumina ce se stinge* (The Light that Is Failing, 1934), and a so-called indirect novel entitled *Şantier* (1935) that consisted of annotated passages from his Indian journal. Other works related to his Indian experiences were *Soliloquii* (Soliloquies, 1932), a small volume of personal philosophy, and his doctoral dissertation on yoga published in French in 1936 under the title *Yoga: Essai sur les origines de la mystique indienne*. Eliade also composed two novels about the younger generation: *Întoarcerea din rai* (The Return from Paradise, 1933) and its sequel *Huliganii* (The Hooligans, 1935). Two fantastic novels appeared in 1937: *Domnişoara Christina,* a story about a female *strigoi* (an amorous ghost figure with an insatiable thirst for blood in order to survive), and *Şarpele* (The Snake), a work that involved Eliade in a pornography scandal and prompted authorities to dismiss him from his university teaching position until his case was finally dismissed by a new Minister of Education. A play entitled *Iphigenia* was published in 1939 and finally staged when Eliade was out of the country. Besides his doctoral dissertation on yoga, the appearance of an article entitled 'Cosmical Homology and Yoga' published in the *Journal of the Indian Society of Oriental Art* in 1937 marked an important point in Eliade's development as an historian of religions because he begins to use the terms sacred and profane in a systematic manner to represent the concrete and real in the case of the former and indicating that the profane represents the insignificant, illusory, and relative. Other themes discussed in this article that have importance for Eliade's later work are chaos, cosmos, and centre symbolism.

After receiving his doctoral degree, Eliade began his teaching career as an assistant to Nae Ionescu, a professor of logic and metaphysics and ideological leader of the Legion of the Archangel Michael (popularly known as the Iron Guard). Acknowledging the growing popularity of the movement in pre-Second World War Rumania, Eliade did not perceive anything sinister about the movement, but rather perceived it as more of a mystical sect than a political movement due to its structure and vocation.[5] Eliade's close association with Ionescu and personal friends in the Iron Guard caused him some personal problems because his apartment was searched in 1938 for incriminating evidence by the authorities. Even though no compromising material was found in Eliade's apartment, he was taken into custody on 14 July and sent to a Rumanian concentration camp for his refusal to denounce the Iron Guard, and he continued to refuse to recant his association with the group or its members during his incarceration: he claimed to be a non-political person and thought that it would be absurd for him to dissociate himself from a movement when he did not believe in the political destiny of his generation.[6]

Due to his newspaper writings and his choice of associates, it is easy to comprehend why the Rumanian authorities would view Eliade with, at least, suspicion and conclude that he was a member of the Iron Guard. In his political writings, Eliade expressed an ambivalent attitude because he criticized Marxism, Fascism, and Democracy for being foreign ideologies unsuitable for Rumania, and yet writes favourably of Mussolini, the Italian fascist leader.[7] He also enthusiastically supported the Iron Guard movement in his periodical compositions, and criticized democratic ideals because of their tendency towards secularization of the absolute, the destruction of individualism by its egalitarian tendency, and its potential to lead in its extreme forms to creations like Communism. In other essays, Eliade applauded peacemaking, espoused non-political social involvement because of the social divisions caused by partisan politics, and indicated that politics compromised spiritual values and one's freedom.[8] The periodical essays in which Eliade's political ideas appear indicates an inconsistent position, although his political conservatism remains constant.

Even before his incarceration, Eliade knew that he would not obtain a position at a university ever again and would be unable to write and publish under the yoke of a dictatorship.[9] What is curious about this episode in Eliade's life, if we take into consideration that the Iron Guard became associated in historical consciousness with terrorism and pro-Nazism, is that he does not admit that he was a member of the movement, even though close friends were members and he was considered to be a member by the national authorities at the time. In his *Autobiography* he does want his reader to believe that he was a non-political person with friends closely associated with the Iron Guard and that it was a benign, patriotic movement that advocated non-violence. He does not tell us directly that he was or was not a member of the movement. In fact, he seems to hint that he was not a full member of the Iron Guard, even though he might have been sympathetic to some of its ideals. Moreover, he is critical of the Legionaries in his *Autobiography* when some of its members resorted to acts of violence.

Eliade's association, either directly or indirectly, with the Iron Guard continued to cause him trouble after the war. Ernesto de Martino, a translator of Eliade's work *Techniques du Yoga*, received several denunciations concerning the author's alleged fascist activity before the war. Eliade surmises in his *Autobiography* that the allegations originated with the Rumanian legation, and he acknowledges that the denunciations functioned to remind him that his 'imprudent acts and errors committed in youth constituted a series of malentendus that would follow me all my life'.[10] Eliade proved to have a prophetic vision because a more recent accuser, namely Ivan Strenski, thinks that Eliade's scholarly work is tainted by his former fascist associations.[11] Should Eliade be condemned for his involvement with the Iron Guard whether or not he was a member of the movement? Should he be criticized for associating with others closely associated with the movement? Should he be censured for the violent activities of others? Although he is not entirely clear in his *Autobiography* about his status in the Iron Guard, he does say that he was a non-political person and that he made some errors while a young man. It is a pernicious characteristic of some academics to be unforgiving for someone who did not have the correct ideology throughout his/her life. Even if Eliade was a hard-core Fascist throughout his life, for which I have not found any evidence, this political ideology did not affect his scholarship to any sinister extent, and it is unjust to taint someone and to judge them guilty by association. How can we come to grips with Eliade's prewar association with the Iron Guard? Before and after the war, it can be concluded, by reading his *Autobiography*, that he was a patriot and a Rumanian nationalist concerned with his nation's historical past, present dictatorial bondage, and uncertain future; he was also concerned with preserving its culture during its period of diaspora for its artists and intellectuals after the Second World War. Eliade's patriotic fervour is evident in his notion of 'Romanianism', a non-political nationalism that embodied a messianic sense of the divinely-chosen nature of the Rumanian nation with a special mission to fulfill in the world.[12]

After his release from the sanatorium of Moroeni where he was taken to recover from an illness contracted while incarcerated in the concentration camp for political dissidents, he returned to his wife, Nina Mareş, and private life until he was appointed cultural attaché to the Rumanian legation in London during the Second World War. With the severing of diplomatic relations between England and Rumania, Eliade was appointed cultural adviser to the Rumanian legation in Lisbon in 1941 where he stayed until September 1945. His exile from Rumania 'possessed the value of an initiation'.[13] Besides the hardships caused by the war and exile from his homeland, Eliade lost his wife who died of cancer on the morning of 20 November 1944. Eliade recalled spending the night by her bedside reading from the Gospel of John and being consoled when she died that she would no longer suffer.[14] After the death of his wife, Eliade was invited by Georges Dumézil to teach at the École des Hautes Études in Paris in 1945.

During the 1940s, Eliade published a number of works including two fantastic novellas in 1940: *Secretul doctorului Honigberger* (The Secret of Dr Honigberger) and *Nopţi la Serampore* (Nights at Serampore). The first novella revolves around the mysterious disappearance of a German doctor who practises yoga. The second work is located in India where the characters are transported back in time 150 years to witness a tragic event. Another novella appeared in 1945 entitled *Un om mare* (A Great Man), while a history of the Rumanian people appeared in 1943 entitled *Os Romenos, Latinos do oriente* (The Romanians, Latins of the East). Other works more directly related to the history of religions began to appear in 1942–43: *Comentarii la legenda Meşterului Manole* (Commentary on the Legend of Master Manole), *Insula Lui Euthansius*, includes some essays on symbolism, a major contribution to the history of religions entitled *Traité d'histoire des religions*, *Mitul reintegrării* (The Myth of Reintegration), a collection of thirteen articles on symbolism, and his major work on his conception of history *Le Mythe de l' éternel retour: Archétypes et répétition* (The Myth of the Eternal Return: Archetypes and Repetition). Although some of his earlier novels were translated into French, they were not very successful either with the critics or the public. The latter part of the decade was a time of considerable poverty for Eliade, who had been deleted from the government payroll and could not return to his homeland because of the unfavourable political climate, but he was able to find some happiness after meeting Christinel Cottesco; they were eventually married in January 1950 before Eliade travelled to Italy to lecture at the University of Rome.

During the summer of 1950, Eliade participated in his first Eranos Conference at Ascona, Switzerland. The shadow of poverty continued to follow Eliade and his new wife, however, and forced them to borrow money from friends in order to survive. Finally, on 9 December 1950, every scholar's dream came true when Eliade received a grant from the Bollingen Foundation of New York for three years which would pay him a monthly stipend of two hundred dollars, enabling him to feel delivered from the nightmare of poverty.[15]

The 1950s marked a change of venue for Eliade from Europe to America. After having given the Haskell Lectures at the University of Chicago on initiation patterns in 1956, and accepting a position as a visiting professor for the 1956–57 academic year, Eliade accepted a permanent position at Chicago in 1957. Additional important works appeared during this decade: *Shamanism*; *Images and Symbols*; *Yoga: Immortality and Freedom*; *The Forge and the Crucible*; *The Sacred and the Profane*; and the novel *Forêt interdite* (The Forbidden Forest). Besides the publication of his many books and articles, Eliade's career reached a milestone when he was awarded the title of Sewell L. Avery Distinguished Service Professor by the University of Chicago in 1962.

But before this award was granted, Eliade suffered an acute attack of rheumatoid arthritis in 1960 which was to afflict him until his death from a stroke on 22 April 1986. Even though he reported having to take six Aspirin tablets daily for the sometimes unbearable pain, his health problems did not hinder his scholarly productivity: he assumed the role of a heroic scholarly figure. Academic institutions around the world recognized his many contributions to scholarship by awarding him honorary degrees. He continued to teach until his retirement in 1983. Eliade crowned his productive career with his three-volume *A History of Religious Ideas* and as chief editor of the multi-volume *Encyclopedia of Religion*. Overall, Eliade's life was dedicated to scholarly and literary pursuits.

Eliade's personal odyssey was not only an exterior journey; it was also an interior voyage. He interpreted his own life as a paradox: an attempt to live in history and beyond it; to be involved in current events yet withdrawn from them; to be a Rumanian and live in a foreign land; to be a literary figure and scholar of religion; to be a representative of a particular national culture and yet be a member of a universal race of beings.[16] Thus he thought that he lived the conjunction of opposites in an existential way. The conjunction of opposites, however, forms a unity. It is this union or centre that Eliade sought throughout his exterior journey and his interior scholarly and creative pilgrimage. The lifelong search for a centre is the over-arching theme of this book which will be tied together in the concluding chapter.

Taking into consideration these many paradoxes, Eliade's life and work can be viewed as an attempted synthesis which he discovered in the unitary world of culture that was ultimately a return to nature.[17] As we will notice in the subsequent chapters, Eliade interpreted modern Western culture as areligious, suffering from alienation, desacralization and demythologization. In one sense, Eliade wanted to reintroduce religious mystery into modern human life. This implies that much of his work was soteriological. In order to achieve his goal of alleviating modern alienation, Eliade returned to religious history for a remedy. The search for meaning and new modes of being in the historical past was a religious experience because the historian of religions must relive the experiences of past cultures.[18] By following this procedure, Eliade wanted to reintroduce religious mystery into the lives of contemporary humans lost in the destructive labyrinth of the twentieth century.

ELIADE'S CRITICS

Eliade's ambitious programme for the history of religions has stirred considerable criticism and given birth to much misunderstanding. His theoretical contributions and methodology have provoked often virulent, vicious and scurrilous attacks by those within the history of religions, anthropologists, theology and even feminists. The criticisms of anthropologists are, for instance, often of a general methodological nature and also of a more particular kind. After chiding Eliade for his anthropological naiveté, Dorothy Libby asserts that an additional difficulty is 'Eliade's apparent assumption of social evolution. Although in one of his summary statements he remarks that one cannot really sketch an evolutionary development where one pattern of initiation rites gives place to another, the book as a whole does seem to reflect this attitude.'[19] Lessa, commenting on another work by Eliade, categorizes his general approach as 'Frazerian',[20] a point also made by Edmund Leach, who furthermore claims that Eliade is an armchair scholar.[21] Considering Eliade's attempt to interpret the significance of the New Year ceremonials among several religious cultures, Wallace finds that his hermeneutic is invented and mystical.[22] Another anthropologist criticizes his theory of initiation as speculative.[23] A work by Saliba summarizes the criticisms of anthropologists and adds some newer ones: the omission of Islam and Chinese religious traditions from his work; the lack of guiding principle in the selection of data; and the accusation that Eliade selects his facts and omits data that negate his generalizations; that Eliade compares outward manifestations and not meanings; that the claim that Eliade's work is scientific and empirical cannot be substantiated by concrete evidence; that Eliade does not distinguish between primary and secondary sources and does not evaluate his sources; and that his work on non-literate cultures is flawed because he applies Western concepts to them.[24]

Not only is Eliade called a Frazerian by some scholars, sometimes he is called a Jungian or too much emphasis is placed on Jung's influence upon his work.[25] After indicating some of the similarities between Eliade and Jung, Ricketts asserts that similarities do not prove that Eliade is dependent upon Jung.[26] Ricketts proceeds to demonstrate some of the differences between Jung and Eliade when he states, for instance, that Eliade does not use the term archetype in the same way as Jung to refer to the archetypes of the collective unconscious, even though Eliade's failure to distinguish his use of the term archetype from that of Jung introduces some confusion into his work.[27] In Eliade's later works, the acceptance of Jungianism ends with the rejection of psychology for its reductionism.

Within the field of the history of religions, most of the criticism tends to focus on Eliade's methodology. Jonathan Z. Smith criticizes Eliade's use of morphology and comparison. According to Smith, morphology, a logical arrangement of particular items organized into a complex whole, assumes an *a priori* 'fitting economy',[28] which ignores the categories of space and time.[29] It thus excludes the historical (a criticism made also by other scholars). The process of comparing data is also non-historical.[30] Rather than a method for inquiry, comparison is, according to Smith, a matter of memory and impression.[31] In a more recent work, Smith calls into question again Eliade's comparative method:

> Comparison requires the acceptance of difference as the grounds of its being interesting, and a methodical manipulation of that difference to

achieve some stated cognitive end. The questions of comparison are questions of judgment with respect to difference: What differences are to be maintained in the interests of comparative inquiry?[32]

Smith's comments suggest that he is interested in differences between religious phenomena, whereas Eliade is overly concerned with sameness to the extent of being blind to their differences. In contrast to Smith's position, Ioan Culianu perceives part of the reason for confusion with regard to Eliade's work to be due to his lack of obsession with methodology.[33] In his work devoted to Eliade's hermeneutics, Marino thinks that comparison aids the integration of phenomena within the same class or category, an operation that guarantees the validity of Eliade's interpretation.[34] With regard to morphological classification, Marino asserts that it is non-diachronic and agrees with Smith that its synchronic character involves an atemporal nature and adds that it originates in phenomenology.[35]

Besides Smith's criticism of Eliade's use of morphological classification and comparison for being non-historical. Ninian Smart also reproaches Eliade for his ahistorical approach by concentrating on archetypes, which devalues historical consciousness.[36] According to a more positive assessment by Marino, archetypes play both an original foundational role and a heuristic role as a paradigmatic hermeneutic instrument. Archetypes have a genetic sense of immanent *a priorism* and serve as dynamic and exemplary.[37] Marino proceeds to argue that the hermeneutic value of the ideal archetype springs from the evidence; its paradigmatic function defines the supreme criteria of an interpretation.[38] On the other hand, Culianu perceives an archetype as an operational category with heuristic value that liberates itself from historical reality.[39]

Along the same line of criticism as that levelled at Eliade by Smith and Smart, Robert D. Baird argues that the phenomenological search for structures is ahistorical. A further problem with phenomenological structures is that they are not historically falsifiable, which implies that any attempt to verify them tends to be more akin to theological verification.[40] According to Baird, Eliade's use of structures also tends to negate the religious individuality of a person, if he/she must be understood in terms of universal structures because one participates in the archetypes to varying degrees and may be unaware, as Eliade affirms, of the deeper meaning of one's symbols, myths, and rites.[41] This unawareness of the transconscious meaning of symbols by the religious individual is criticized by Guilford Dudley because it insulates Eliade's interpretation of archetypes against empirical testing.[42] Dudley, Baird, Smith, and Smart seem to agree that Eliade's approach to religious phenomena is both ahistorical and even anti-historical. This line of criticism along with Eliade's emphasis on phenomenology leads da Silva to conclude that Eliade is a phenomenologist of religion and not a historian of religions.[43] In contrast, Marino asserts that Eliade does, in fact, emphasize that human acts and behaviour are historically conditioned, and that religious phenomena are manifested in history, limited by it, and conditioned by it.[44] Marino admits that the relation between archetypes and history is ambiguous, yet they are real, objective and profoundly significant. In a certain sense, the archetypes represent, according to Marino's interpretation of Eliade's hermeneutic, the skeleton of history.[45] Toward the end of his career, Eliade attempted to respond indirectly to his critics by publishing his three-volume *The History of Religious Ideas*. It is doubtful, however, that this three-volume work would placate his critics.

Because Eliade's archetypal structures cannot be verified empirically according to Dudley, his research is not free of values, and his theories are not based on inductive reasoning.[46] This implies that Eliade's method is not based on empirical procedures for testing the verification of his data. Thus Eliade does not construct tentative hypotheses to explain the facts. Moreover, there seems to be a mere acceptance of facts by intuitions. From a more positive perspective, Marino thinks that the use of intuition in Eliade's hermeneutics produces an operative heuristic scheme in the sense that a totality is realized intuitively by the sudden revelation of the total structure being interpreted.[47] According to another critic, Eliade exposes himself to attack by empiricists for methodological heresy and dogmatism.[48] What is interesting about this attack on Eliade by his critics is the latter's naive comprehension of science. I will deal more fully with this type of criticism in the next chapter.

Eliade's concept of the sacred is attacked for hermeneutical reasons. According to Smart, a systematic phenomenology of religion does not need to be grounded on the sacred–profane polarity and its concomitant world-view, a procedure that is then imposed on other world-views that do not reflect the fundamental polarity.[49] Another writer thinks that religious patterns need not be traceable to the sacred, which might be more aptly reducible to the naturalistic account of the origin and structure of their meanings.[50] Such a naturalistic approach presents the danger of explaining away or glossing over the essential religious feature of a phenomenon. The polarity of sacred and profane space, for example, does not help us to comprehend the space occupied by modern human beings. Lived space is not without structure, amorphous and chaotic like that of the profane space described by Eliade; it is neither sacred nor profane, but should be comprehended as human and not as a polarity between sacred and profane.[51] Furthermore, if a ritual object, for instance, becomes sacred by the attention focused upon it in a given situation, Smith argues that such activity suggests that there is no inherently sacred or profane nature of an object.[52] Sacred and profane are not substantive categories. If sacrality is a category of emplacement, where something is sacred or profane depends on the situation because 'sacred and profane are transitive categories; they serve as maps and labels, not substances; they are distinctions of office, indices of difference.'[53]

The ontological status of the sacred is also called into question by critics. If myth and symbol are the language of the sacred, Eliade's assertion that myths decay, symbols can become secularized, and that they never disappear because they are embedded within our unconscious is based on an implied ontology, which is not philosophically defended.[54] Thus Eliade merely assumes an ontological status of the sacred. In fact, his ontology forces his work beyond mere descriptive analysis into the domain of philosophical anthropology by making normative judgements about the general mode of human nature and condition.[55] Eliade thinks that he is justified in following this path because he perceives his work as a foundation for philosophical speculation. In his early contribution to the study of Eliade's works, Altizer implies that Eliade does not manifest the same openness to the profane as he does to the sacred.[56] Eliade replied several years later: 'In all my "scholarly" studies I attempted to illustrate a rigorous and relevant hermeneutics of the sacred. I did not intend to elaborate a *personal* philosophical anthropology.'[57]

Eliade is also attacked on feminist grounds. Reviewing Eliade's discussion of female and male initiation rites, Saiving accuses Eliade of sexism and androcentrism because of his inconsistency when viewing women as sacred in the context of their own rites and as profane in the context of male rites.[58] After reviewing Eliade's contribution to the phenomenon of initiation, it can be stated that he does equate the maternal world with the profane.[59] But he is primarily interested in the transition from the profane or break with childhood and female realm by a male novice being initiated to the sacred world of responsibility, knowledge, and adult sexuality. He writes, 'In short, through initiation, the candidate passes beyond the natural mode – the mode of the child – and gains access to the cultural mode; that is, he is introduced to spiritual values.'[60] This position is not intended to denigrate the role or status of women in traditional cultures. In fact, Eliade makes clear later in his study of initiation that certain myths indicate 'an avowal of the original superiority of feminine sacrality'.[61] With respect to the charge of androcentrism, Eliade's remarks must be understood in their context. He is discussing initiatory ordeals like subincision and the significance of bisexuality for a male novice. If the segregation of the male symbolizes his asexuality, the ritual ordeal represents a transition to totality and perfection represented by one's androgynous condition. 'The androgyne is considered superior to the two sexes just because it incarnates totality and hence perfection.'[62] Thus, it is not a matter of preferring one sex to another; it is rather a means of achieving symbolic perfection.

Another critic claims that Eliade is insensitive to culture.[63] A Buddhist scholar objects to Eliade's connecting of the Buddha with shamanistic traditions.[64] A scholar of myth dismisses Eliade's own study of the same subject as repetitive.[65] Furthermore, the quality of Eliade's thinking is called into question by another critic: 'Instead of resolving difficulties earnestly and directly, he often evades problems by resorting to paradoxes, metaphors or other literary devices. Part of this is owing to his literary method of writing.'[66] What makes Eliade such a target for the scholarly animosity of others? Although there are some problems with his theories and methodology, he provokes strong reactions from others by his courage to venture and to take scholarly chances, by the universalism of his vision, by his overt criticism of other methods and their shortcomings, by the audacity of some of his claims, by his encyclopedic approach to religious phenomena, by his particular interpretations, and by his own methodology.

From a more oblique perspective, we can view Eliade's critics as ancient Getae, worshippers of the deity Zalmoxis and ancestors of the modern Rumanians. According to the ancient Greek historian Herodotus, in order to communicate with Zalmoxis, a messenger is chosen and dispatched every four years to inform the deity of the needs of the people, an activity that assumed the form of a human sacrifice. After being chosen, seized by his hands and feet, swung aloft and hurled on to the raised spear-points held by other men, the messenger is hopefully killed and his soul travels to Zalmoxis to give the message of the people.[67] In a less serious vein, have Eliade's critics not impaled another Rumanian messenger without telling him what they want to tell the god?

As stated above, this work is an attempt to understand Eliade's many contributions to the study of religion not simply as a historian of religions, although we will investigate his contributions to his chosen field throughout this study. This book also intends to look at his contributions to theology and philosophy. Even though there is a certain amount of overlap, Chapters 4, 5 and 6 tend to emphasize the theological aspects of his work and Chapters 7, 8 and 9 highlight the philosophical side of his work. This approach will be attempted by considering the more mature works of Eliade from 1937 when his concept of the nature of religion begins to more nearly resemble his later contributions to the nature of religious phenomena. Due to Eliade's interest in the concept of time in both his religious scholarship and novels, we will be able to integrate to a some degree his literary accomplishments into this work. Furthermore, we will be able to view Eliade as an ecumenical thinker engaged in an inter-religious dialogue with other religious traditions. Thus, this study is not confined to Eliade as simply a historian of religions: one purpose of this work is to comprehend the theological and philosophical implications of his scholarship. In order to comprehend the theological and philosophical aspects of his work, this study will compare Eliade with other thinkers. Some of these thinkers will be so-called postmodernist. The intent of this comparative approach is similar to what Charles Tilly calls individualizing comparison, 'in which the point is to contrast specific instances of a given phenomenon as a means of grasping the peculiarities of each case'.[68] Another purpose of this book is to examine the significance of finding the centre of existence, a theme that runs throughout Eliade's life and work.

2 *Religionswissenschaft*

The German term *Religionswissenschaft* (science of religion) has been a concern of some religious scholars since the nineteenth century and a current source of disagreement and confusion among scholars of religion. The possibility and plausibility of a science of religion has attracted scholarly concern for over a hundred years. If we briefly review and contrast the introduction of the term *Religionswissenschaft* in the nineteenth century with the contemporary comprehension of the term, we discover divergent views about the nature of a science of religion.

Friedrich Max Müller (1823–1900) is given credit for initiating a call for a science of religion. But what did he mean by the term? What was the purpose of this science? Were natural science and its methodology a model for Müller?

He understood *Religionswissenschaft* to mean comparative religion in which no given religion can claim a privileged position.[1] By comparing religions with each other, one will gain higher knowledge because one will be using the widest possible evidence to make inductive, impartial judgements.[2] Writing from a Western context, Müller thought that this new science, the last science that humans are destined to elaborate, would enable Christianity to assume its rightful place among the great religions of the world, demonstrate the meaning of the fullness of time, restore the sacred character of the history of the world, change one's views of other religions, allow one to perceive common ground between religions and enable one to better comprehend one's own religion.[3] In order for comparative religion to achieve its many goals, Müller chose comparative linguistics, a successful new discipline, as his methodological model, and rejected the model provided by natural science.

Differing methodologically from Müller, the Dutch scholar Cornelis P. Tiele (1830–1903) conceived of the science of religion as having a philosophical character, including phenomenology and ontology as its initial two stages. Within the flux of historical change, ontology was a study of that which was permanent, and consisted of a phenomenological–analytical aspect and a psychological–synthetic part. Tiele understood science to mean a sound and critical method with its own independent rank among other types of disciplines.[4] Excluding the methodological applicability of natural science to *Religionswissenschaft*, Tiele argued for a deductive approach which begins 'from the results yielded by induction, by empirical, historical, and comparative methods'.[5] The science of religion would investigate religious phenomena and seek to penetrate to their foundations and to the ground of religion itself. Besides his concern for the permanent aspect of religion, Tiele perceived the need for morphology, a study of the changes and transformations that are a result of a continuing development or evolution.

Another Dutch scholar, Pierre D. Chantepie de la Saussaye (1848–1920), comprehended *Religionswissenschaft* as a discipline of the classification of religious phenomena. Presupposing a unity of religion in its diverse forms, Chantepie de la Saussaye established his science of religion on the following basis: an increasing knowledge of empirical data, a philosophy of world history, and a unifying philosophical concept of religion.[6] The history of religion, an aspect concerned with the various manifestations of religion, was divided into ethnographical study, providing details of tribal religions, and historical work, which was concerned with more civilized nations and the subjective and objective sides of religion, respectively the psychological and metaphysical aspects.[7] If the history of religion was concerned with the manifestations of religion, the philosophy of religion was devoted to determining the essence of religion.

This brief review of three nineteenth-century religious scholars enables us to grasp *Religionswissenschaft*, a synonym for comparative religion and a historical–philological science, as part of what German thinkers call *Geisteswissenschaft* in contrast to *Naturwissenschaften*.[8] Without being modelled on the natural sciences, the German term *Wissenschaft* (science) includes humanistic and social studies which are regarded as rigorous scholarly sciences, whereas the English usage tends to refer to the natural scientific model. Thus, the German term *Wissenschaft* (science) is much wider in meaning and scope than the English term. As Kitagawa observes, Müller's ambiguous use of the term *Religionswissenschaft* influenced the field of religion, and the ambiguity of the term science continues to the present time.[9]

The ambiguous use of the term 'science' initiated by Müller in the study of religion can be found in some recent articles in Western journals.[10] Using natural science as their model, Penner and Yonan emphasize the need for valid definitions, the construction of theories, and criticize the use of understanding as a method because it is not a procedure that can be used to gain knowledge.[11] The operation of understanding is merely a preliminary technique, and should not 'be confused with the logical procedures of validation and justification inherent in any scientific method'.[12] Following Michel Foucault, Wiebe argues for an *episteme*, a historical *a priori* that delimits a body of knowledge within the totality of experience. What constitutes knowledge and what is knowable are communally determined and constitute the necessary conditions for a particular science.[13] Wiebe calls for a 'positivist ethos', which would include 'a close analysis of facts, the construction of tentative hypotheses and theories to explain the facts and a methodical empirical objective (i.e. intersubjective) set of procedures for testing the hypotheses and theories'.[14] By following the suggested 'positivist ethos', religious scholars could avoid the dogmatism of having others simply accept the individual intuitions of scholars about the essence of their research. Another call for a science of religion comes from Ninian Smart, who distinguishes it from the social sciences and theology. According to Smart, his vision of a science of religion, which is not completely developed, does not reduce religion away, needs to correspond to its object, and must take into account the inner feelings of religious persons.[15] Smart provides a general outline for his science of religion: it is aspectual or treats religion as an aspect of existence; it is polymethodic or uses different methods of disciplines; it is pluralistic because there are many religions to consider; it is without clear boundaries because it is not possible or realistic to generate lucid definitions of religion.

Recent historians of religion and phenomenologists of religion continue to insist, as did Müller, Tiele and Chantepie de la Saussaye in the nineteenth century, on the scientific character of discipline.[16] Probably the most well-known historian of religions, Mircea Eliade, insists that his discipline is scientific.[17] Due to Eliade's importance as the leading international advocate of the history of religions and the vehement criticism of his work by other scholars for being unscientific, the remainder of this chapter will try to elucidate several items: (1) the criticism of Eliade's method for its alleged lack of scientific rigour; (2) the understanding of science by some contemporary philosophers of science; (3) Eliade's own comprehension of science and its relationship to his scholarly discipline. This procedure will enable us to see that Eliade's critics tend to have a rather naive comprehension of the nature of science and its method. Furthermore, since Eliade's critics use the positivistic model of science, it seems wise to consider alternative opinions about the nature of science from philosophers of science who do not share the positivistic model of the discipline.

ELIADE'S CRITICS

The basic presupposition of Eliade's critics is that science, by which they tend to mean natural science, is the acme of intellectual and methodological integrity, authority and certainty. The critical assessments of Eliade's contributions to the history of religions based on scientific grounds are generally the following: Eliade's theories cannot be empirically tested or verified; his research is not value-free; his use of sources is rendered questionable by its selectivity; his work lacks inductive reasoning; his use of imagination and intuition are unscientific. In short, Eliade's critics are saying that his methodology lacks scientific rigour. These serious charges need to be examined in greater depth in order to discern the critics' rationale.

Dudley, Saliba and Baird criticize Eliade's work for its inability to empirically test or verify its conclusions. Eliade's interpretation of hierophanies, symbols and archetypes cannot be empirically tested, according to Dudley, because symbols, for instance, have a transconscious meaning of which an individual within a given religious tradition may be unaware. This presupposition of a transconscious or unconscious meaning of a symbol tends to insulate Eliade's interpretation against empirical tests.[18] Saliba, who examines Eliade's works on the religions of non-literate people in the light of contemporary anthropological studies, argues that Eliade does not test, for instance, his hypothesis that initiation rites foster an ontological change in the status of novices.[19] Baird argues that phenomenological structures cannot be historically falsifiable and thus cannot be subject to verification.[20]

Eliade was a signer of the Marburg statement in 1960 which demanded of historians of religions that they adopt a value-free scientific approach detached from theological or philosophical questions; but Dudley claims that Eliade's research is not value-free.[21] This criticism implies that Eliade's conclusions are affected by his value-laden methodology. At best, this is a spurious attack because scientific research is itself not value-free, as we will make clear shortly.

Eliade is also criticized for his use of sources. On the one hand, Dudley criticizes Eliade for not focusing on a more limited ethnographic area to allow for more adequate empirical testing controls.[22] On the other hand, Saliba accuses Eliade of being too broad with his use of sources, a procedure that tends to suggest a Frazerian approach.[23] Saliba also attacks Eliade for selecting certain facts and neglecting others that might negate his generalizations.[24] There is a tendency in Eliade's use of sources to neglect differences among like phenomena and to search for similarities, a position that implies that differences are not very important. Eliade's comparative approach is mainly concerned, according to Saliba, with 'the outward manifestations of things rather than their meanings'.[25] Furthermore, Eliade fails to distinguish between primary and secondary sources because his use of ethnographical works is based on secondary sources.[26] This point echoes Edmund Leach's caricatures of Eliade as a man on a ladder with his scholarly feet off the ground or an armchair anthropologist.[27] By failing to distinguish between primary and secondary sources in his use of anthropological writings, by not evaluating his sources, and by grouping together sources without the application of any recognizable criteria, Eliade fails to use his sources correctly.[28] Besides Saliba's presumptuous attitude to be speaking for the whole of anthropology, he is mistaken in his assertion that secondary sources are more interpretative. For example, the Synoptic Gospels of the New Testament are generally considered to be primary sources for early Christianity. And yet they are certainly interpretations of the life, ministry and teaching of Jesus.

Another line of criticism levelled at Eliade from a scientific perspective is his lack of inductive reasoning. This type of attack is best exemplified by Dudley: 'Empirical data for Eliade is never raw, but "pre-valued" and "pre-viewed" from his general world perspective.'[29] Rather than beginning with the given data of religious experience or phenomena, Eliade deduces certain assumptions about religious beings and these conjectures hinder any inductive process. As we will see when discussing certain philosophers of science, the scientific method is not or does not necessarily have to be inductive to be successful. We will also note that the scientific method is not value-free nor without its own assumptions. Thus, Dudley's charge[30] that Eliade's methodology is a heresy from an empiricist's viewpoint is off-target because Eliade is not a scientist in any positivistic way, although he can be considered scientific in the German sense of *Geisteswissenschaft*. Therefore, Eliade is not engaging in the same kind of activity as an empirical scientist.

Due to his use of imagination and intuition to interpret a given religious phenomenon, Eliade is accused of being speculative. Agreeing that imagination and intuition can be useful devices for the historian of religions, Saliba asserts that they must be guided by objective criteria.[31] The role of imagination, intuition and other criticisms will be examined within science in light of some selected philosophers of the discipline. And then we will examine what Eliade might say to his critics.

PHILOSOPHERS ON SCIENCE

Before considering what Eliade means by science and the role of the history of religions in humanistic studies, we will pause to consider some selected prominent philosophers of science and what they have to say about empirical testing and verification, value-free scientific research, use of sources by scientists, inductive reasoning and the scientific use of imagination and intuition. By following this procedure, we will see that the positivist model of science is a fallacy, at least according to some philosophers òf science, and expose the scientific naiveté of Eliade's critics. Although the philosophers chosen – Kuhn, Popper and Polanyi – demonstrate a diversity of opinion about the method and nature of science, they tend to share an attitude towards science in which science is not what many have presumed it to be, possesses its own methodological problems, and does not possess the highest authority.

The assertion that theories must be empirically tested or verified is not universally accepted by philosophers of science. Karl R. Popper, who proposes a critical rationalism in his works, states that scientific theories, universal statements and systems of signs or symbols, are not verifiable or justifiable, although they are capable of being tested by experience.[32] A given theory can be tested by using some criteria of demarcation, which must exclude anything metaphysical and represent a world of possible experience. The criterion of demarcation, for Popper, is falsifiability, whose aim is to reject untenable theories and to find the fittest system, 'by exposing them all to the fiercest struggle for survival'.[33] If conclusions are falsified, then their falsification affects the validity of the theory, assuming that one accepts the fundamental statements that contradict a theory. Even if conclusions to a theory cannot be falsified, this positive result provides merely temporary support for a theory because it is possible that its conclusions could be falsified by future tests. If a hypothesis is more falsifiable, it is less probable. Since there can be no scientific assertions that cannot be tested and none that cannot in principle be refuted, there are no ultimate statements in science.[34] But this is not an occasion for despair by a scientist.

If a hypothesis proves itself by continually surviving the process of falsification, it can be provisionally accepted by what Popper calls corroboration,[35] the process of tests, trials and fitness to survive attempted refutations. The degree of corroboration is greater to the extent that the hypothesis is falsifiable. If a theory survives serious attempts to falsify it, it can be provisionally accepted but not conclusively established.

The critics of Eliade and others advocating a scientific methodology in the study of religion imply that the scientific method will lead to certain knowledge because the researcher can personally verify his/her findings. Popper's argument suggests that we can never attain absolute certainty or truth. According to Popper, there are many sources of our knowledge and none possesses absolute authority or certainty.[36]

Another assumption of Eliade's critics is that scientific research is value-free and objective. Thomas S. Kuhn demonstrates that scientists accept and value certain paradigms and not others. Paradigms provide scientists with a map and direction for map-making. Kuhn writes, 'In learning a paradigm the scientist acquires theory, methods, and standards together, usually in an inextricable mixture.'[37] Thus paradigms represent an entire constellation of beliefs, values and techniques shared by the members of a given commu-nity.[38] A given scientist makes choices in terms of what he/she thinks is valuable to learn or what problems are worthwhile to solve. Polanyi writes about scientific passions, which have a logical function and are not a mere psychological by-product of scientific work: 'Passions charge objects with emotions, making them repulsive or attractive; positive passions affirm that something is precious. The excitement of the scientist making a discovery is an *intellectual* passion, telling that something is *intellectually* precious and, more particularly, that it is *precious* to science.'[39] These scientific passions serve as a guide to what is of greater or lesser interest. Polanyi also asserts that the alleged complete objectivity of natural science is a delusion.[40] In fact, personal judgements and guesswork play essential roles in science. Polanyi writes, for instance, 'Scientists – that is, creative scientists – spend their lives in trying to guess right.'[41] Thus scientists act on the basis of a guess, or what Popper calls a subjective belief, or what appears to be promising.[42]

We have noted that Eliade is criticized for carefully selecting his sources in order to support his theories. Scientists are also selective. According to Polanyi, scientists frequently ignore evidence which appears incompatible with their accepted theories. It is their hope that any conflicting, new evidence will prove false or irrelevant.[43] As Kuhn notes, scientists may conclude that new findings render a solution to a problem impossible and set aside for a more propitious time an unsolvable dilemma.[44] Even the alleged empirical observation is selective because it depends on the scien-tist's point of view, theoretical interests, conjectures and anticipations, and horizon of expectations.[45] Since the body of scientific knowledge is so vast and a single individual can know but a small fragment of the knowledge comprised by science, a lone scientist cannot judge the validity of all scientific results personally. Thus individual scientists must rely on the findings of others in the overall field. This means that a given scientist must rely on the authority of opinions accepted at second hand.[46] Similarly, historians of religions can usually only master one or two religious traditions on an intimate basis and must rely on the expertise of other scholars more familiar with other traditions. Scientists and historians of religions are both limited and must trust to a certain extent the authority of others.

At least one philosopher of science does not accept the assertion that the primary method of science must be inductive, a result of observations or experiments on particulars to universal statements in the form of hypotheses or theories. Following the philosophical lead of Hume, Popper argues that an observation or experimental result can only be a singular statement and not a universal one.[47] Thus no amount of collected observations will verify a general statement. Since the principle of induction does not provide an adequate mark of the empirical, it is not a suitable criterion of demarcation or falsifiability, and must be a synthetic statement; it cannot be based on experience because it leads to an infinite regress.[48] The actual procedure of science is to operate with conjectures or to leap to conclusions.

Although knowledge cannot begin from nothing, neither can it start from observation. Popper asserts, 'The advance of knowledge consists, mainly, in the modification of earlier knowledge.'[49] This statement implies that tradition is the primary source of our knowledge, although it is not the ultimate source of it. In fact, there are no ultimate sources of knowledge.[50] Our knowledge is finite and human, which implies that it is 'mixed with our errors, our prejudices, our dreams, and our hopes; that all we can do is grope for truth even though it is beyond our reach'.[51] For Popper it is our ignorance which is infinite, not our knowledge.

We have noted that Eliade is accused of being too imaginative and intuitive with his method, which implies that there are no empirical constraints on his conclusions. This type of criticism seems to suggest that imagination and intuition are foreign to the scientific enterprise. This is, however, not the case, as Popper and Kuhn make clear.

Although observation and reason cannot be ultimate authorities of our knowledge for Popper, intellectual intuition and imagination do have a role to play in science. They are, however, unreliable because they can mislead us, even though they may enable us to see things clearly.[52] For Kuhn, intuition can come to the scientist as flashes of insight that enable a new paradigm to be formed. These new intuitive insights depend upon previous experience gained from the old paradigm.[53] These newly-discovered intuitions are scientifically communal because they are shared and tested by others within the group. Thus intuitions, non-individual and shared possessions, are analyzable.[54] If one assumes a scientific posture, this is not sufficient rationale for rejecting the use of intuition and imagination in one's methodology.

We referred earlier to Wiebe's call for an *episteme*, an absolutely certain, demonstrable knowledge. This old scientific ideal is, according to Popper, a false idol because scientific knowledge can never assert that it has gained truth nor even probability, a possible substitute for truth.[55] Popper writes, 'Only in our subjective experience of conviction, in our subjective faith, can we be "absolutely certain".'[56] If the aim of science is not indubitable knowledge, towards what should it strive? Popper answers: To strive for knowledge and to search for truth.[57] In a later work, he discusses the aim of science as an attempt to find satisfactory explanations or solutions to interesting problems.[58] To strive for final answers is an illusory goal. Science can advance by new and deeper discoveries, finding new problems, and submitting one's tentative solutions to continuous and rigorous testing. The criticisms of Eliade's work for not being scientifically rigorous, those raising the possibility of a scientific approach to religion, and the call for scientific certainty are misled by the idol of a false science. The insights of the three philosophers of science that we have utilized have presented a very different view of the scientific method and the knowledge based on its procedure. Although the views of our three thinkers are far from universal acceptance by other philosophers of science, like the early Rudolf Carnap, Ernst Mach, and Carl Hempel, and even demonstrate philosophical differences among themselves, those within religious studies who advocate a *Religionswissenschaft* on the English empirical model, should pause to reconsider these three thinkers' arguments which have been available for some time. At the very least, the advocates for a scientific approach to religion would gain food for thought and might possibly rethink their positions. We are not affirming that Eliade's work is scientifically rigorous and without problems. We are rather asserting that he needs to be fairly criticized based on what he claims to be doing, which is what we need to examine next.

ELIADE AND *RELIGIONSWISSENSCHAFT*

As Eliade tells us in his autobiography, he was an avid amateur scientist in his early teens. He was an enthusiastic entomologist, botanist, geologist and chemist, turning his attic bedroom into a small laboratory. Even though he seems to have practised the scientific methodological data–hypothesis–verification model in his early life, he discovered the humanist aspect of *Wissenschaft* in his later life, using Goethe as his intellectual hero.

In his mature years Eliade assumes a critical posture towards natural science and those who uncritically embrace it. Referring to fellow humanists ashamed to admit that they read poets or mystics, Eliade writes in his journal on 26 June 1963, 'They try to appear "serious," "scientific". They imitate the objectivity of the scientists. Actually, they are timid and sterile. Their absence of curiosity is a proof of impotence and mediocrity.'[59] If Eliade deplores the timidity, lack of daring and failure of historians of religions, it is in the opinion of Charles H. Long a result of methodological tensions within the discipline: 'These tensions arise because the data with which the religious historian deals tend to undercut any systematic methodology.'[60]

This explains the failure to develop a science of religion or a total hermeneutics.

It is Eliade's conviction that no humanistic discipline should conform to models taken from the natural sciences. In fact, many of these borrowed scientific models are obsolete.[61] (A point that our chosen philosophers of science seem to suggest.) Even his research into ancient alchemy that could be considered a scientific enterprise, Eliade confesses to be more philosophical and religious in nature because he is more interested in the metaphysical and soteriological implications of these traditional scientific techniques.[62] Even though Eliade demonstrates a critical attitude toward the natural scientific model as a methodological tool, *Wissenschaft* in the broader German sense of the term as humanistic studies does play a role in his methodology.

Religionswissenschaft or the history of religions, as Eliade refers to it, uses an empirical method of approach. Attracted to both the history and meaning of religious phenomena, the historian of religions tries to systematize the results of his/her findings and reflects on the structures revealed by the phenomena. This historical aspect of the work of the historian of religions is completed by phenomenology or philosophy of religion.[63] But why is the historian of religions concerned not only with the historical becoming of a religious phenomenon but also with its structure? Eliade answers, 'For religious forms are non-temporal, they are not necessarily bound to time.'[64] Thus the historian of religions must go beyond the ordinary historian. Rather than reconstructing an event, the historian of religions 'must trace not only the history of a given hierophany, but must first of all understand and explain the modality of the sacred that that hierophany discloses'.[65] Before the historian of religions can isolate and comprehend the structure of a religious form, he/she examines all the historical examples possible. Thus the history of religions is by nature an encyclopedic approach to its subject. In his journal, Eliade acknowledges the difficulty: 'The history of religions is an impossible discipline; one must know everything, consult at least a dozen auxiliary disciplines (from prehistory to folklore), always chase after genuine sources and forever be consulting specialists of all types.'[66] Thus Eliade understands the science of religion in a very broad sense of the term because it also embraces phenomenology and philosophy of religion without neglecting the historically concrete.[67]

If one's approach must be encyclopedic, there is always the danger that one could get lost in the labyrinth of material from different cultures and historical periods and conflicting interpretations by scholars. The historian of religions must be guided by the sources or texts of the traditions that he/

she is studying. In an autobiographical admission, Eliade relates how he was misled by one writer's stories about certain Indian religious figures, which proved to be a decisive lesson for him, because it demonstrated the importance of going to the sources themselves.[68] Even after reaching the sources, the scholar's imagination and intuition play an important role. The imagination opens up creative possibilities beyond the historical level. Eliade perceives a structural analogy between scientific work and literary imagination. He quotes with approval the American physicist Jacob Bronowski: ' "The step by which a new axiom is addressed cannot itself be mechanized. It is a free play of the mind, an invention outside of the logical process. This is the central act of imagination in science, and it is, in all respects, like any similar act in literature." '[69] Thus Eliade approves of a systematic and rigorous science that allows and even encourages the use of the imagination. There is, however, an inherent danger in this attitude because an unchecked imagination can lead to fictitious interpretations and the impossibility of verifying one's findings. Another danger is the potential manipulation of historical details to conform to a predetermined synthetic pattern.[70]

The role of intuition in Eliade's work can be observed in the very nature of symbols, which have the ability to reveal a perspective through which religious phenomena can be grasped and articulated into a system. The symbolism of night and darkness, for instance, reveals the structural solidarity between precosmic and prenatal darkness and death; it also demonstrates the symbolism of rebirth and initiation. This renders possible an intuition of certain modes of being; it gives one a comprehension of one's place in the world and one's human condition.[71] Eliade is suggesting that the religious phenomena themselves demand an imaginative and intuitive approach.

CONCLUDING REMARKS

Based on Eliade's understanding of the scientific nature of the history of religions, it becomes evident that he comprehends his discipline in terms of what the Germans call *Geisteswissenschaft* and not *Naturwissenschaft*. The terminological ambiguity inherent in the German usage and the contrasting English understanding of the term science is not recognized by Eliade's critics and some advocating a science of religion, who have failed to see the important methodological distinctions between *Naturwissenschaften* and *Religionswissenschaften* inherited from Max Müller and other nineteenth-century figures. Although there are problems in Eliade's method, it can be asserted that he should not be criticized for something he is not trying to do, that is, scientific research based on the positivistic model.

As we have seen, Popper, Kuhn, and Polanyi give us a different view of science. Their view demonstrates a discipline that follows paradigms, accepts certain presuppositions, uses imagination, intuition and guesswork, lacks absolute certainty, allows for passions and value, openness, selects sources, and uses a debatable, at least according to Popper, inductive process. Our philosophers of science enable us to see the naiveté of Eliade's critics and those who call for a science of religion. They are naive because they fail to see the actual workings of science and the various problems inherent in the scientific model. They have failed to perceive that scientists are also human beings who bring to their work presuppositions, emotions and what Polanyi calls tacit knowledge.

Assuming that our three philosophers of science are correct in their observations about the nature and aims of science, or nearly on target, can we use the empirical scientific model for humanistic research? If the nature of the scientific enterprise is even close to what our philosophers have asserted, it appears that we are obliged, at the very least, to reconsider or even to discard the scientific model for the study of religion. The philosopher Richard Rorty makes us pause to reflect because he indicates that hermeneutics is peculiarly suited to the study of human beings, whereas the scientific method is appropriate to nature. Rorty thinks, however, that it would be better to drop the spirit–nature distinction.[72] Those advocating a science of religion are conforming to the scholarly norms of the day by trying to adhere to the scientific model. The attempt to be scientific or of choosing one method over another is confused because evaluative terms cannot be segregated in a language. If we use a term to describe a human being, this given term becomes an evaluative term.[73] Even though scientists may perceive a correspondence between their mathematical vocabulary and the reality of nature, this does not mean that we must comprehend science as a discipline moving toward a correspondence with reality. It would be better to affirm that one vocabulary works better than another for a particular purpose and that knowledge is a means of coping with reality and not representing it.[74] Although Rorty does not think it would do any harm to keep the term hermeneutic, Charles Taylor is more emphatic in his insistence upon retaining the term because common and intersubjective meanings are not captured by social science.[75] Taylor's argument is sharply distinguished from Rorty's position because: (1) Taylor wants to retain the Diltheyan distinction between the natural and human sciences that Rorty finds useless; (2) Taylor views hermeneutics as a special method, whereas

Rorty views it as looking for a helpful vocabulary; (3) Rorty claims that Taylor's search for internal explanations of social contexts is the mistaken use of civility as a method. If hermeneutics is best suited for the study of human behaviour, it is, then, wise to retain the term. Our three philosophers of science and Rorty enable us to see that the *Natur/Geisteswissenschaften* distinction is not as helpful as in the past. Although hermeneutics facilitates a useful vocabulary, it also represents a special method or methods that must take the historical and social contexts into account. Because the historian of religions is dealing with different material than is the laboratory scientist, the socio-historical experience embodied in the evidence that he/she uses cannot be transformed into a science by the natural scientific inductive procedure because the hermeneutic knowledge gained by the historian of religions is fundamentally different in character and intention from the natural sciences.[76] Due to the problems inherent within the use of either *Naturwissenschaften* or *Geisteswissenschaften*, it is wiser to acknowledge that *Religionswissenschaft* is an unrealizable ideal, and that it is necessary to give up the false idol of the scientific method.

If we need not adhere blindly to the scientific model, this does not mean that religious research cannot be systematic and rigorous. Since religious phenomena are complex, we need to use tools more appropriate to their multifarious nature. Some of these tools are currently being used by scholars in the field. We are advocating an approach that would be comprehensive and interdisciplinary.[77] Whatever final form this type of approach takes, it is still important to acknowledge that the interpretations of a historian of religions can never be final in any absolute sense. Newcomers to the field of the history of religions will bring new questions and provide new answers to old material and problems. This is a never-ending process of question and answer, of search and discovery, and finding and interpretation.

3 The Fore-structure of Hermeneutics

In Eliade's novella 'The Secret of Dr Honigberger', mystery and its interpretation play major roles in the work. The narrator of the story, a young Indologist, is invited to discuss India with a Mrs Zerlendi, who asks the young man if he is familiar with the life and writings of Dr Johann Honigberger, a Transylvanian German doctor from Brashov, court physician, pharmacist and adventurer. The German doctor is important to the mystery because Dr Zerlendi, as his daughter relates to the Indologist, was busy researching a book on the life of Dr Honigberger when he disappeared from his home without taking anything – clothing or money – with him. Prior to his disappearance, Dr Zerlendi had cut himself off from his family and the world, working in his office simply dressed, and spending time meditating in his bedroom. After accepting the challenge from Mrs Zerlendi to unravel the mystery of her husband's disappearance, the young Indologist discovers a revealing notebook written in a foreign script, which he successfully interprets to mean that the doctor has found, by means of imitating the yogic techniques used by Dr Honigberger, a method of becoming invisible. The story ends in a surrealistic way. After the Indologist returns to Mrs Zerlendi's home to convey his discovery to her about her husband, he discovers that neither she nor her daughter recognize him because 20 years have mysteriously passed. In this novella the narrator uses his hermeneutical skills to unravel a mystery and functions much like a detective.

Like the young Indologist of the novella, it is the task, at least partially, of the historian to reconstruct an event of the past or a sequence of events, much as a police detective investigating a murder, in order to discern what happened at a given time or to retrieve the sociological, economic or political contexts of past events. According to Eliade, it is the work of the historian of religions to go beyond the detective work of the historian based in the social sciences and to understand and explain the manifestations of the sacred. In other words, the historian of religions is concerned with meaning by which he/she seeks to identify and elucidate the circumstances that prompted or rendered possible the hierophanies expressed by supernatural beings, symbols or myths. Therefore, the historian of religions encounters a series of messages waiting to be deciphered and comprehended.[1] By the nature of his/her discipline and the type of phenomena encountered, the historian of religions is necessarily an interpreter. Thus the problem of hermeneutics is at the very core of Eliade's own scholarly work. Like other aspects of his immense contribution to the cross-cultural study of religion, Eliade's hermeneutics have been criticized by others as noted in the first chapter. Without completely reiterating the criticism discussed in the first chapter, we can acknowledge that the most insightful and persuasive criticism of Eliade's hermeneutics comes from Jonathan Z. Smith. Taking a cue from Kant, Smith states that morphology, for instance, presupposes a 'fitting economy', which involves the notion that natural laws observe a certain economy that to human judgement is fitting and understandable. Due to the empirical law of economy, there are, for instance, a limited number of archetypes, although there may possibly be a large number of manifestations. Thus comparison is strictly limited in procedure, not in scope, because one can only compare within a system or an archetype. The crux of Smith's criticism is the following: 'Comparisons within the system do not take time or history into account; comparisons between the pattern and manifestation are comparisons as to the degree of mani-festation and its intelligibility and do not take historical, linear development into account.'[2] In another work, Smith refers to comparison as a matter of memory and impressionistic rather than a project for inquiry or a method.[3] Along slightly different lines of criticism, Baird laments the way individuals lose their religious individuality and how secondary rites and symbols develop because the universal structures have supremacy.[4] According to Saliba, the comparative method is used defectively by Eliade because material from different historical periods are collected and grouped together in a style reminiscent of Frazer's corpus.[5] (It should be noted that when Eliade's critics want to denigrate him and his work, they often connect him with a style of scholarship that has already fallen into disrepute and label him Frazerian, which serves as a kind of shorthand for what critics do not like. Unfortunately, this label is not very informative.)

In a sense, Eliade agrees with his critics that morphological classification is atemporal. It is non-historical by definition because religious forms are non-temporal by necessity, transcending the realm of history.[6] Eliade still insists, however, that morphology must be inferred from history and particular historical examples and experience. An excellent summary statement on the transhistorical aspect of his interpretative work is found in the preface to his book on shamanism: 'In other words, the historian of religions makes use of all the *historical* manifestations of a religious phenomenon in order to discover what such a phenomenon "has to say"; on the one hand, he holds to the historically concrete, but on the other, he attempts to decipher whatever transhistorical content a religious datum reveals through history.'[7] The non-historical structures revealed by the method of morphology manifest the basic unity among similar phenomena, but if the meaning of a structure depends on the real, there must be a concealed relation between structure and history.[8] From another perspective, morphological classification is a rationalization which synchronically organizes material spread over vast expanses of time and space. Eliade's use of morphology seems to suggest that he assumes that all diachrony can be eventually synchronized.

Although Eliade collected his share of criticism, he also accumulated his defenders.[9] Eliade's.critics would be astonished to read, however, the work of Adrian Marino, who claims that Eliade rediscovered all the classic positions and solutions of hermeneutics, resolved all the basic hermeneutical problems, and enriched and developed a method character- ized by an intuitive, direct experience with historical texts.[10] Besides someone being able to find antecedents to Eliade's method in nineteenth- century figures, like Max Müller, Cornelis P. Tiele and Pierre D. Chantepie de la Saussaye, Marino's assertions suffer from scholarly hyperbole and false praise.

Marino's work, the contributions of other defenders of Eliade, and the barbs of his critics, all make one pause to reconsider his hermeneutics. With the exception of Marino, what previous writers have neglected to address is the fore-structure of Eliade's hermeneutics. By investigating the fore-structure of his hermeneutics, we will be able to see the implications that it holds for his interpretation of the sacred, the continuity of religious attitudes, and the hermeneutical problems presented by distance, situation and horizon. Since other writers have reconstructed his hermeneutics,[11] this chapter intends to focus rather on the neglected fore-structure of Eliade's hermeneutics. Taking a hint from the work of Hans-Georg Gadamer because of his important contribution to the problem of the fore-structure of inter- pretation,[12] this chapter seeks to review the 'projects', which include the presuppositions, prepossessions, pre-understandings and anticipations of Eliade's hermeneutics. According to Gadamer, projects are structures which will anticipate what will be discerned in a given object under investiga- tion.[13] In other words, we want to determine to some degree the types of presuppositions and anticipations that Eliade brings to his interpretative task. This chapter will also serve as a supplement to Marino's study of Eliade's hermeneutics where the author discusses the following: the origi- nal moment within the hermeneutical circle; intuition and reflection; induction and deduction; analyses; part and whole; past and present; and sacred and profane.[14] Although there will be some overlap with Marino's examination of Eliade's presuppositions, I want to draw attention to the following items and their implications for the fore-structure of Eliade's hermeneutics: sacred language; the unity of his methodology and how it bridges the problem of distance; situation and horizon; and the problems associated with a total hermeneutics.

By following this procedure, we will not give a systematic account of Eliade's hermeneutics, but we will determine some of the intellectual presuppositions that he brings with him in order to interpret religious phenomena. We also want to include a comparison of Eliade and Jacques Derrida, the most renowned deconstructivist. From Derrida's perspective, Eliade's hermeneutic is a *pharmakon*, both a poison and a medicine. It can thus cure or destroy; it can also help us to understand, or confuse us.

SACRED LANGUAGE

Human beings are born into a culture which represents a pre-given body of material that the culturally-bound members will eventually learn and incorporate into their natures. Gadamer uses the German term *Bildung* (culture) to describe the result of a process of becoming that possesses no goals outside itself.[15] As cultural beings, we discover given institutions, customs and, most importantly, language as part of the humanly-constituted world in which we find ourselves.

For Eliade, the world reveals itself as language, which implies that it needs to be interpreted.[16] Eliade is mainly concerned with the secret language of the world, that is, symbol and myth, the basic components of a primary religious language. Through symbol and myth, a narrative form of symbolic expression, the world reveals itself not objectively but in a deeper and more fundamental way.[17] The symbol may reveal a condition of the world ordinarily inaccessible to us, a world pattern or unity or a paradoxical situation. Myth, a primordial event that occurred at the beginning of time, may reveal the sacred as historical and real by describing the irruptions of the sacred into the world. The sacred may reveal itself as, for example, supreme beings, moral laws, symbols, myths and other complex modalities of manifestation.

In contrast to Eliade's position, Derrida does not affirm that the world reveals itself as language, but he suggests that language traces the world. By using language, human beings also erase it. From a slightly different perspective, language inscribes the world and leaves an inscription as a trace, which serves to trace the origin of all knowledge. The trace – a presence– absence – represents a reserve, which implies that it is an indeterminate medium that opens up the world, but it does not indicate anything in particular.[18] Continually overflowing itself, a trace is supplementary by nature, but it only supplements itself. With regard to the sacred language of myth, Derrida could reply to Eliade that the distinction between signifier and signified is a product of consciousness, which only deals with signs. The signified is a signifier because the former is not independent nor superior to the latter. As language reveals itself, it conceals and erases itself.[19] How is it possible to interpret that which erases itself? By reading the language that reveals itself and at the same time conceals itself, one signifies, writes and interprets and thus produces, for instance, a different myth.

For Eliade, an individual becomes aware of the sacred because it reveals itself to him or her as wholly different from the profane.[20] Although the sacred shows itself as something that does not belong to our world, it manifests itself through objects that are an integral part of our natural profane world. A stone, for instance, will not be worshipped because it is a mere stone, but may be adored because it reveals the sacred, a hierophany that designates an act of manifestation of the sacred.[21] This hierophany is paradoxical because a given object not only reveals the sacred and becomes something else; it also continues to remain itself.[22] In other words, a stone, even though it reveals the sacred, continues to participate in its surroundings with other stones, trees, dirt and so forth. While on vacation in 1937, Eliade noticed a large stone on the edge of the lake, half in the water and half on the beach, and what occurs when an object loses its sacred character. He observed couples climbing on top of the stone, while someone took their picture. 'Thousands of years ago such a stone would have been worshiped for its supposed magical or sacred virtues. It is too strange, too different from all the others, half in the water as it is. Today, "the peculiar" attracts the attention and devotion of people in another way: couples photograph one another. . . . The mystique – or, if you will, the magic – of the stone has remained the same.'[23]

In order to grasp the meaning of the sacred revealed in the world, its original intentionality must not be lost by reducing it to something else. Throughout Eliade's work, we find a polemic directed against reductionism that provides a negative foundation for his hermeneutics, which is aptly expressed in the following statement:

Indeed, there is no such thing as a 'pure' religious fact. Such a fact is always also a historical, sociological, cultural, and psychological fact, to name only the most important contexts. If the historian of religions does not always insist on this multiplicity of meanings, it is mainly because he is supposed to concentrate on the religious signification of his documents. The confusion starts when only one aspect of religious life is accepted as primary and meaningful, and the other aspects or functions are regarded as secondary or even illusory. Such a reductionist method was applied by Durkheim and other sociologists of religion.[24]

Thus if we reduce a sacred phenomenon to a psychological, sociological, or historical statement, we will lose the original intention of the sacred and fail to understand it as a religious phenomenon.

Since the sacred is unique and irreducible, it must be granted an original ontological status because it possesses such an original status when it is manifested to a believer. When interpreting the sacred one must not impose norms foreign to the object, but rather one should attempt to grasp it on its own level as something religious.[25] Although Eliade does not admit it, to try to grasp something as religious is to have already begun to interpret a given phenomenon. For Eliade, the task of the interpreter must be to recreate imaginatively the conditions for the sacred appearance. In other words, the historian of religions must relive a multitude of existential situations and unravel a number of pre-systematic ontologies. By assuming that an interpreter can move back in time to relive another existential situation, Eliade places himself at odds with Derrida who asserts that one can only experience in the present: 'The absolute impossibility of living other than in the present, this eternal impossibility, defines the unthinkable as the limit of reason.'[26] From a different perspective, Gadamer warns that psychological empathy (*Einfuhlen*) and reenactment (*Nacherleben*) are confused with true understanding which involves deciphering the meaning of a non-datable, publicly communicable message. Once the message is understood, it acts as a bridge linking interpreter and text.[27]

For Eliade, it is not, however, sufficient to comprehend the sacred as an irreducible form because understanding must be accompanied by the technical attempt to grasp its intentional mode. In contrast, Derrida would deny that it is possible to grasp the intentional mode of the sacred or a sacred body of literature like a myth. The intention of a mythmaker, for instance, is insignificant because the deconstructing method is not concerned with this type of literature on its own terms. The true intentionality of the sacred, according to Eliade, can be captured by the dialectic of the sacred, which refers to the fact that there are always profane things besides the sacred. And that the sacred manifests itself through objects, myths or symbols – all something other than itself – but never completely or directly.[28] For example, not all stones are sacred and thus venerated. 'The dialectic of a hierophany implies a more or less clear choice, a singling-out.'[29] The chosen object is separated, because it manifests the sacred, from everything else around it. And since religious experience presupposes a bipartition of the world into the sacred and the profane, the latter is transmuted into the former by the dialectics of hierophany. The various processes of desacralization, on the other hand, retransforms the sacred into the profane.[30]

When reflecting on Eliade's position, as explicated above, it is evident that he brings to his method a basic presupposition: unity. The fundamental unity of his methodological stance is to be found within human consciousness. Rather than a stage in the history of consciousness, the sacred is a structural element of human consciousness.[31] In a more recent work, Eliade expresses the fundamental unity of religions as based on the 'indivisible unity of the history of the human mind'.[32] Thus there is a basic unity underlying all religious experience. This unity grounded in consciousness possesses implications for religious continuity because almost all religious attitudes have continued to exist since prehistoric time without a break to the present.[33] Likewise, the dialectic of the sacred remains one and allows for the spontaneous and complete rediscovery of ancient religious values regardless of the historical period.[34] This pre-given unity allows Eliade to state the following: 'The dialectic of the sacred belongs to all religions, not only to the supposedly "primitive" forms.'[35] An implication of the unity of the dialectic of the sacred is that it tends indefinitely to repeat itself in a series of archetypes, 'so that a hierophany realized at a certain "historical moment" is structurally equivalent to a hierophany a thousand years earlier or later.'[36] In conclusion, Eliade presupposes a unity of the history of the human mind, which will have important implications for other aspects of his hermeneutics.

Rather than the unity discovered by Eliade, Derrida stresses difference in his philosophy in a very special sense. Derrida emphasizes the ambiguity of the verb 'to differ' because in some cases the verb signifies non-identity and in other cases it refers to the sameness of things; it also can refer to a present distinction or a delay, an interval of space and time.[37] To capture the sense of 'differing' as spacing and temporalizing and to indicate the sameness that is non-identical, Derrida uses the term *différance*. The *ance* ending of *différance*, marked by a silent *a*, indicates that it is not simply a word nor a concept; it is neither existence nor essence; it is neither active nor passive because the perceiving subject is similarly constituted.[38] *Différance*, a necessarily finite movement, is what precedes and structures all opposition. In other words, it comes before all differences, and represents the play of differences. *Différance* makes possible, for instance, the opposition between presence and absence because it also produces these differences. It cannot be exposed because it cannot become manifest in a present moment and never produces presence itself, whose structure is constituted by difference and deferment.[39] In contrast to Eliade, for Derrida the mind is not the locus of unity because *différance* is also the structure of the mind or psyche. Because of his use of irony and his articulation of both pro- and anti-aspects of every philosophical stance, Derrida does not argue any thesis nor adopt any philosophical position for long, due to the workings of negation within his method. Thus, there can be no unity because no unifying factor exists and nothing unified is to be discovered. The work of the historian of religions is, then merely prefatory within the context of Derrida's notion of *différance*; it can never become final in any sense because we can never arrive at the truth.

In sharp contrast to Derrida, Eliade's projection of unity on to the history of religious phenomena tends to bridge the problem of distance and con-temporaneity in his hermeneutics. When trying to interpret an ancient religious text that is culturally and historically remote from his or her own situation, an interpreter encounters the hermeneutical problem of temporal distance, which appears as a gulf that needs to be bridged. The unity of religious consciousness, for Eliade, is more a support for the hermeneutical process than a temporal gulf that separates the interpreter from a religious text or artifact. Just as *homo religiosus* can repeat and relive the para-digmatic events of the divine beings and cultural heroes by repeating the origin myths and rituals that took place *in illo tempore* (in the beginning of time), the historian of religions can also encounter and relive the same myths and rituals of a foreign culture, an ability that allows the historian of religions to understand religious phenomena and behaviour from within, like an actor assuming a dramatic role, and not as external, remote forms.[40] Past religious phenomena and events are always potentially contemporary for us because they are also given in consciousness, which enables an object to become present to us no matter how remote it is to us. In a journal entry of 1962, Eliade writes, 'No religious behavior, however, archaic it may be, is ever definitively abolished.'[41] This allows Eliade to think that the re-construction of original circumstances is not limited by the historicity of our being because we can always recover the past to a great extent.

From the perspective of Derrida, spatial distance is both active and passive; spacing is a force that relates and separates concepts from one another.[42] The distance created by spacing allows elements to enter into relation without letting them coincide. Derrida also states that '*spacing* designates *nothing*, nothing that is, no presence at a distance.'[43] What Derrida leaves us is a synthesis without reconciliation.

SITUATION AND HORIZON

According to Gadamer, one can never gain complete knowledge of one's situation by means of reflection because of the nature of one's historical being.[44] Thus one's situation is a standpoint that limits the possibility of one's reflective vision. Eliade agrees that a finite being finds him- or herself in a situation. This is not, however, a limiting condition due to one's historical nature as Gadamer claims. The individual, for Eliade, can know other kinds of situations:

> Although it is true that man is always found 'in situation,' his situation is not, for all that, always a historical one in the sense of being conditioned solely by the contemporaneous historical movement. The man in his totality is aware of other situations over and above his historical condition; for example, he knows the state of dreaming, or of the waking dream, or of melancholy, or of detachment, or of aesthetic bliss, or of escape, etc. – and none of these states is historical, although they are as authentic and as important for human existence as man's historical existence is.[45]

Eliade sounds like an Upanishadic sage at this point because of his emphasis on other states of consciousness and their non-historical nature.

Derrida would agree with the implications of Eliade's position that we must beware of a metaphysical concept of history: 'The history of meaning developing itself, producing itself, fulfilling itself.'[46] If we must overturn the metaphysical concept of history, we are also obliged to mark the interval and beware that it is not reappropriated. The truth is no longer to be found within the historical realm because of the withdrawal of presence. With the withdrawal of the origin of presence, a basic condition for the manifestation of truth, non-truth becomes truth and non-presence is presence. What is the reason for this situation? Derrida answers, '*Différance*, the disappearance of any originary presence, is *at once* the condition of possibility *and* the condition of impossibility of truth.'[47]

As part of the fore-structure of Eliade's hermeneutics, there is his pre-understanding that myths and rites disclose *homo religiosus* as not only in a historical situation but as also involved in a boundary situation. He defines it as follows: 'A boundary situation is one which man discovers in becoming conscious of his place in the universe.'[48] These boundary-like situations – birth, initiation and death – demand to be understood and interpreted, so that one can grasp the existential situation that made a given religious action possible. This is not only a challenge for the historian of religions; it is also an existential demand to decipher and to elucidate these crucial situations. The process of hermeneutics requires one to place oneself in the situation of other beings in order to understand their condition. From another perspective, Derrida perceives his own philosophy as on the boundary or a marginal endeavour, which is given emphasis by his notion of play. In the to-and-fro movement of play, presence is disrupted by play, a movement of absence and presence.[49]

An important part of the notion of situation is the related concept of horizon, a 'range of vision that includes everything that can be seen from a particular vantage point'.[50] If one possesses a horizon, one is not limited to what is nearest, but one can rather see beyond it. The horizon of the interpreter is never closed. Gadamer asserts:

> The historical movement of human life consists in the fact that it is never utterly bound to any standpoint, and hence can never have a truly closed horizon. The horizon is, rather, something into which we move and that moves with us. Horizons change for a person who is moving. Thus the horizon of the past, out of which all human life lives and which exists in the form of tradition, is always in motion.[51]

Thus we can move with our historical consciousness into the past of another religious culture and shape a common horizon. In fact, the horizon of the present needs the horizon of the past in order to be formed. And the fusion of these horizons represents understanding.[52]

In an earlier work, Eliade is not quite as optimistic as Gadamer about our ability to broaden our historical horizons. Eliade makes a distinction between modern *homo religiosus*, who cannot experience, for instance, the sacred in matter, and archaic *homo religiosus*, whose thinking is dominated by cosmological symbolism formed by a vastly different experience of the world. For the archaic religious person, this world is alive and open, and an object is not simply itself but can function as a sign for something else. Modern *homo religiosus* is only able to know matter as a natural phenomenon, although such a person might be capable of achieving an aesthetic experience.[53] Whereas Eliade perceives limitations in understanding religious phenomena due to the irreligious attitudes of modern humans, Gadamer thinks that when our historical consciousness moves into another horizon, this does not mean that we are moving into an alien world unconnected with our own. The coming together of another horizon and our own forms a single horizon that moves beyond the frontiers of the present moment.[54]

The historian of religions, for Eliade, can widen his/her horizons by elucidating a wide number of existential situations unfamiliar to a person of the West. The broadening of horizons by the historian of religions renders possible three positive results: it gives one a deeper knowledge of human nature, enables one to transcend cultural provincialism and one can encounter others from different types of archaic and foreign cultures in a way that is culturally stimulating.[55] With the knowledge and enriched experience gained from such a widening of horizons, Eliade controversially claims that this can form the basis for the eventual development of a new, universal humanism.

In order to understand the past, we must possess an historical horizon, an ability to see beyond what is near at hand and to perceive a larger whole. In fact, to place ourselves into the situation of another person, we must already have a horizon.[56] Eliade thinks that religious phenomena cannot be understood outside their historical context because outside history there are no pure religious and human data.[57] Thus we must listen to the past and always take into consideration the historical context of what we are investigating and trying to understand.

By listening to the messages of the past, the interpreter tends, as part of the fore-structure of his/her hermeneutics, to assimilate the past to his/her own expectations of meaning. We find this expectation of meaning in the work of Eliade, who asserts that every religion possesses a centre, a central conception which informs the entire corpus of a religious culture's myths, rituals and beliefs. Another expectation is that with any investigation of sources there is always an irreducible kernel reflecting a situation of *homo religiosus* that defies explanation and is not solely historical.[58] Thus no history of a religious phenomenon can reveal all its meaning. Eliade's distinction between modern and archaic beings fails to be reciprocal because it does not make apparent the assumed world-views of each party. There is a danger that Eliade's theory of religion and its expectation of meaning espouses a certain world-view. This presents a potential methodological problem because his world-view of authentic *homo religiosus* is used to evaluate other world-views.[59] And Eliade tends to favour the archaic, religious world-view in a nostalgic way as that which is lost to modern beings. Another meaningful expectation that Eliade brings to his task is his conviction that myths decay and symbols become secularized, although they never disappear and can be revived. As Baird makes clear, these assertions are based on an implied ontology of the sacred and its structures.[60] Another important aspect of the fore-structure of his hermeneutics is Eliade's call for a creative hermeneutics that involves certain risks for an interpreter.

TOTAL HERMENEUTICS

The history of religions, for Eliade, is a total hermeneutics, 'being called to decipher and explicate every kind of encounter of man with the sacred'.[61]

Eliade calls for a creative hermeneutics, which reaches beyond simply interpreting and understanding the religious facts to thinking about them. By allowing for the stimulation of philosophical thought, creative hermeneutics leads to a change in human beings and a source for new cultural values.[62] Besides its creative potential for the hermeneutist and as a revelation for non-apparent values on the level of immediate experience, creative hermeneutics can enable one to discover one's place in the world. If one grasps, for example, the symbolism of the cosmic tree, Eliade relates that, 'He is making a discovery that is important for his whole life. From that point on, when he looks at certain trees, he will see them as an expression of the mystery of the cosmic rhythm.'[63] This is a good example of Eliade's aesthetic vision of religion with an existential dimension.[64]

There are problems, however, with trying to execute a creative hermeneutics. There is initially a risk to the interpreter of potentially fragmenting oneself and also becoming obsessed, tempted or trapped by the subject matter that one is studying. Due to the psychic dangers confronting the interpreter, his/her activity can be compared to a quest through a labyrinth, a kind of initiatory ordeal.[65] Another obstacle for the interpreter is camouflage, the hiddenness of the sacred in the ordinary.

The theme of Eliade's novella 'The Cape', a title symbolizing covering, protecting, or shrouding in mystery, is about camouflaging meaning. In this surreal story, the Rumanian Communist Party newspaper called *Scinteia* is antedated by exactly three years with a single word changed in its logo, reading 'Dreamers of all countries unite!' This falsification causes the secret service to investigate the motivations and goals of the organizers of this perfidious plot. The secret service investigators, by practising a hermeneutics of suspicion, assume that real human motives are always hidden or camouflaged. To uncover hidden meaning one must be able to detect clues and reconstruct the actual situation. In summary, the call for a creative hermeneutics, the personal risks to the interpreter and the camouflaging of the sacred are all further evidence of the fore-structure of Eliade's hermeneutics.

Although the sacred is hidden within the world, it does reveal itself to the sensitive inquirer, who must recognize it and recover its meaning. Due to its dialectic nature, the sacred also hides itself in the very process of its revelation. The initial task of the hermeneutist is to grasp the intentional structure of the sacred by imaginatively recreating the conditions of a sacred manifestation. Since a sacred manifestation tends toward an archetype, the next task of the interpreter is not reduction but rather eidetic reintegration.[66] This implies that understanding does not occur by the reconstruction of a particular phenomenon but rather by the reintegration of a given phenomenon into its system of associations through the use of morphology. Thus a phenomenon of a given type or structure tends toward a system into which the elementary hierophanies fit. This system is always greater than the elementary hierophanies.[67] Thus the initial structure – archetype – tends towards a larger context of structural associations. As a result of this, a given archetype is not understood in terms of itself, but only occurs when the total system of associations is uncovered or reconstructed.[68] This necessarily involves comparing a single phenomenon with many similar or dissimilar phenomena until one situates it into its proper place.[69] The task of comparison is to find the universal element in the particular manifestation.[70] Thus comparison helps to elucidate the meaning that is no longer obvious due to cultural camouflage.

According to Derrida, the existence of an archetype and the activity of comparison are impossible because of the theme of *différance* in his philosophy. An archetype is too static, ahistoric, and synchronic to be compatible with the transformative nature and generative movement of *différance*, the systematic play of differences and traces of differences.[71] It is also impossible to compare religious phenomena because Eliade possesses nothing stable with which to work, since he is basically a scholar dependent upon texts. There are only ever different repetitions, a double movement of negation and affirmation. Repetition makes the presence-of-the-present possible. The phenomena that Eliade finds in religious texts are, from the viewpoint of Derrida, constituted by the play of identity and difference.

Since there are no expressions of religion to be found in a pure state, and since religious historical data survives by chance and comes to us from many different sources, the task of the historian of religions is not an easy one, a partial rationale for Eliade to call the discipline mysterious and absurd.[72] The historian of religions must not only trace the history of a particular hierophany; he/she must also understand and explain the modality of the sacred that the hierophany discloses.[73] Eliade suggests that we can only understand a given phenomenon when we are able to grasp it within its structural whole, whereas Derrida suggests that we can only understand what we deconstruct or breakdown and rebuild.

As part of the fore-structure of his hermeneutics, Eliade brings certain assumptions with him to his task. He presupposes a danger in reduction: 'Reducing historical phenomena to lower "conditioning" is to empty them of all exemplary meaning: thus, everything that is still valid and significant in human history disappears.'[74] In fact, as Fenton argues, all methods are reductive to some extent and Eliade's hieromorphic interpretations of religions are also reductionistic because 'they oversimplify the complex phenomena of religious history'.[75] Eliade also assumes and never proves that there is something irreducibly real in the world. He begs the question by stating, 'It is impossible to imagine how consciousness could appear without conferring a meaning on man's impulses and experiences. Consciousness of a real and meaningful world is intimately linked with the discovery of the sacred.'[76] Thus the world and human existence are meaningful, and the task of human beings is to search for meaning by means of hermeneutics, a recreation and discovery of meaning. According to Derrida's notion of dissemination, it is impossible for an interpreter to return to a rediscovered unity of meaning. Whatever meaning is generated it is always already divided or spilled in advance.[77]

If the dialectic of the sacred tends to repeat a series of archetypes for Eliade, the indefinite repeatability of hierophanies enables the historian of religions to understand them. This understanding is made possible by the objective nature of religious symbols and the autonomous, coherent, universal systems of symbolic associations.[78] Since hierophanies are historical manifestations, they are historically conditioned. Yet Eliade claims that structures remain the same and seek to reveal the sacred in its totality, a part of the presumed unity of religious phenomena discussed previously.[79] This permanence and continuity of archetypes enables us to participate in the religious world of another culture and interpret religious phenomena objectively.[80] Although he does not address the hermeneutical problem, Eliade implies in his work that there is no complete gap that separates the interpreter from his/her object of study. In other words, there exists no alienation between the meaning of a foreign religious text, for instance, and the understanding that an interpreter brings to a text.

There is evidence of certain anticipations in Eliade's theory of religion due to his definition of *homo religiosus*. The myths of *homo religiosus* suggest, for instance, that he/she resides in an open cosmos and is reciprocally open to the world. These dramatic narratives also convey messages about how *homo religiosus* actively communicates with divine beings and shares in the sanctity of the world. Because of the basic dichotomy between the sacred and profane ways of life, it is possible to anticipate that it necessarily follows that profane people live in a closed cosmos unable to communicate with any potentially higher beings and are separated from the holiness of the world. This kind of anticipation about profane persons is grounded in Eliade's acceptance of the basic distinction between the sacred and profane, which causes some problems with his concept of *homo religiosus*. To assert that a profane person is without transhuman meaning because such a person empties him- or herself of all religion is to oversimplify such a person's status. There are always those individuals in any religious tradition that accept some elements of belief and/or practice and do not adhere to other aspects of the tradition. We will see in Chapter 7 that Eliade's concept of archaic *homo religiosus* varies considerably from discoveries made by anthropologists.

A fundamental ontological presupposition made by Eliade, which involves the priority of being, also contains important implications for his concept of *homo religiosus*. In other words, there is nothing antecedent to the question of being. With this basic presupposition shaping his own mind and hermeneutical approach to religious phenomena, Eliade claims that *homo religiosus* possesses an ontological thirst for the real and sacred. In fact, Eliade equates religion with ontology. Besides its inherent nature, other reasons for the priority of being are its link with the cosmos and meaning. If the question of being possesses priority, if being is intertwined with the cosmos and meaning, and if *homo religiosus* yearns for being, Eliade concludes that *homo religiosus* can only live meaningfully in a sacred world. By contrasting the life of *homo religiosus* with its opposite, it necessarily follows that profane, non-religious persons do not live an authentic style of life, do not dwell in a real world, are separated from that which is real, and lead an illusory and meaningless form of existence. From a critical perspective, it can be affirmed that it is conceivable for someone to feel related, for instance, to a transhuman, non-religious, meaningful, universal force and think that one's life is meaningful.

The fore-structure of Eliade's hermeneutics influences his method of interpretation. He is accused of making normative judgements and not simply describing what manifests itself when he distinguishes authentic from inauthentic religious experience.[81] He suggests a distinction between normative and cognitive functions. By distinguishing between them, he tends to separate two functions in the process of understanding which, according to Gadamer, belong together.[82] In this process, the horizon of Eliade becomes decisive and predominant over the religious phenomena that he attempts to interpret. The hermeneutical danger is that the original intended meaning could be lost. Wilfred Cantwell Smith offers a verification principle: 'No observer's statement about a group of persons is valid that cannot be appropriated by those persons.'[83] This means that no statement about another religion is true unless members of that faith accept it. It is doubtful that Eliade would accept such a principle due to his understanding of the dialectic of the sacred. Smith's verification principle suggests that members of a religion are fully cognizant of the meaning of their religion, and this seems to be assuming too much. Hermeneutics is always a recreation and rediscovery of that which is hidden or forgotten.

CONCLUDING REMARKS

If we divorce ourselves from our discussion of Derrida for the moment, the hermeneutics of Eliade suggests overall three impressions. By his emphasis on the hermeneutical importance of archetypes, Eliade seems to imply that he is not overly interested in the intended meaning, for instance, of the author of a religious text. It is not a particular author's intended meaning that is ultimately significant, but it is rather the universal elements in a religious text that must command our attention. His hermeneutics seems to be more concerned with what is unexpressed by a text. By reliving imaginatively and emphatically the religious behaviour of another, his work also suggests that he is validating the religious experience of another person or group and coming into possession of a remote and foreign experience. And since we have been shaped by hermeneutics, we are compelled to engage in a hermeneutical adventure, an initiatory journey through a labyrinth of possible meanings. We have been shaped by hermeneutics in an existential manner and will continue to be so formed in the future.[84] Therefore, we have no choice and must continue to be part of this continuing process.

By an investigation of the fore-structure of his hermeneutics, we have noted that Eliade brings a considerable amount of pre-understanding with him to his interpretative task. The foundation of the fore-structure of his hermeneutics is his conviction that there exists a historical unity of human consciousness in which the sacred is a structural element. Since there is a basic unity underlying all religious experience, this fact involves further implications: religious attitudes form a continuity throughout history; the dialectic of the sacred is a unity, universal, repeats itself in archetypes and allows for a rediscovery of religious values; unity alleviates the hermeneutical problem of distance and the possibility of contemporaneity because an interpreter can recover past religious behaviour and can reconstruct the original circumstances of such action.

The fore-structure of Eliade's hermeneutics also possesses implications for situation and horizon. Situation does not impose a limit on the interpreter's imaginative vision. Thus Eliade is unwilling to accept the interpreter's historical conditioning and limitations as a finite historical being. Eliade's optimistic stance continues with his comprehension of horizon because we have the ability to widen our horizons by elucidating a wide number of existential situations. This ability of the interpreter involves a few important implications: we can deepen our knowledge of human nature; we can transcend cultural provincialism; we can be culturally stimulated; and we can move towards a new humanism. A danger in Eliade's hermeneutics is, however, that his normative judgements render his own horizon predominant over that of his subject matter. Thereby, there is also the possibility that the original intended meaning of a religious person or group could be lost.

An important aspect of the fore-structure of his hermeneutics is his call for a creative hermeneutics with its risks for the interpreter and the problem presented by the camouflaging of the sacred. We noted that Eliade perceives his creative hermeneutics to lead to philosophical reflection, to human transformation, to new cultural values and to greater ontological awareness. With the maximum effort necessary for knowledge and understanding on a worldwide scale, creative hermeneutics leads to a new humanism, a personal transformation of the individual as a universal norm.[85]

Eliade's hermeneutic also presupposes the danger of reductionism, and that there is something irreducibly real in the world. Another presupposition is that meaning is given or can be expected to be discovered in the world and human existence. Since archetypes remain the same, Eliade implies that there is not complete alienation between a religious text and an interpreter.

Although certain criticisms have emerged in the course of this chapter, some of the pre-understanding and assumptions that Eliade brings to religious texts and behaviour may be valid. It is, however, beyond the scope and intention of this chapter to determine which presuppositions might be valid. By attempting to retrieve the fore-structure of his hermeneutics, we have tried to throw further light upon Eliade's hermeneutics by viewing what he brings with him to his interpretative task.

With relation to our discussion of Eliade and Derrida, it should be very obvious that they are philosophically very far apart in their respective hermeneutical positions. Without repeating points already made in the preceding paragraphs, we can indicate a few of their fundamental differences.

Eliade and Derrida have very different attitudes toward the evidence that a scholar encounters and the intention of the author of a text that they might be reading. If a signifier points to merely another signifier for Derrida, and if writing represents an absence of signifier and referent, it is impossible to have evidence. From these philosophical convictions, Derrida denies the significance of an author's intention, whereas Eliade is convinced that an author intentionally places a core meaning within a text that can be deciphered by an intelligent reader without any need of sophisticated hermeneutical tools. While Eliade is on a quest for the truth, Derrida, the consummate ironist, claims that his works are nonsensical and even meaningless and are merely prefatory to the disclosure of the truth.

With his emphasis on morphological classification, Eliade can be categorized as a kind of rationalist. In contrast, Derrida subordinates rationality to spontaneity. Derrida also attacks subjectivity because there can be no point of reference for his philosophy. No position is allowed to become permanent because all positions are erased as soon as they become established, through Derrida's use of negativity. While Eliade makes use of the dialectic of the sacred and profane in his theory of religion, Derrida employs a kind of anti-dialectic by using a fourth moment, a deconstructive instant, that destroys the movement of the dialectic. By his use of morphological classification, Eliade brings diverse religious phenomena together into a meaningful whole, but Derrida's concepts continually fall apart into a multiplicity. If Eliade is concerned with finding similarities between religious phenomena, Derrida is certain that there is only *différance*. Rosen critically observes, 'Where there is only *différance*, there is no difference.'[86] What Rosen means is that if there is only Derridean *différance* all distinctions disappear and end in identity.

This general comparison of the respective positions of Eliade and Derrida enables us to understand that a conceptually constructed theory of hermeneutics is an impossibility for the latter thinker. To interpret a text for Derrida means that the interpreter produces his/her own text. This radical position sets Derrida at insurmountable odds with Eliade who is convinced that one can understand a text and capture the original author's intentions without altering the text. Besides the basic philosophical differences between these two thinkers, the lack of agreement between them cannot be traced directly to their hermeneutics but rather to their politics. Rosen makes an interesting assertion: 'Every hermeneutical program is at the same time itself a political manifesto or the corollary of a political manifesto.'[87] Derrida's radical political agenda is reflected in his anti-hermeneutical stance, whereas Eliade's emphasis on order and unity tends to expose his much more conservative position.

4 Theology of Nostalgia

As previously suggested, the history of religions is a discipline that Eliade understands in a very broad sense. It is not only concerned with the interpretation of symbols, myths and various forms of religious behaviour, but also represents the occasion for philosophical reflection. According to Eliade, a hidden agenda of his conception of the history of religions is that it embodies a theology. This chapter examines what Eliade claims is a camouflaged theology within his work.

In his journal entry of 8 November 1959, a note referring to his work *Patterns in Comparative Religion*, Eliade makes his commitment plain:

> I wonder if the secret message of the book has been understood, the 'theology' implied in the history of religions as I decipher and interpret it. And yet the meaning emerges rather clearly: myths and religions, in all their variety, are the result of the vacuum left in the world by the retreat of God, his transformation into *deus otiosus*, and his disappearance from the religious scene.[1]

In another journal entry later the same year on 5 December Eliade cites the need to isolate and identify '*the presence of the transcendent in human experience*'.[2] From a methodological perspective, these might seem to be remarkable admissions for an acknowledged historian of religions or someone involved in *Religionswissenschaft* (the science of religions). Some would argue that theology is an illegitimate task for an historian of religions, who is supposed to be concerned with an unprejudiced, empathical, objective comprehension of various kinds of religious phenomena. On the other hand, David Tracy calls attention to Eliade's work as an achievement that 'paradoxically serves a prophetic religious role to challenge the dominant prophetic, ethical, historical trajectory of Western religion in favor of its grounds in the power of manifestations'.[3]

We will not be overly concerned with the legitimacy of such an implied theology for a historian of religions. Rather we will concentrate on elucidating Eliade's implied theology by proceeding along the following path: his comprehension of the human situation; understanding of God; what he calls cosmic Christianity; and the nostalgia for paradise. This chapter does not claim that Eliade is a systematic theologian or a theological poet like Kierkegaard, a spy for the eternal. Eliade's works are, however, full of theological reflections and implications which do bear some relation to each other. We will argue that the key to understanding Eliade's theological reflections is the essential role that nostalgia plays in his ruminations. This chapter will also include a comparison of Eliade and the deconstructive a/theology of Mark C. Taylor, whose major contribution to deconstructive theology is entitled *Erring: A Postmodern A/theology*, a work that is divided into two parts. In the initial part of his book, Taylor unravels the Western theological system by means of his deconstructive method. The second part of his work – a deconstructive a/theology – represents a restoration of the first part of his book, a reformulation of theology in postmodern terms. When comparing Taylor to Eliade we will have to note what Taylor takes away in the first place of his book and what he restores in the second a/theological part of his work. A/theology is an inherently ambiguous endeavour because it represents the liminal thinking of marginal thinkers.[4] It can be construed as a cancelling of what Eliade conceives as the theological venture due to its transgressive and subversive nature, which enables a/theology to bring about change. From another perspective, a/theology is the end of theology itself.

HUMAN SITUATION

In a manner reminiscent of Tillich's method of correlation, Eliade takes religion to be the solution to every existential crisis in life because it offers exemplary, transcendental patterns.[5] The transcendental patterns act as a magnet drawing individuals out of their crucial, personal situations, and challenges them to overcome their contingent and particular condition and to adhere to the universal patterns: 'The religious solution lays the foundation for an exemplary behavior, and, in consequence, compels the man to reveal himself as both the real and the universal.'[6] Religion is a reply to the fundamental question concerning the meaning of existence.[7] Since modern beings are involved in religious crises that involve an awakening to an awareness of the absence of meaning, we must determine more fully the human situation as conceived by Eliade.

Eliade does not treat the basic human condition as characterized by sin because it is not a topic that interests him, a point he acknowledged in response to a question about original sin in a seminar of Norman O. Brown.[8] Eliade prefers to discuss the human situation in terms of fallenness. The concept of fall is used by Eliade in three basic ways but not necessarily in the Judeo-Christian sense of the concept. The initial sense of the fallenness of the human condition represents a fall from paradise, a loss of primordial perfection and a disaster. Eliade equates the fall from paradise with the rise of religion:

Religion is indeed the result of 'the fall,' 'the forgetting,' the loss of the state of primordial perfection. In paradise, Adam knew nothing of religious experience, nor of theology, that is, the doctrine of God. Before 'sin,' there was no religion.[9]

Human beings feel torn apart and separated from perfection and that which is powerful and utterly different from themselves. Thus the human condition after the fall from paradise is characterized by dissatisfaction, forgetfulness of a timeless, paradisaical condition, and separation from that which is utterly holy. This separation represents a fissure within human beings and the world.[10] Thus this initial fall involves an ontological change within beings and the structure of the world. From a mysterious unity, human beings have fallen into disunity. Within their condition of dissatisfaction, separation, forgetfulness, ontological fissure and disaster, human beings are nostalgic for their lost paradise, a paradoxical state in which contraries exist in unity.

For Taylor, we cannot begin with a fall from paradise because we must begin where we are located at the present moment. If we deconstruct Eliade's nostalgia for a lost paradise, we find ourselves in the postmodern period, a discovery that engenders in us a sense of irrevocable loss and incurable fault.[11] The time and space in which we find ourselves can be characterized as liminal in the sense that it is a time between times and a place that is no place.

The second sense of fall for Eliade corresponds to the death of God as proclaimed by Nietzsche in the nineteenth century. This prophetic proclamation means that modern beings have lost the possibility of experiencing the sacred at the conscious level.[12] The religious affection is driven into the unconscious level of existence. In his journal, Eliade reports reading Dietrich Bonhoeffer's *Letters from Prison* with approval. Bonhoeffer desperately searched for religion in everything natural, profane and rational, whereas Eliade locates religious significance in the unconscious which alone remains religious.[13]

According to Taylor, modern humanistic atheism is incomplete and inadequate because it is only a partial nihilism, which is a sign of weakness; it 'never reaches the extreme point of questioning the function of truth and the value of value'.[14] Other problems associated with humanistic atheism are its attachment to the psychology of mastery, becoming bound to an economy of domination and its irrevocable narcissism of which self-deification is its most extreme form.[15] If humanistic atheism is incomplete, inadequate and replete with problems, when did it go wrong? It did not go far enough because the humanistic atheist fails to recognize an important implication of the death of God, that is, if God is deceased so is the self.[16] Another sense in which Eliade uses fall is to refer to the fall into history or time. The fall into history reflects the awareness by modern human beings of their conditioning and victimization by the brute forces of history.[17] From another perspective, the fall of beings into time commences with the secularization of work: 'It is only in modern societies that man feels himself to be the prisoner of his daily work, in which he can never escape from Time.'[18] Thus it is history that creates obstacles for modern beings on the path to salvation, an existential problem that is expressed as the terror of history. The drama of history is devoid of enduring meaning and value because modern beings know only profane time and not the time sanctified by the incarnation of Christ.[19] As beings suffer without grasping the meaningfulness of their pain, history comes into focus as an absurd, cruel, authentic hell that provokes human despair. The only adequate response to the terror of history is faith, the highest form of freedom, because it can defend beings from the rapacious character of historical forces and enable beings to grasp sacred time or time made meaningful by the Incarnation.[20]

Taylor shares with Eliade a grim comprehension of history. History entails repression because it is connected with the denial of death by human beings.[21] Thus, history is partly the product of a negative utterance, which is the propellant power that drives history. Repression, aimlessness, unhappy consciousness, struggle against Chronos, and domination are all part of the narrative of history. With the death of God, the disappearance of the self, and the overcoming of unhappy consciousness, history, a plotless and meaningless narrative, comes to an end. The end of history is merely a play about terminating endgames. But the end of the endgame is really the commencement of a never-ending game. As part of this meaningless end-game, human beings finally affirm the end of history by a 'denial of the denial of death'.[22] If history begins with a negative utterance, it ends with the coincidence of the affirmative and negative utterances. Humans are now free to live in the present, which also involves a path of dying, because they are liberated from any neurotic obsession with past and future modes of time. Possessing the fortitude to die and thus live, it is now possible to embrace death as 'mazing grace'.

Without embracing death, Eliade deepens the tension within the terror of history by making a distinction and implied comparison between profane, non-religious beings and *homo religiosus* of archaic traditions. The profane being assumes a new existential situation by regarding oneself as the sub-ject and agent solely of history and refusing transcendence, whereas *homo religiosus* seeks to live in close proximity to the sacred. By accepting no paradigmatic models beyond humanity, a profane being makes oneself and desacralizes both oneself and the world. Such a person leads a tragic existence:

> The sacred is the prime obstacle to his freedom. He will become himself only when he is totally demysticized. He will not be truly free until he has killed the last God.[23]

As a product of the desacralization of human existence and the world, the profane being forgets that one is still a product of religion, something that *homo religiosus* never forgets. By trying to be empty of all religion, the profane being loses all transhuman meaning.[24] Although the profane person opposes *homo religiosus*, such an individual remains an inheritor of religion because one remains a product of the past and cannot abolish history.

Not all profane beings are completely irreligious. They do not lose their religious inheritance and they continue to cling to pseudo-religions and degenerate mythologies and rituals. There are, for instance, the festivities connected with the New Year celebration, the revelry of a marriage or the birth of a child, the pseudo-religion of Marxism, the private mythologies of dreams and fantasies, the escape from time provided by reading and the nostalgia for paradise exemplified by nudism. The cinema often utilizes the mythical battle motif of a struggle between a paradigmatic hero and monster, as in *Star Wars* or the Indiana Jones films. In contrast to such profane beings, *homo religiosus* of archaic traditions lives on a twofold plane: 'It takes its course as human existence and, at the same time, shares in a transhuman life, that of the cosmos or the gods.'[25] Living in an open cosmos and open to the world, *homo religiosus* is accessible to cosmic experiences. This means that *homo religiosus* is in active communication with divine being and shares in the sanctity of the world.[26] *Homo religiosus* is comfortable in the cosmos because such a person lives at the centre of the world: 'To attain to the centre of the World means, therefore to arrive at the "point of departure" of the cosmos at the "beginning of Time"; in short, to have abolished Time.'[27] By periodically abolishing time through the repetition of cosmogonic acts, *homo religiosus* defends him- or herself against time, devalues time, manifests an anti-historical attitude, does not accept him- or herself as only a historical being and lives in a constant present.[28] *Homo religiosus* lives at the juncture of the *axis mundi*, the meeting-point of heaven, earth and hell. By being at the centre of the world, *homo religiosus* is near to heaven, can move from one cosmic region to another, can communicate with divine beings, and lives in the sacred zone of absolute reality.[29] In contrast to profane beings, life for *homo religiosus* is meaningful. Eliade's understanding of *homo religiosus* betrays a nostalgic attitude towards archaic religious beings. In fact, Kenneth Hamilton accuses Eliade of a theological bias precisely because he appeals to archaic and Oriental cultures in order to demonstrate the poverty of modern religious experience.[30]

The human condition of the profane person is best expressed, according to Eliade, as a series of initiation trials or ordeals, that is, of deaths and rebirths.[31] From one perspective, initiation trials represent a search for a centre, a repository of the sacred. Since the path to the centre is guarded by demonic beings or defended by labyrinths, it is a dangerous journey.[32] The search for the centre and the prototype for modern beings, for Eliade, is Ulysses:

> His journey was a journey toward the center, searching for Ithaca – which is to say, searching for himself. He was a good navigator, but fate – in other words, the ordeals of initiation he had to go through – forced him again and again to defer to his return home. I think the myth of Ulysses is very important for us all. We shall all of us turn out to be a little like Ulysses, seeking for ourselves, hoping to reach the end of our journey, and then, when we reach our home and homeland once again, no doubt discovering our selves. But, as with the labyrinth, as with every quest, there is a danger that we may lose ourselves. If one does succeed in emerging from the labyrinth, in finding one's way back home, then one becomes another being.[33]

How do we reach our homeland? In a sense, we are already there because the homeland, for every exile, is language.[34] Since there is no tension or contradiction between the world and homeland, the centre is where one finds oneself in language. 'As long as you are in that center, you are at home, you are truly in the real *self* and at the center of the cosmos.'[35] This road home to our centre is arduous and fraught with dangerous perils. In his autobiography, Eliade refers to his own personal experience:

> The last events in Bhawanipore now seemed to me like a long wandering in a labyrinth. I felt that I should not be able to get out of that labyrinth until I should have returned to the 'center.' I must at all costs 'concentrate' myself, regain my true center.[36]

The profane, illusionary, and phenomenal existence of modern individuals can be transformed into a new, real, enduring form of life, from profane to sacred, from religious death to life.

If the search for one's centre is a journey to find one's true self, for Eliade, it suggests that there might be something substantial and real to be discovered. According to Taylor, the search for the self leads to the discovery of the absence of self, which cannot become totally present to itself because the presence represents a trace. Why is this the case? Any trace is a result of the interplay of identity and difference. Therefore, within the presence there is always absence. If God can be conceived as the absolute centre of existence, and if God is dead, this absence means that there cannot be an absolute centre for Taylor.[37] Furthermore, the self cannot achieve authentic selfhood because it can never be itself due to the absence of the absolute other. Moreover, if it is necessary for the self to become present to itself in order for it to become itself, any achievement of genuine selfhood is a re-presentation because identity entails repetition.[38] This means that the self can only become itself by doubling itself and becoming itself the same. The self-presentation of the self to itself is a duplicitous endeavour because: 'There is always difference *within* identity and absence *within* presence.'[39] Instead of self-presentation, repetition and re-presentation result in a depresentation that leads to disruption and dislocation, which suggests that within this scenario one cannot possibly secure self-presence. Repetition and a re-presentation that turns out to be a de-presentation suggest that one's search must necessarily lead to the discovery of the absence of self.

After shattering the concept of the self, one is left with a mere trace, an opening of space for Taylor. 'Within the space of the trace is inscribed a cross that marks the site of the disappearance of the self.'[40] Self-presence is forever haunted by the ominous shadow of eternal death, the absence and outside that is always also respectively present and inside. In other words, eternal death is the coincidence of opposites, the unity of identity and difference. The cross that marks the absence of the self is not connected to any christological symbolism; it rather signifies death of the self, which cannot find its identity due to the absence of relationship to a transcendent being. The cross also suggests preeminence of the mark of death upon the living present.

In contrast to Taylor, Eliade depicts a more hopeful scenario. Although the road to the centre or home is arduous, the rite of passage that symbolizes the journey of life ends on a hopeful note for Eliade, who is confident in the creative power of the mind. This creative power enables one to remain free in any circumstances.[41] To be cognizant of one's freedom means to be a creative spirit, unleashed from the crush of industrial society, morally regenerated, existentially reborn and hopeful.

DEUS OTIOSUS

That a man who holds opinions like these should be regarded by some (Altizer is a good example)[42] as an atheistic theologian or a death-of-god theologian seems preposterous, yet such has been Eliade's fate at the hands of some of his colleagues. When they correctly see that Eliade has an implied theology, how can they misread him so badly? The interpretations are so patently extreme that, with Ricketts[43] but drawing upon subsequent material as well, one simply cannot resist an extreme response. Not only are such attitudes far from products of new insights but they represent a stance toward the sacred which Eliade has treated and refused as simply another version of the *deus otiosus*, the remote, withdrawn deity.

It is necessary to look at what Eliade says rather than at what one might attribute to him for as little reason as deconstructionists often offer. He enumerates three basic characteristics of the *deus otiosus*: (1) God withdraws to the sky after creating the world and human beings; (2) this withdrawal is sometimes accompanied by a disruptive break in communication between one cosmic region and another; (3) since the withdrawn deity is forgotten by humans, its place is taken by various divinities closer to human beings.[44] Having lost religious actuality and significance, the withdrawn deity plays no part in the cults and myths of the religious culture.[45] God's remoteness and non-actuality are equivalent to his death. Nevertheless, this withdrawal of God from contact with the world and its inhabitants inaugurates true religion because the vacuum created by God's withdrawal is filled by other divine beings.[46]

The divine withdrawal and remoteness expresses historically the increasing interest that humans take in their own religious, cultural and economic discoveries. The discovery of agriculture, for instance, transforms human economy and attitudes towards the earth and its fertile, life-giving powers by *homo religiosus*. 'Religious experience becomes more concrete, that is, more intimately connected with life.'[47] This implies that *homo religiosus* in turn withdraws from the remote, transcendent deity and is more concerned with the concrete aspects of religion. Although the withdrawn deity disappears and is essentially forgotten, its memory survives and is camouflaged in myths and symbols. Sky symbolism manifests, for instance, the sacred divinity in height, ascension and centre symbolism.[48]

By reviewing the characteristics of the *deus otiosus*, it is evident that the death of God is not a recent phenomenon acknowledged only in the works of philosophers and theologians nor is it some type of radical innovation. Death-of-God pronouncements are surely an unconscious revival of the *deus otiosus* known in the history of religions, an excellent example of the process of desacralization, the final camouflaging of the sacred and its complete identification with the profane. The death-of-God theology is a drastically secularized version of the myth of the *deus otiosus*.[49]

If the death of God is not a new phenomenon in the history of religions for Eliade, it is not fully adequate for Taylor because humanistic atheism never goes far enough. Humanistic atheism fails to perceive the implications of the momentous news of God's death because it does not comprehend that the death of God involves at the same time the death of the self, the end of history, the closure of scripture, and the meaninglessness of life. Humanistic atheism also fails to recognize that, by experiencing God as death rather than as life, the atheist is actually denying death: 'If God is death, then the murder of God seems to be the denial of, or flight from, death.'[50] The wholly other, master of human slaves, does not manifest itself as spirit, august, nor *mysterium tremendum* because the death of God suggests not only the personal death of God or a tragedy that God alone suffers. In other words, the death of God signifies something more. Taylor seems to suggest that the death of God is a symbol of something more awesome: the equivalence of God's death and death itself. Thus, the death of God is more than the sorrowful demise of an ultimate being because God becomes death. It is death/nothingness that now assumes dominion as the absolute master.[51] And from this eternal shadow of death, humans flee and give up their struggle to gain their autonomy. The humanistic atheist's flight from eternal death represents a feeble effort to deny death. A direct result of the death of God is that the highest values devalue themselves.[52] Thus one is left with the ominous spectre of eternal nothingness.

As stated earlier, Eliade was placed within the death-of-God group by Altizer, an identification that Eliade rejects explicitly in his works. In his journal for 13 May 1966, Eliade acknowledges reading Altizer's book entitled *The Gospel of Christian Atheism*, but tells us that the book did not initially take hold of him for some unknown reason.[53] Not until almost a year later does Eliade provide an answer in his journal with an entry on 4 April 1967:

> Have I already noted these lines from Heidegger's *Holzwege* that Tom Altizer should meditate on? In any case I'm recopying them here: 'Hier stirbt das Absolute. Gott ist tot. Das sagt alles andere, nur nicht: es gibt keinem Gott.' (This is where the Absolute meets death. God is dead. And this means everything except 'there is no God!').[54]

This implies that Eliade cannot accept the death of God and its radical implications for human existence. If God is dead, according to the deconstructionist theology of Taylor, the self is absent, history is ended, scripture is closed and life is meaningless. In contrast, Eliade cannot accept these implications because human existence implies the search for meaning and meaninglessness is anti-human.[55]

Eliade is not, however, a theologian or philosopher in the traditional sense. Unlike Anselm, Aquinas, Descartes and Kant who tried to prove the existence of God, Eliade's attitude does not suggest that he favours a philosophical proof. Eliade refers to the definition of God given by Saint Sylvester, that is, God is like an onion because He is good and makes you cry. According to Eliade, this is a good illustration of negative theology: that nothing can be affirmed of God. Since God is indefinable, we can say anything whatever about Him, even that He is like an onion.[56] Proofs are naive and dangerous because one might falsely imagine that one knows a specific item about God. It is far better to leave everything in suspension and to be content with personal certitudes.[57] Why should we leave talk about God in this condition? Eliade seems to suggest that if we could clearly define God we would lose the mystery.

Although Eliade is opposed to the classical arguments for God's existence, he does prefer a way of referring to God, who can be defined as the *coincidentia oppositorum*, the co-existence of contraries. An archaic formula for wholeness and the conjoining of male and female sexuality is expressed, for instance, by androgyny, a symbol of perfection, autonomy, strength, and union of opposites. Another example is, of course, Jesus Christ, the God-man and most perfect hierophany. The *coincidentia oppositorum* formula is the best way to understand God because it lucidly demonstrates that God can only be grasped as a paradox that is beyond rational comprehension and ultimately represents a mystery.[58] Since the *coincidentia oppositorum* defies rational comprehension and leaves only a mystery, the union of opposites is a symbolic way of referring to God. And this symbolic expression often becomes a nostalgic wish by human beings to recover a lost unity or a nostalgia for a lost paradise.[59]

According to Taylor, due to the death of God and the disappearance of the transcendent being, an opening is created that allows the word embodied in scripture to fill the vacuum. This vacuum-filling word is the incarnational-divine word that enables us to realize the death of the transcendent God, the wholly other. This radically incarnate word represents an inscription, a script to be enacted. The embodied word, forever liminal and playful, is 'a play within a play, a play that is forever an interplay'.[60] The play of the incarnate word represents a play of differences that joins and separates opposites, and that both forms and reforms the word itself.

COSMIC CHRISTIANITY

As we have noted, religion begins with a fall from original paradise for Eliade. Humans become forgetful and are ontologically separated from the holy and themselves as they fall into disunity. Regarding themselves as solely historical beings and wishing to live in a desacralized world, modern beings have lost touch with the sacred. With the death of God, humans cannot experience the sacred on a conscious level and only the unconscious remains religious. Because humans have fallen into history, they are subject to its brutal forces and must confront the terror of history, a living hell that provokes despair. Christianity is the religion of fallen humans because modern beings are irremediably identified with history and progress and a rejection of the paradise expressed in archetypes.[61] Although Western Christianity is too deeply rooted to be shaken by criticism, Eliade feels distant sometimes from its spirit.[62] Eliade does, however, express a nostalgia for what he calls cosmic Christianity or cosmic religion.

As humans journey through the labyrinth of history, they search for a centre by following an initiatory pattern. According to Eliade, we find our centre in cosmic Christianity, a place where, unlike the *deus otiosus*, Jesus is not remote. There is no possibility of finding one's centre in cosmic Christianity or any other entity in Taylor's theology because the self is decentred, an occurrence caused by the death of God. Taylor's decentred, deindividualized self is co-relative and codependent and finds itself within a web of multiple and constantly changing relations.[63] Once the self-identical self is deconstructed, what kind of self appears for Taylor? He answers that it is a 'subject that is formed, deformed, and reformed by the eternal play of differences'.[64] Having lost its identity, the self is a mere trace – both present and absent – and bears the marks of marginality: centreless; abnormal; errant (e.g. self is a trickster or thief); and anonymous.[65] Since the deconstructed self is a mere trace within an ever-changing network of traces, it is caught in a marginal, nowhere land of liminality where one is an anonymous, impersonal entity. In sharp contrast, cosmic Christianity, a natural religion as conceived by Eliade, developed from the interaction between Christianity in Central and Western Europe and folk religions of rural areas. In tune with the cosmic rhythms, this popular religion perceived nature as the good work of God and not as a realm of sin. Agricultural peasant gods and heroes are transformed into saints, the fertility goddesses are assimilated to the Virgin Mary or female saints, religious behaviour is celebrated in the feasts of the Church and incorporated into the cult of saints.[66] The dogmatic teachings of the Church play a minor role, and history is ignored. Nature is more important and a source of goodness because it is sanctified by the presence, death, and resurrection of Jesus, giving living matter, life and the world a religious dimension.[67] The Christ of the peasants of Eastern Europe is non-historical, participates in the mysteries of life, and is present in the sacraments. This cosmic Christianity is not a new form of paganism, not a pagan–Christian syncretism, nor a paganization of Christianity, it is rather the impregnation of the peasant ancestral religion by the Christian spirit.[68]

The aura of nostalgia pervades cosmic Christianity because a nostalgia for a sanctified nature made sacred by the presence of Jesus dominates the attitudes of the peasants. There is also a nostalgia for paradise, a place apart from the terrors of history.[69] These nostalgic attitudes are examples of a passive revolt against the cataclysmic tragedies and injustices of history. Within this religion, our nostalgia for the mystery of God is satisfied by the sanctification of nature made by the presence of Jesus. Our nostalgia for the lost unity of the *coincidentia oppositorum* is also satisfied as we rediscover a unity with nature.

Eliade intimates in his works that he shares the nostalgias of the Rumanian peasants. He knows, however, that cosmic Christianity does not only exist in places like rural Rumania, but is also to be found in India, in Mediterranean religion, in Negro spirituals, and even in urban centres because, even though urbanites no longer share the values of agricultural society, the rhythms of nature – day and night and the change of seasons – still prevail.[70] Therefore, cosmic religion remains a concern for modern individuals. The best contemporary exemplification of cosmic religion is the theology of Teilhard de Chardin, which represents a resanctification of the world, life and matter.[71] Thus Eliade perceives a spiritual connection between a Christian theologian and Rumanian peasants. The mystery and holiness of nature is rediscovered in modern art by Chagall, who does not lose the sacred, primeval and maternal aspects of nature.[72]

If the Christian faith with its emphasis on the significance of history fails to answer our existential needs, is the cosmic Christianity of European peasants, even if such a religion is as idyllic as Eliade seems to imply, a viable alternative? It is highly doubtful that European peasants would admit to living in anything near a paradisaical condition. Since agricultural work is laborious and success uncertain because of natural forces beyond one's control, it is uncertain that any great number of people would perceive cosmic Christianity as a viable option and anything more than an unrealistic fantasy. Eliade's nostalgic theological reflections are shaped by a vision of a rustic past of peasants living in harmony with nature and a view of archaic *homo religiosus* that is of questionable authenticity.[73] Moreover, it seems unlikely that modern beings shaped by the historical events of the twentieth century and technological advances could recapture an agricultural frame of mind. Since humans cannot go back to an idyllic agricultural age, we seem to have two choices: either going forward with purpose and courage or aimlessly wandering through the labyrinth of human existence.

In contrast to Eliade, the marginal, wandering, erring individual of Taylor's conception roams within a divine milieu, a complex web of inter-relations, that marks liminal space and time.[74] Within the divine milieu, all is relative, nothing is itself, nothing possesses self-identity or presence, everything is subject to eternal recurrence and time becomes eternity and vice versa. Due to its liminal and marginal nature, it is paradoxical and cannot be captured by extremes, which suggests that it represents a middle way.[75] The divine milieu, a medium of all presence and absence, of a/theology, is also an acentric totality because it never had a fixed centre and never will.[76] Taylor equates it with scripture and writing, which implies that it is a kenotic process, an emptying of absolute self-identity and self-presence that suggests it cannot be an absolute point of origin.[77] From this a/theological perspective, Taylor appears to have eliminated any possibility of nostalgia. Moreover, the divine milieu is an eternally recurring drama that is creative and destructive.

NOSTALGIA FOR PARADISE

Can we return to an idyllic age? Eliade seems to think we can. He thinks that *homo religiosus* of archaic religions lived in a kind of paradise where communication existed between heaven and earth. The encounter with divine beings was made 'possible by the ascension to heaven, and one was friends with the animals and possessed a knowledge of their language. The archaic individual was also in harmony with nature, which created in one a sense of cosmic relatedness. In one's mystical solidarity with nature, one was comfortably at home in the world and enjoyed a spiritual plenitude. By an indefinitely repeated invocation of archetypes, *homo religiosus* could remain near the real and meaningful. According to Eliade, modern beings would like to recapture and relive the paradisaical state summarized in the preceding assertions. To return to a primordial period and to an original plenitude, freedom and beatitude are the ardent wish of modern beings overwhelmed by the meaninglessness of profane existence. Such a concrete paradise can be gained in the present moment on earth. Eliade observes:

The longing for Paradise can be traced even in the most banal actions of the modern man. Man's concept of the *absolute* can never be completely uprooted: it can only be debased. And primitive spirituality lives on in its own way not in action, not as a thing man can effectively accomplish, but as a *nostalgia* which creates things that become values in themselves: art, the sciences, social theory, and all the other things to which men will give the whole of themselves.[78]

By returning to the beginning to find one's roots, one demonstrates a desire to begin anew and to regain the lost paradise of the primordial period. On what basis does Eliade make this claim for modern beings? The foundation for his observation is grounded in his understanding of the nature of the sacred. The dialectic of the sacred reveals the nostalgia for paradise.[79] Eliade's convictions about the nostalgia of modern beings for paradise are also based in his own personal experience.

In his autobiography, Eliade acknowledges his pride that he is only three generations removed from Rumanian peasants, which made him feel close to the soul of the country.[80] Descended from a family of Moldavian yeomen, he would remind himself of his family heritage when he experienced moods of deep melancholy in adolescence.[81] Thus Eliade's own personal nostalgia for paradise – the cosmic Christianity of Rumanian peasants – is by his own admission precious to him. One wonders, however, whether a commitment with so few experiential roots can suffice to ground a theology. Eliade was born in Bucharest and lived most of his life in the city, within its literary and scholarly milieu, with time out for adventure in India. Although he refers to the pleasure of hiking and climbing mountains in the summer, most of his life was spent in just this urban environment. Therefore, he really does not claim any first-hand knowledge of peasant culture, in fact, he tells us in his autobiography that his most experiential connection with the life-world of Rumanian peasants resulted from talking and making friends with Rumanian males while in the army. Even were Eliade nearly correct about the modern individual's quest for paradise, much of what he reports suggests that he discusses more about his own nostalgia than about any general human nostalgia.

Eliade suggests that he knows this. He is much too good a scholar not to recognize the diaphanous character of his nostalgia. We would do him greater justice if we understood his nostalgia as the occasion for achieving a new maieutics, a giving birth to ideas latent in the mind, in order to awaken and renew human consciousness to the archaic symbols and archetypes living or dormant in the mind of all humankind.[82] He perceives the nostalgia for paradise as an ancient archetype hidden within the human mind trying to come forth. This new maieutics, or the more comprehensive term metapsychoanalysis, is envisioned as giving birth to a new authentic and complete human being, becoming conscious of a common spirituality, and rescuing one from cultural provincialism and historical and existential relativism.[83] This vision is a proposal for a resacralization and remythologization of contemporary culture.[84] It is within the context of these goals that the nostalgia of paradise must be understood. Eliade's theological reflections suggest that they are the product of his religious imagination shaped by his understanding of archaic religion as well as by a nostalgia for paradise. Due to his cosmopolitan background, his criticism of cultural provincialism and his existential relativism, Eliade's theological reflections and nostalgia for the cosmic Christianity of Rumanian peasants is open to suspicion and suggests a possible camouflaging of his own theological position. Eliade's mind and body are in the twentieth century, but his heart is in the *illud tempus* of archaic religion.

Rather than nostalgically wishing for a return to a lost origin, Taylor claims that for an a/theology to be affirmative it must proclaim play in a careless manner. The unending game that represents play can be witnessed in the drama of the death of God, loss of self, end of history and the play of differences characteristic of scripture. Play is purposeless, meaningless, useless and non-serious.[85] Although a player needs no goals, play involves risk and insecurity, features that dramatically manifest themselves when the player experiences loss of self.[86] The completely gratuitous and frivolous nature of play disseminates by means of the incarnate word and creates a delirium that in turn generates a world of carnival, an inverted liminal space and time.[87] Traditional values, hierarchies, and meanings are inverted and upset and, if radicalized, become a perversion that is subversive.[88] Within the frivolity of play, Eliade's distinction between sacred and profane, for instance, would be subverted and inform one that nothing is forever sacred and simply profane. In other words, the sacred would become irreducibly ambiguous because it could be holy and filthy. The free play of erring helps one to realize 'mazing grace'. It is to be bewildered, delirious, and deluded. It is also to erringly wander through a never-ending labyrinth that is by nature an abyss.[89] Taylor's emphasis on play, carnival, carnality and mazing are reasons for wonder. What kind of life emerges from the spirit of play? With his conservative inclinations, Eliade might ask about ethics and might also indicate the potential danger of play turning into a hedonistic style of life. If the whole of historical existence is without purpose, meaning, centre or telos, any kind of decadence is permissible.

CONCLUDING TRACES

For Taylor, history possesses no pure origin, no final end, and no centre.[90] The end of history marks the beginning of erring and vice versa. The serpentine wandering characteristic of the path of erring means that one is always tracing and retracing the margin. This wandering inexorably leads one astray and thus to a state of failure. Unlike the straight path of Quranic Islam, erring is a roaming that eventuates in deviating from one's intended path and causing one to miss one's intended mark.[91] If Eliade's nostalgic vision embodies a settled, pastoral kind of existence, Taylor is convinced that we are condemned to a nomadic form of existence in which there is no absolute beginning or ultimate end. The nomad's task always remains unfinished because such an individual continues to fail, to blunder and go astray.[92] The nomad is forever homeless, rootless, without ground or map because he/she cannot find his/her centre of existence. Taylor's position suggests that deconstruction saves one in order to wander, which is an inversion of the Protestant ethic of work as salvation.

Taylor's a/theological self, a marking and a trace, is a perfectly adequate concept for a nihilistic philosophical position because his notion of the self is Kafkaesque in its emphasis on the impersonal nature and non-uniqueness of the self. In Taylor's world we would all be Kafka-like numbers without personal identity. To be a bit more frivolous or a/theological, only a nihilistic mother could love Taylor's self. Anyone convinced by Martin Buber's assertion that one achieves real being within the primal reality of the *Zwischenmenschliche*, the 'between man and man', where dialogue and love arise, cannot be enamoured with Taylor's concept of the disappearance of the self. There does not seem to be any possibility for meaningful encounters or dialogical exchanges with such a silent, wandering trace. If there can be no meaningful exchange of messages between unique selves, there seems to be little hope of attempting to solve the problems of society. Within this bleak type of scenario, suicide, an embrace of death by which Taylor is so fascinated, becomes the only authentic, nihilist option. Moreover, if there is no self, Taylor can have no knowledge with which to write any type of theology.

Although we can characterize Eliade's christology as heterodox, Taylor's radical christology is heretical because the embodied word is not a singular event for all time, is restricted to a specific space and time, and is not restricted to a particular historical person. Taylor envisions christology as a continual process.[93] Therefore, the Christ-event is not unique in world history. Taylor would agree that his heretical christology is a real possibility of travelling the erring path. Just as God and self disappear and history ends,

Christ must pass away. Why? If the radical incarnated word embodies presence and absence, the word can only appear by disappearing.[94] Therefore, the process of kenosis can only become complete when the divine incarnation empties itself.

The theological efforts of both Eliade and Taylor produce theologies or an a/theology in the latter's case without love. Whereas nostalgia seems to take the place of love for Eliade, Taylor's a/theology is bereft of love but contains a plethora of negativity by its very nature. Taylor gives the impression of being enamoured of death, formerly God, and recalls the character Aimee Thanatogenos (as her name indicates, a lover of death with a very bad memory for living faces) of Evelyn Waugh's disparaging and irreverent novel about the death-industry in America entitled *The Loved One* with its supercilious characters. Taylor offers others a twisted path of no love or salvation for the post-theistic period.

Taylor's deconstructive a/theology represents the dissemination of Derrida's philosophy into the sphere of theology. According to Derrida, to disseminate is to spill in advance and to scatter the seed or sperm without an initial insemination because primal insemination is already dissemination.[95] Since Taylor's deconstructive a/theology represents a dissemination of Derrida's thought, his a/theology can be construed as a rapidly wiggling sperm anxiously looking without success for a womb to fertilize. Wandering endlessly like a sperm/serpent without hope of finding a centre/womb, Taylor is condemned to travel on a meaningless quest for traces without the comfort of knowing that his seed will help create further theological life. But this is exactly his nihilist point: this is the end.

5 Dialogue and the Other

From a small village in central China to a mansion in West Palm Beach, Florida on the north American continent, modern technology continually brings all the inhabitants of the world closer together. The morning and evening television newscasts inform Americans, for instance, what important events are occurring in Japan, India, Russia and the Middle East. International commerce, diminishing natural resources, and politics bind all global residents into a smaller unity. A more dramatic form of world unity is created by the awesome threat of a nuclear war. If we recall the nuclear plant disaster at Chernobyl in Russia and the spread of its radiation to many parts of the world, it does not take much imagination to concoct a more disastrous scenario for nuclear warfare. In the worst-case scenario, a nuclear war could be the ultimate holocaust. Therefore, all humankind shares potentially a common calamitous fate.

Our interconnected, shrinking world and the fact of religious pluralism have awoken a more global ecumenical consciousness and alerted world inhabitants to the need for religious dialogue. Many Western thinkers have joined in the dialogue with Eastern religions through participation in international conferences and sharing of ideas through books and essays on the subject. The need for ecumenical dialogue has been addressed on a larger scale by the World Council of Churches and after Vatican II by the Roman Catholic Church.

A variety of learned opinions recognizes the need for cross-cultural dialogue. Gordon D. Kaufman, a Protestant theologian, asserts that dialogue is necessary because no individual of any religious tradition possesses absolute truth. We have insights and understandings inherited from our religious ancestors, which are finite, limited, relative and imaginative constructions.[1] Hans Küng, a renowned Catholic theologian because of the controversy that his work sparked with the Papacy, agrees with Kaufman that no one person possesses the full truth. Thus we need to be on our way to a greater truth by means of a mutually responsible dialogue.[2] However, Wilfred Cantwell Smith finds dialogue inadequate because it is too polarized and merely represents a transition stage. He prefers the term 'colloquy' because it is less confrontational and connotes more a sense of mutually confronting problems.[3] Nonetheless, colloquy still implies conversation between participants.

If it is granted that there is a need for dialogue or something similar to it, what should its aim and nature be? According to Jürgen Moltmann, the aim of dialogue is to create a climate for a life of fellowship in which mutual participation, exchange, and cross-fertilization become possible.[4] Although not necessarily disagreeing with Moltman, most thinkers tend to agree with Raimundo Panikkar that the aim of dialogue must be understanding:

> The aim of the intrareligious dialogue is understanding. It is not to win over the other or to come to a total agreement or a universal religion. The ideal is communication in order to bridge the gulfs of mutual ignorance and misunderstandings between the different cultures of the world. . . .[5]

Ninian Smart agrees that mutual understanding does not necessarily involve increased agreement among the partners.[6] If most would agree that mutual understanding is a desirable goal, there is less agreement among ecumenical writers as to the exact nature of dialogue.

Donald K. Swearer sets forth certain requisites for a dialogue: (1) being engaged by the faith of another; (2) an awareness of the uniqueness of one's own faith.[7] On the other hand, Hans Waldenfels claims that dialogue cannot be made to conform to a plan with deliberate advanced programmed results. By entering a dialogue selflessly and not intending to win, participants should simply allow the truth to emerge.[8] Winston L. King calls dialogue an attitude that includes the following elements: (1) an empathetic approach to another religious tradition; (2) some component of experiential encounter (e.g. shared worship, meditation); (3) the opening of oneself to spiritual change through existential contact.[9] In the twilight of his career, Paul Tillich enumerated four presuppositions that must be met for an authentic dialogue: (1) acknowledgement of the value of each religion by the participants; (2) serious confrontation with total conviction; (3) common ground; (4) openness to criticism.[10] Although our common humanity as religious beings is sufficient reason for engaging in dialogue grounded in respect, John B. Cobb, Jr, the Whiteheadian process theologian, calls for us to go beyond dialogue by means of dialogue in order to avoid a stagnant dialogue.[11] In fact, Cobb suggests that authentic dialogue embodies a dynamic nature that transports us beyond itself because real 'dialogue changes its participants in such a way that new developments beyond dialogue must follow.'[12]

In contrast to Cobb's position, Raimundo Panikkar calls for a dialogical dialogue, a relational witnessing to the truth. He explains, 'Dialogue does not seek to be primarily *duo-logue*, a duet of two *logoi*, which could still be dialectical; but a *dia-logos*, a piercing of the *logos* to attain a truth that transcends it.'[13] Dialogue is not a pair of speeches; it is a process of transcending the *logos* (thought) by going through it to the *pneuma* (unthinkable spirit).[14] The goal of dialogical dialogue is understanding, which necessitates judging the other's view to be somewhat true. 'Accordingly, to understand is to be converted to the truth one understands.'[15] Panikkar is making a huge leap from understanding to conversion to the truth, a leap that a thinker like Eliade would not make. Listening, observing, correcting, and being corrected are all part of the dynamics of dialogue.[16] Panikkar refers to this dialogue as 'intra-religious' instead of interreligious dialogue. The former represents an inner dialogue within oneself when one enters a religious dialogue by questioning oneself and one's beliefs, accepting the challenge of possible change and risking one's traditional way of life.[17] Thus dialogue involves understanding the other and oneself.

Panikkar's dialogical dialogue is rejected by Carl A. Raschke, who contends that it represents an intention rather than a deliberate method.[18] Instead, Raschke proposes a hermeneutical dialogy, which embodies a definite theological dimension. Hermeneutical dialogy, an intuition of unity through diversity, seeks to widen parameters, integrate findings, and cut through the sedimented layers of language and experience to get to that which is ontologically prior to representations. Raschke explains:

> A hermeneutical dialogy transcends mere dialogue in as much as it is fundamentally a project of interpretative disclosure. It is not simply conversation, but an adventure with *logos*. It is the opening of dialogical speech to the event of presencing that activates religious language. It is a clearing away of semantic space for the emergence of divine 'truth' as *alētheia* (literally, 'unconcealment').[19]

Following Heidegger's notion of 'thinking the unthought', Raschke wants to think the event of divine manifestation, a form of incarnate thinking.[20] This implies exposing the unthought meaning of truth, or embodied, interpersonal, dialogical witness to *logos*.

The dialogic encounter is not without its dangers and problems. There is the potential danger of polemics and proselytizing, if one figure claims superiority for one's religion.[21] A very subtle rendition of such a pretentious claim is the position of Karl Rahner and his assertion that non-Christians are anonymous Christians because there are grace-filled elements in non-Christian religions, exposing their members to the influence of divine grace.[22] The Protestant theologian Wolfhart Pannenberg states that the single God of Jesus is revealed in all religions. As part of his programme to stress the process of change throughout history, Pannenberg affirms that non-Christian religions perceive the revelation of the one God only in a fragmentary way.[23] Or the claims by Panikkar that Christians and Hindus only meet in Christ because within Hinduism itself is the presence of Christ in so far as it is a true religion. Thus a genuine Hindu is only saved by

Christ and not by Hinduism, and Hinduism culminates in Christianity.[24] Linbeck criticizes such assertions: 'There is something arrogant about supposing that Christians know what nonbelievers experience and believe in the depths of their beings better than they know themselves, and that therefore the task of dialogue or evangelism is to increase their self-awareness.'[25] The professions of superior truth follow the 'dungeon' approach, according to Paul Clasper, that lends itself to authoritarianism and dogmatism.[26] Clasper prefers the metaphor of the round table with its open discussions. A former missionary himself, Clasper would add a hearth to the room with a round table in order to emphasize the sharing aspect of dialogue. Another problem, according to King, is that Buddhists, for instance, seem largely uninterested in Christian doctrine and experience.[27] Since dialogue must be a mutual encounter, a lack of participation by one party leads to only a monologue. Although he claims that his endeavour is merely a beginning of dialogue, the intended dialogue between Hans Küng and other German scholarly experts representing Islam, Hinduism and Buddhism is a failure because the book does not include believing representatives of the non-Christian traditions.[28] It is also a failure at dialogue because, although Küng responds to the European scholar's positions, the selected experts do not respond to Küng. There is thus none of the give-and-take which is characteristic of genuine dialogue. Another problem inherent in cross-cultural dialogue is language. John Hick argues, for instance, that God, the Eternal One, is perceived in diverse cultures under personal and non-personal forms. Although he asserts that he is using the term God in a non-theistic sense, Hick claims, 'God is neither a person nor a thing, but is the transcendent reality which is conceived and experienced by different human mentalities in both personal and non-personal ways.'[29] If Hick insists on using the term God, a dialogue with representatives of Advaita Vedānta Hinduism or non-devotional Buddhism would appear to be difficult, although not a total impossibility.

In the remainder of this chapter I want to examine Eliade's contribution to cross-cultural dialogue and what he means by hermeneutical dialogue. The work of Eliade is not usually thought of as being concerned with cross-cultural dialogue. In fact, his work in the history of religions is permeated by an ecumenical spirit, and he perceives his own work as dialogical in nature. It can be fairly stated that he is a neglected contributor to cross-cultural dialogue, and this aspect of his work needs to be acknowledged and examined.

We also want to compare Eliade's grasp of the nature of dialogue with the more recent theories of Julia Kristeva, a postmodernist thinker, and the later work of Jürgen Habermas, a prominent second-generation representative of the Frankfurt School of thought, on his theory of communicative action, in order to make clear the unique features of the contributions of all three thinkers. Although the philosophies of Kristeva and Habermas are very different, they do seem to share the opinion that Marx and Freud are complementary. Whereas Kristeva uses Freudian insights as developed by Jacques Lacan to provide the ground for her theory of linguistics, Habermas uses psychoanalysis as a more meta-theoretical model. In order to rehabilitate Marx, Habermas strips the Communist theorist of his connection to the philosophy of consciousness, leaves him with little theory of value, and denudes him of a theory of history, whereas Kristeva tends to favour the Maoist direction of Marxist theory. Besides comparing what these three thinkers have to say about dialogue, we will also be concerned to learn what role the person spoken to, or the other, plays in their concepts of dialogue. Moreover, by comparing Eliade with Kristeva, we will be able to continue his conversation with postmodernism. And by examining his thought with that of Habermas, we will be able to compare Eliade to another thinker that is grounded in the tradition of *Geisteswissenschaften* and its unifying notion of *Verstehen* (understanding).

NATURE OF DIALOGUE

Eliade conceives of the history of religions as, at least partially, paving the way for religious ecumenism within Christianity and between it and other world religions.[30] In an entry in his journal on 3 January 1963, Eliade imagines that by means of his scholarly work he is opening windows to other worlds for Westerners in order for them to carry on a dialogue with foreign cultures. This image holds true even if those cultures are long dead.[31] Thus the very nature of the history of religions embodies an ecumenical and dialogical spirit.

A basic presupposition of Eliade's position is that the world is becoming a planetary unity, which implies the need for ecumenical dialogue between religions at the current time. If the world is becoming a more unified entity, the dialogic encounter between cultures is an absolute necessity in order for us to better understand each other. From a more contextual posture, Eliade thinks that there is a danger that Western culture will decline by falling into a sterile provincialism. Such a possibility may become a reality if Western culture neglects a dialogue with other cultures.[32] What other kinds of benefits would result from a dialogic encounter with other cultures? It helps a Westerner to better understand oneself and enriches one's consciousness by exposing one to foreign modes of thought.[33] An encounter with other cultures will also oblige one to delve into 'the history of the human spirit, and will perhaps persuade him to admit that history as an integral part of his own being'.[34] The Oriental ideas of death and resurrection can, for instance, be of interest to Westerners because they reveal crucial human situations. Even though Westerners may feel that the Oriental solutions are unusable and may not want to borrow them, Oriental concepts of death and resurrection can be used by Westerners to meditate on them and to try to decipher them. This process could stimulate philosophic thinking.[35] Eliade suggests that we listen to the message of other cultures as they relate to us their inner history, bear witness to their own meaning and value, and inform us about possible solutions to the crucial problems of life. But this does not explain how one can begin to decipher elements of another culture and how to enter into dialogue. What is the proper response?

In order to enter into dialogue with other cultures, Westerners must, according to Eliade, come to know and understand these cultures. Thus hermeneutics is the proper response and place to begin dialogue.[36] If Westerners are to encounter and understand the values of foreign cultures, hermeneutics is an indispensable tool. We must understand each other before we can have an intelligent dialogue. This path of encounter leads to a total knowledge and new humanism, which is not simply a replica of the old form of humanism in the West. In order to arrive at a total knowledge characteristic of this new humanism, it is necessary to integrate the research of several disciplines: orientalists, depth psychologists, ethnologists, and historians of religions.[37] Moreover, Eliade envisions dialogue by means of hermeneutics to lead to a new type of religious experience, which he suggests would be more universal. In other words, Eliade suggests that we can be transformed by the truth.

Another thinker concerned with the truth is Habermas, who defines the search for the truth within what he describes as the lifeworld (*Lebenswelt*). When individuals communicate with each other and arrive at understanding, they interreact within the horizon of a lifeworld, a concept that Habermas finds complementary to that of communicative action.[38] The lifeworld, which consists of language, culture, society and the person, forms the overall context within which our communicative utterances are fixed. Habermas clarifies his position by stating:

> Communicative actors are always moving *within* the horizon of their lifeworld; they cannot step outside of it. As interpreters, they themselves belong to the lifeworld, along with their speech acts, but they cannot refer to 'something in the lifeworld' in the same way as they can to facts, norms, of experiences.[39]

Although Eliade does not use the same terminology, he agrees with Habermas that we communicate within a lifeworld. For Habermas, the lifeworld is the context for the objective, subjective, and social realms of linguistic usage in which the social being achieves its identity. Thus the lifeworld is more of a linguistic concept for Habermas where language and experience intertwine throughout the various forms of life, whereas Eliade would perceive the lifeworld in a more ontological way because the world of *homo religiosus* is always modelled upon a sacred archetype that is saturated with being.

A rather different understanding of communication is offered by Kristeva, who is concerned with texts and their ability to communicate with a reader by transforming three closely related parts – dialogic, temporal, and political – from the linguistic theory of Mikhail Bakhtin. Rather than investigate the complex psychoanalytic structure that she builds upon her revision of Bakhtin's linguistic theory, we will concentrate on what she means by dialogue.

According to Kristeva, there are three aspects of dialogue or dimensions of textual space: writing subject, addressee, and exterior texts. These aspects can be explained by the linguistic distinction made by Saussure between synchronic and diachronic features of language. With respect to the latter horizontal aspect of language, an utterance belongs to both the writer and the person to whom a word is directed. From the synchronic perspective, an utterance is vertically directed toward an anterior literary structure.[40] These aspects form a horizontal axis composed of the subject and addressee and a vertical axis comprised of the text and context that coincide with each other. This structure manifests an intersection of words or texts. Instead of dialogue resulting in the intersubjectivity envisioned by Eliade and Habermas, the notion of intertexuality replaces intersubjectivity for Kristeva. Moreover, the materialistic aspect of Kristeva's theory is evident when she refers to a word as spatial and the internal structure of a text as temporal.[41] This tends to suggest that dialogue is also temporal, possibly ephemeral, and without any lasting significance for her.

DIALOGUE AND THE OTHER

By its very nature, dialogue implies a subject who communicates and someone spoken to or an other. As we noted in Chapter 4, the self is in a fallen condition for Eliade. From an original unity, the self falls into a condition of separation, forgetfulness, and ontological fissure. The fallen condition of the self also includes the death of God and the fall into history. Although the self is ontologically split for Eliade, it is possible for it to find the centre of its existence within a religious context.

In sharp contrast to this metaphysics of presence from a postmodernist perspective, Kristeva conceives of a heterogeneous and decentred self that is engaged in a process of development, a position that is not all that different from Eliade's perspective at this point. But unlike Eliade's position, Kristeva asserts that the self is unable to be present to itself, which implies that subjects cannot be present to one another and cannot communicate adequately with each other. As the subject develops or in the act of dialogue, the subject splits apart into a subject who speaks and the subject who is addressed or the other.[42] The combined voices of the dialogical partners represent the internal life of the speaking subject and include its unconscious experience. This internal life is a temporal process that enables a variety of selves to emerge. What Kristeva means is that a self is not ontologically signified nor is it fixed as a linguistic object, but it is instead an infinite series of signifiers that are in a continual state of flux.

In contrast to the process of splitting apart that Kristeva finds in any dialogical interaction between a subject and the other, Habermas discovers a consensus derived through rational discussion, mutual understanding, and common recognition that the other possesses a right to engage in a given dialogue as an equal participant. And Eliade thinks that the rapture and terror, although caused by one's encounter with the sacred, are sublimated into the binding force of dialogue. Therefore, in sharp contrast to Kristeva, Eliade and Habermas think that dialogue possesses a binding power.

Not only is the subject split in the process of dialogue for Kristeva, the other also experiences a splitting because it is both 'signifier in his relation to the text and signified in the relation between the subject of narration and himself.'[43] From a more primordial and psychological perspective, Kristeva claims that once the dependence on one's mother is ended, it is transformed into a symbolic relation to an other, which is absolutely necessary for any communication.[44] Before a subject reaches this point, it must pass through a signifying process that includes a mirror stage, a spatial intuition that allows a child to be distinct from its unified image, and a discovery of castration, a completion of the process of separation that finally signifies the subject as a separate entity detached from dependence on its mother.[45]

Instead of finding the roots of communication in the pre-Oedipal drives of the self as Kristeva does, Habermas finds the roots of what he calls communicative action in the propositional, illocutionary, and expressive speech acts.[46] Assuming that these three structural components of speech acts are integrated into a grammatical unity in every speech act, they can function to symbolically reproduce the lifeworld, serve to transmit cultural tradition, enchance individual socialization and social integration.[47]

In sharp contrast to Kristeva, Eliade and Habermas believe that it is possible to relive or reenact (*Erlebnis*) the attitude of the other, which would seem to be impossible for Kristeva's ever-transitional and dividing other. To assume the attitude of the other for Habermas depends on how the other responds to one's own physical or vocal gesture: 'Once the first organism has learned to interpret its own gesture in the same way as the other organism, it cannot avoid making the gesture *in the expectation* that it will have a certain meaning for the second organism.'[48] Once this change of consciousness occurs and affects the attitude of one person for another, the initial organism encounters the other as a social object and not merely as a reaction to one's gesture but as an interpreter of that gesture. The other also changes because it appears to the first person as an interpreter of the latter's behaviour. The participants become hearer and speaker when they assume the attitude of communicating with each other and themselves. In a similar manner Eliade discusses the need to assume the role of the other in other to grasp that person's religious world.[49]

From a more instinctual level of existence for Kristeva, another significant aspect of the development of the self is its experience of rejection, a signifying process that tends toward death.[50] Although death is deferred by the body in order to prevent its own destruction, it still reinscribes rejection as a sign, forming a mark that 'thwarts rejection in order to reactivate it and defers rejection so that it will return to divide and double the mark in turn'.[51] This does not mean that Kristeva understands rejection as simple destruction; it is rather an excessive kind of renewal that destroys presence that results in the disappearance of object and subject. The only thing left is what Kristeva calls the 'motility of the *chora*', a location where a subject is repeatedly both generated and negated.[52] Upon its arrival, the *chora* produces a separation from the object and absence, an establishment of the real.[53] For Kristeva, the subject is without presence: 'The *subject* is only the *signifying process* and he appears only as a *signifying practice*, that is, only when he is absent *within the position* out of which social, historical, and signifying activity unfolds.'[54] And the other is split from the divided self by rejection, coinciding with the plurality of the natural and social world.[55] This lack of definite presence by a subject and other is totally unsatisfactory to Eliade and Habermas because of their own metaphysical presuppositions that directly conflict with those of Kristeva. Moreover, Habermas sees the possibility and need for an intersubjectivity, while Eliade perceives a common ground between himself and members of other cultures because they create just as he does.[56] Habermas and Eliade both assert that speakers express their intentions to others in the dialogical encounter, whereas Kristeva claims that intentions are only possible because a subject goes beyond its own intentions and meanings.

DIALOGUE AND UNDERSTANDING

With Eliade's polemic against reductionism providing a negative foundation for his hermeneutic, it is his conviction that the original intention of a sacred phenomenon is lost, if it is reduced to psychological, sociological, or historical statements.[57] Thus a religious phenomenon must be interpreted as a religious form in order not to miss the sacred, a unique and irreducible element. If the sacred must necessarily be granted a primary ontological status, external norms foreign to it must not be imposed upon it. Eliade is insisting on a phenomenological *epoché* at this point. He wants to empathetically place himself in the context of *homo religiosus* in order to grasp the meaning of a sacred phenomenon.[58]

It is, however, insufficient to relive the appearance of the sacred manifestation by imaginatively recreating the conditions for its appearance. The phenomenologist must focus on its intentional mode, which is accomplished by grasping the dialectic of the sacred: the sacred is qualitatively distinct from the profane.[59] In fact, there is a paradoxical relationship between the sacred and profane:

> What is paradoxical is that an ordinary, finite, historical thing, while remaining a natural thing, can at the same time manifest something which is not finite, not historical, not natural. What is paradoxical is that something transcendent, wholly other, infinite, transhistorical, limits itself by manifesting itself in some relative, finite, historical thing.[60]

Thus the sacred does not manifest itself in an ordinary manner. Moreover, Eliade's phenomenological *epoché*, grounded in his negative dialectic, posits the sacred by a process of negating the profane. Due to the nature of his hermeneutics and the dialectic of the sacred, Eliade's conception of dialogue is itself dialectic.

In contrast to Eliade's conception of dialogue, Kristeva, as influenced by Bakhtin, finds that all language and speech possess a fundamentally dialogical character. This basic bivalence originates in a carnivalesque tradition, which itself is essentially dialogical.[61] The carnivalesque feature of dialogue refers to a play of language composed of some of the following characteristics:

spectacle, game, contradiction, and relativization. The carnivalesque nature of language possesses important consequences for someone who enters into dialogue:

> A carnival participant is both actor and spectator; he loses his sense of individuality, passes through a zero point of carnivalesque activity and splits into a subject of spectacle and an object of the game. Within the carnival, the subject is reduced to nothingness, while the structure of the *author* emerges as anonymity that creates and sees itself created as self and other, as man and mask.[62]

The carnivalesque nature of dialogue is revolutionary for Kristeva because it is rebellious in its challenge to any social law, authority or God. The results of a carnivalesque structure are anti-Christian, an unacceptable consequence from Eliade's perspective based on what he affirms about cosmic Christianity, and anti-rationalistic, a position certainly untenable for Habermas.[63]

For Eliade, understanding cannot occur by a simple reconstruction of a particular phenomenon because it must be reintegrated within its system of associations, a procedure that can be called eidetic reintegration.[64] In other words, after uncovering the intentional mode of a sacred phenomenon that tends toward an archetype, it must be reintegrated into its proper system by morphological classification which allows one to discern its meaning. If a given phenomenon tends toward a larger context of structural associations, a particular archetype, an initial structure of the sacred, cannot be comprehended by itself, but can only be understood when the total system of associations is reconstructed and grasped. Morphological classification possesses a distinct advantage for hermeneutical dialogue because the archetypes, although grounded in history, are non-historical and transcend historical particularity. Another advantage is that an earlier manifestation of a sacred phenomenon cannot be considered inferior or superseded by a later manifestation because all sacred manifestations have value and meaning. This allows participants in a hermeneutical dialogue to meet as equals. Moreover, the comparative aspect of Eliade's hermeneutic embodies within itself an ecumenical spirit by its very nature.

On the other hand, Habermas conceives of understanding, from his rationalistic perspective, as a means for speaking individuals to reach an agreement concerning the validity of an utterance.[65] If a speaker does raise a validity claim, the other can either accept, reject, or remain undecided about it. Habermas clarifies his position by stating that 'A *validity claim* is equivalent to the assertion that the *conditions for the validity* of an utterance are fulfilled.'[66] According to Habermas, an agreement on the validity of an utterance is intersubjective, a position not that far different from that of Eliade, although Eliade would not stress its rationality and would instead emphasize its more ontological nature. Habermas is more empathic than Eliade when he stresses that the inner goal of human speech is gaining understanding.[67]

Other aspects of Eliade's hermeneutics enhance dialogue in different ways. Eliade perceives a fundamental unity of all humankind. This unity is located in the human mind, which contains the sacred as a structural element.[68] This gives all religious history an indivisible unity and provides a common ground from which to begin cross-cultural dialogue. By means of the implications of his position, Eliade can claim that Western Christians share a common ground with Hindus, Buddhists, Taoists, Muslims, members of tribal religions and with religious cultures long since deceased. In short, all gaps of understanding can be bridged.

Instead of the common ground and unity discovered by Eliade that enhances the possibilities for cross-cultural dialogue, Kristeva finds a disunity among participants because it is not possible for a speaker to understand the other as he/she understands himself/herself. The reason for one's own limitations is tied to the other's inability to completely understand himself/herself. This problem can be traced back to the self's lack of inherent unity and inability to be present to itself, which Eliade does not perceive as a problem.

Due to the unity of religious consciousness throughout history and diverse cultures, the hermeneutical problem of temporal and spatial distance is overcome by Eliade. The historian of religions is able to recapture the spirit of a religious milieu, relive and understand it. The historian of religions occupies a given situation, but this fact does not limit one from grasping the meaning of a foreign situation.[69] By interpreting the existential situations of other beings, one can widen one's own horizon and transcend cultural provincialism.[70] If the sacred forms part of the structure of human consciousness, archetypes, initial structures of the sacred, are the same, which implies that they are permanent and continuous. This enables the dialogic partners to participate in the religious world of each other. Therefore, there is no unbridgeable gap and no inherent cultural alienation that needs to be overcome by those engaged in dialogue.

Eliade's hermeneutical dialogue suggests a procedure advocated by John S. Dunne who refers to a process of 'passing over'. Dunne defines it as follows:

It is a method of entering sympathetically into another person's auto-biographical standpoint, seeing the whole world anew as that person sees it, and then coming back enriched to one's own standpoint and to a new understanding of one's own life. The technique of passing over is based on the process of eliciting images from one's feelings, attaining insight into images, and turning insight into a guide of life.[71]

According to Dunne, one will return with new understanding of one's religion and culture by encountering a foreign religion. And it is necessary to come back in order not to lose one's own religion, culture and identity.[72] Dunne comprehends this process as proceeding indefinitely because one can never know everything.[73] Although he does not explicitly refer to the same process as Dunne, Eliade is engaged in a similar endeavour with his dialogue *via* hermeneutics. Along similar lines, Habermas discusses relating to more than one world, and when dialogical participants move to a mutual understanding about something in one world this indicates that 'they base their communication on a commonly supposed system of worlds'.[74] This direction of thought is not, however, shared by Kristeva.

By encountering another culture and returning to one's own cultural milieu, it is not necessarily possible that one gains anything from Kristeva's perspective. Even though a given utterance is made in a dialogical situation and expresses a clear literal meaning to another person, this utterance is still burdened with ambiguities because the rhythm of my speech may vary, my tone of voice may cause confusion, and my bodily gestures may not be synchronized with my communicative intentions, which all contribute to create an unintended heterogeneity of my utterance's meaning.[75] If what I have to say possesses a multiplicity of intended and unintended meanings that are laden with ambiguities and incoherences, this would certainly be the case to an even greater degree with someone from another culture. Furthermore, what one can say to another is often limited to some degree by the language-ability and capacity for understanding of another person.

In the actual execution of his hermeneutical dialogue, Eliade tends to stress the common pattern to be discovered in a cross-cultural encounter. Moreover, he tends to emphasize what diverse cultures have in common. When discussing the phenomena of magic flight, for instance, in the Middle East, China, India, and Oceania, Eliade cites the examples of kings who were carried shoulder-high like gods flying through the air. After citing other examples of magic flight, Eliade offers an interpretive generalization: 'They all express a break with the universe of everyday experience; and a dual purposiveness is evident in this rupture: both *transcendence* and, at the same time, *freedom* are to be obtained through the "flight".'[76] The same search for common patterns exists in other forms of hermeneutical dialogue.

If it is agreed that certain religious experiences possess common features cross-culturally, what accounts for the different types of experiences? According to Eliade, one must try to grasp the intentionality of a religious phenomenon within a cultural context. If a given experience is placed within its religious context, *homo religiosus* discovers what he/she is preconditioned or predisposed to uncover.[77] In other words, the religious conditioning of one's cultural milieu influences what type of religious experience or phenomenon one discovers. Thus one's cultural predispositions determine and give shape to the experience of *homo religiosus*. In another context Eliade seems to suggest that one can transcend one's existential situation and one's pre-given world. He states in an interview that 'It seems to me that messages emanating from the fundamental symbols reveal a world of meanings that is not reducible simply to our historical and immanent experience.'[78] While discussing the work of the French anthropologist Griaule and the claim that he appeared after his death to his Dogon and European friends meeting to celebrate his birthday, Eliade replies, 'These things are possible when the people to whom they happen belong to a certain spiritual universe.'[79] These examples suggest that Eliade does not believe that we are simply confined to the world in which we find ourselves. In contrast, Habermas is more consistent than Eliade in his position on this point. Although the situations in which we find ourselves may change, we can never transcend our lifeworld for Habermas.[80] On the other hand, Habermas does share with Eliade the presupposition that participants in communication encounter one another in a horizon of unrestricted possibilities of mutual understanding,[81] whereas Kristeva perceives limitations on our understanding because of the nature of language itself. In fact, she equates language with the process of rejection by calling language a substitute for rejection.[82]

Unlike the philosophical position of Kristeva, a basic tenet of Eliade's hermeneutical dialogue is that any encounter with another religion leads to a more lucid understanding of one's own situation.[83] This suggests that Westerners have much to learn from foreign cultures. If dialogue is an event that connects speaking and hearing, as Ricoeur asserts,[84] Eliade would agree and add that we speak by asking questions concerning our existential situation. What we hear are the messages and solutions offered by other cultures to similar situations. Assuming that we listen attentively, a dialogue with other cultures can enable us to find old solutions to new problems and open our perspective and religious horizon to new possibilities. From Eliade's viewpoint, an authentic East–West dialogue can bring practical benefits and improve our quality of life.

From Kristeva's perspective, it is extremely difficult to understand one's own situation or that of another person because of the way that a typical person expresses himself/herself. Without intending a certain result, I might express a given desire by making an aberrant gesture or expressing an inappropriate tone of voice giving another person the wrong impression about my original intention. Moreover, with its incoherent, multiple desires, the self is a play of differences that possesses a tendency to attach several meanings to a given thing, although lacking an awareness of these layers of meanings or how they interconnect.[85] Drawing upon an implication from her writings, we can state that Kristeva is strongly suggesting that it is very difficult to understand another person or culture, especially if we cannot even comprehend ourselves, whereas Eliade is more optimistic about one's ability to understand the sacred and broaden one's horizon because the sacred itself is an element in the structure of human consciousness.

CONCLUDING REMARKS

By comparing the philosophies of Eliade, Habermas, and Kristeva on the various aspects and problems associated with dialogue, we have discovered many differences. Eliade and Habermas agree that we communicate within a lifeworld that is primarily linguistic for the latter and ontological for the former, whereas Kristeva grounds communication in texts. While Kristeva understands the nature of dialogue as intertextual, Habermas grasps it as intersubjective, and Eliade perceives it as dialectical in character. With relation to our discussion about the status of the subject and the other, we noted that for Eliade both are fallen and searching for their centre of existence, an achievement that is an authentic possibility; that Kristeva asserts the heterogeneous and decentred nature of the subject and other without ontological signification nor a fixed linguistic position; and that Habermas thinks we can assume the attitude of the other and encounter it as a social object who can interpret a subject's gesture or utterance. With respect to the problem of understanding, Eliade perceives a unity and common ground between participants in a dialogue, Kristeva sees only disunity, and Habermas thinks that rational agreement is possible because rationalization is a process built into society itself, which implies that individuals can communicate in any type of context. For Eliade and Habermas, mutual understanding and intersubjectivity are possible, whereas Kristeva thinks that it is very difficult because of the nature of dialogue. Many of the differences that we have summarized can be traced to what these thinkers find in speech itself: Kristeva discovers herterogeneity and/

or difference; Habermas finds rationality inherent in speech, and the revelation of being is revealed to Eliade.

If we were to take Kristeva outside the context of intertextuality, it could be asked: is an interpersonal dialogue really possible, based on her grasp of the problem? Her splitting subject and other, rejection of intersubjectivity, prevalence of heterogeneity, disunity, and the anti-rationalistic structure of the carnivalesque nature of language suggest that an interpersonal and meaningful dialogue would be difficult, if not impossible. Kristeva seems to be stuck in the text of which she is so enamoured because of her presupposition that writing possesses chronological priority over speech. In fact, there is a crisis of language that is captured for us in the literature of abjection that embodies a threatening horror.[86] Following the lead of Nietzsche, Kristeva thinks that our culture is founded on a horror that represses us, and can be expressed through a language of abjection with its source in the repressed unconscious. According to Kristeva, communication leads to pain and death.[87] If Eliade sees ecumenical dialogue on the horizon in spite of what he calls the 'terror of history', and if Habermas perceives rationality within society, Kristeva foresees rather an apocalypse of horrified laughter, a comedy of abjection.

In his work entitled *Der philosophische Diskurs der Moderne*, Habermas devotes a chapter to a critical discussion of Derrida's philosophy. Even though Habermas directs his criticism at the thought of Derrida, the same critical perspective could be directed at Kristeva for being captive of a philosophy of the subject which constrains her though[88] Kristeva's materialistic and textualizing approach, similar to Derrida's concretizing/ textualizing of Being, is insignificant from Habermas's perspective because neither thinker is well-served by their inheritance of a metaphysics weakened by its intentions of a first philosophy.[89] Moreover, with her leftist political agenda, Kristeva is a negative extremist who is anarchist in her intention from Habermas's viewpoint. And based on his autobiographical and literary works that reflect his attitude toward the repression of totalitarian Communism in his own country, Eliade would have little empathy with Kristeva's naive Maoist sympathies.

Eliade would also be critical of Habermas for neglecting the role of sexuality in his social theory. From Eliade's viewpoint, Habermas does not give sufficient emphasis to the irrational in human affairs and history, a power that the former finds lurking within history.[90] Another problem that Habermas must address is the role and significance of the unintended consequences of our actions for history and society. After a critical look at Kristeva and Habermas, it is appropriate to take a similar view of the work of Eliade on dialogue.

There are some essential features of genuine dialogue that Eliade fails to address. Although one can end a dialogue because a sufficient discussion takes place or the partners run out of things to discuss, a break in dialogue possesses an intrinsic relation to its resumption. As Gadamer observes, every dialogue possesses an inner dynamic, an internal infinity and no end.[91] The end of a dialogue is merely a break in a continual process. If listening, observing, speaking, correcting and being corrected are all part of the dynamics of dialogue, this characteristic of give-and-take of dialogic encounter is missing from Eliade's hermeneutical dialogue. Genuine religious dialogue is risky because one takes a chance that one's beliefs could be modified.[92] Eliade's conception of dialogue is too limited because the representatives of other cultures are not at risk.

Since religious pluralism is a reality in the modern world, cross-cultural dialogue is a wise and necessary course of action. There is much that dialogical participants can learn from each other. We can broaden our religious horizons, possibly find solutions to our problems, better understand each other, and overcome our provincialism. But we need to be more circumspect. Although Eliade recognizes the nature of pluralism throughout the world, he fails to acknowledge the pluralism within religious traditions when engaging in dialogue. There is, for instance, a considerable difference between devotional and Advaita Vedāntic forms of Hinduism. And there is a gap between a monk practising Theravāda Buddhism in Sri Lanka and a Japanese follower of Pure Land Buddhism.

Another shortcoming of Eliade's hermeneutical dialogue is that the participants do not mutually benefit by sharing understanding. His dialogical encounter is, too, one-dimensional because Westerners have much to learn from other religious traditions, but there is nothing said about what the East might learn from the West. Eliade seems to suggest that the West is morally and spiritually bankrupt, with nothing worthwhile to offer others. Even if one agrees with Eliade's implied assessment of the spiritual condition of the West, without a crossing-over by both partners into each other's religious traditions, dialogue breaks down in Eliade's hermeneutical dialogue. Since dialogue presupposes at least two participants, Eliade's hermeneutical dialogue is closer to a monologue because Westerners receive but do not give anything. There is an artificiality that pervades his dialogue, which lacks openness, caring, sharing, spontaneity and gradual unfolding of the truth. The great danger in a monologue is that one presents oneself as a communicating being, but one does not communicate anything to others.

We have noted that Eliade perceives a unity within living and deceased religions. This unity is discovered in the sacred, which is an element of all human consciousness. In contrast, Smith conceives of the unity among religions as grounded in their history.[93] In other words, what religions share in common is their historical interconnections. However one conceives of the unity of religions, Eliade seems overly concerned with finding commonality among religions. By stressing common patterns and abstracting from the particulars of history, Eliade is less able empirically to distinguish between superficial and essential commonalities. Moreover, the differences between religious traditions are also important and instructive. Furthermore, an implication that Eliade's hermeneutical dialogue does not foresee is that, by entering into cross-cultural dialogue with other religious traditions, there is a danger that the authority of the sacred could be gradually replaced by the authority of an achieved consensus or mutual understanding.

Further criticism is levelled at Eliade by Raschke, who proposes an alternative to Eliade's hermeneutics: 'An authentic hermeneutics of religion *in toto* must consist in more than a structural exegesis of religious facts; it must penetrate beyond symbolic givens to lay bare the originary meanings that constitute ever fecund semantic potentials for interpretation.'[94] Raschke claims that Eliade's hermeneutic is overly concerned with historic and phenomenological considerations. The former part of Raschke's criticism is a bit odd because Eliade has been accused of being anti-historical.[95]

Three final problems with Eliade's hermeneutical dialogue need to be mentioned. If one is not talking to another person because the historian of religions is addressing an entire religious tradition or a religious archetype, this renders dialogue impersonal. There is no give-and-take with hermeneutical dialogue such as is characteristic of normal interpersonal encounter. Related to its impersonal tone, Eliade's dialogue lacks a sense of being-together and sharing in order to overcome solitude. Moreover, there does not seem to be an inner dialogue taking place within the individual historian of religions with Eliade's method.

Although one can agree with Eliade that the history of religions embodies an ecumenical spirit, we need to correct the various shortcomings of his hermeneutical dialogue and move forward to a more genuine form of dialogue. On the positive side, Eliade's vision does help us to perceive that the religious world is composed of many voices. Finally, by grounding his conception of dialogue in his theory of hermeneutics, Eliade suggests that hermeneutics is a universal principle of philosophy.

6 Sacred Language and Soteriology

In her work on the history of linguistics, Julia Kristeva makes an interesting assertion: if the Renaissance replaced the cult of an almighty God with a new cult of man, a new revolution in our era is replacing the Renaissance cult of man with that of language.[1] From her perspective, into the complex and imprecise sphere of human activities, a science is introduced because language lends itself to scientific analysis. An important form of language that suggests the possibility of scientific analysis for Eliade is myth, a phenomenon that attracted the attention of many thinkers prior to Eliade's important contributions to the subject.

Intellectuals of the eighteenth century generally tended to disparage myth and treat it with contempt. According to Voltaire (d. 1778), myth was nothing more than superstition and historical distortion. Taking into consideration present and past religious cultures, Voltaire concluded that myths are senseless and absurd fables.[2] Along similar patterns of thought, David Hume (d. 1776) was also embarrassed by myth, which, he thought originated in human fears. Within the world in which we find ourselves, the causes of events are concealed from us, and we are powerless to prevent the evils that continually threaten us from these unknown causes, which become an obsession of our hopes and fears. While we face events with anxious expectation, we employ our imagination to form ideas of higher powers on which we imagine ourselves to be dependent.[3] Hume concludes, 'The primary religion of mankind arises chiefly from an anxious fear of future events; and what ideas will naturally be entertained of invisible, unknown powers, while men lie under dismal apprehensions of any kind, may easily be conceived.'[4] Not all eighteenth-century intellectuals shared the negative perception of myth of Voltaire and Hume.

An exception to the negative attitude towards myth, although not the only example in the eighteenth century, was the work of Vico (d. 1744), who was probably the first modern thinker to seriously consider the importance of myth, in his work entitled *The New Science*. In Vico's scheme of history there were three ages of humankind: the prehistoric age of the gods, the age of heroes, and the age of man. These ages represented a gradual growth of maturity and rationality until a final stage of decline. The infancy of humankind was the age of myth, a time in which humans had not discovered themselves because they attributed all causal action to supernatural beings and expressed their understanding about the divine beings and their relations to them in oral narrations. As the ages unfolded, myths were subject to evolution and degeneration, but the original myths embodied a true account of the experience of humans which were later misappropriated, misunderstood, corrupted and falsified.[5] Thus the original, primal myths were a direct narrative of the spirit of humankind in the first age. In order to understand myths, they must be placed in their historical context and reconstructed by semantic, etymological analysis by the interpreter. For Vico, human culture was a unity represented by the triad of language, art, and myth.[6] He comprehended his task as an attempt to go beyond the story of a given myth by grasping the kernel of truth that lay inside it.

In contrast to the rationalists of the eighteenth century, the romantic thinkers of Germany, like Herder (d. 1908) and Goethe (d. 1832), recognized myth as creative wisdom and a form of truth. In fact, Goethe proceeded to create a poetic revitalization of myth, which he conceived of as a symbolic expression. Called the apostle of a new religion by Novalis (d. 1801), Friedrich Schlegel (d. 1829), a revolutionary literary critic, understood myth as a unity of thought, art and belief. Because myth is a form of art, it formed an inseparable unity with poetry.[7] Schlegel called for a new mythology because of the creative and dynamic nature that he perceived within it. He summarized its importance:

> Mythology is such a work of art created by nature. In its texture the sublime is really formed; everything is relation and metamorphosis, conformed and transformed, and this conformation and transformation is its peculiar process, its inner life and method, if I may say so.[8]

Myth possessed the ability to transform and transfigure the objective world in which we lived. Not far removed from the spirit of Schlegel, Schelling (d. 1854) exhibited an even more exalted view of myth because of its perceived metaphysical importance by serving as the key to the purposes of the Absolute Spirit. In Schelling's posthumously published work entitled *Einleitung in die Philosophie der Mythologie*, myth reconciles the finite with the infinite and gives the individual an initial glimpse of the pre-established harmony of the real and ideal worlds because it corresponds to the lower principle in God.[9] For Schelling, myth, an intuition of spiritual harmony, represents a condition for one's striving to regain the centre from which one is created. As long as the individual remains at the centre of the Godhead, one is able to view things as interpenetrated and interconnected with each other. But to leave one's original centre means that one sees things in a confused manner in which unity becomes chaotic and disunited.[10] In comparison to history, myth is primary and history is the derived factor. Moreover, myth is something experienced and lived.[11] According to Schelling, the mythical process is a systematic unfolding of the truth, a recreating of truth, and truth realizing itself.[12] Furthermore, Schelling argues that the truth contained in this process represents a universal truth.[13]

A much less favorable view of myth was provided by David Friedrich Strauss (d. 1874), who equated it with non-historical and unnatural events. Although he generally considered myths as fictions, Strauss also recognized historical myths, a distinct event or fact that takes mythic form with the idea of Christ as its focus, evangelical myths, narratives dealing with Jesus conceived as an idea by his disciples, and pure myths in which Jesus embodied Hebrew traditions. For the most part, myth was not a conscious and intentional invention; it was rather 'a production of the common consciousness of a people or a religious circle . . .'.[14] On the other hand, Strauss qualified this statement when he indicated that myths could be conscious and intentional inventions, if one considered the writer of the Fourth Gospel. The author of this work has related what he thought was true and not the truth of what actually happened.[15] The work of Strauss and his understanding of myth anticipated the twentieth-century scholarship of Rudolf Bultmann; but before Bultmann's concept of demythologization, other figures played an important role in developing a theory of myth.

In his earlier works Friedrich Nietzsche (d. 1900) wanted to return to myth, as illustrated by his emphasis on Apollonian and Dionysian ways of life, and he hoped for a rebirth of myth by using Wagner. Why was myth so important for Nietzsche? He thought that a culture began by believing in myth, which creates a unity within a culture by offering it an image of the world. Without myth a culture loses its creativity and powers of imagination.[16] By becoming trivialized, myth begins to die, its transcendent meaning is lost, and it ceases to be a living reality within a culture. The waning of myth in Greek culture was arrested by the Dionysian musical artist, who revitalized the old myths and transformed them into a creative way of Dionysian wisdom and helped them attain their highest form in tragedy.[17] With the demise of tragedy, myth also died, bringing to an end its resurgence. In contrast to Greek culture and the central role of tragedy, modern culture is anti-mythical because of its rational, sceptical and critical nature. Modern culture, adrift and unprotected from the temporal process, lacks a common myth that would give it a foundation. The need for remythifying of Western culture is evident in Nietzsche's later works and the role played by his prophet Zarathustra, who introduced myths of the future to save Western culture from the advent of nihilism. The most significant myth introduced by Zarathustra was the myth of the eternal return that turned out to be a nightmare.

Defining myths as stories dealing with gods, Friedrich Max Müller (d. 1900) attempted to trace the origin and meanings of myth, using comparative linguistics and etymology. The rationale for his approach was made evident in the following statement: 'Mythology is only a dialect, an ancient form of language.'[18] For Müller, myths represented a disease of language, and this negative assessment of myth was carried forth by some late nineteenth-century anthropologists. For Lévy-Bruhl (d. 1939), myth was a product of a prelogical mind, whereas Edward B. Tylor (d. 1917) in his *Primitive Culture* perceived myth as an attempt by early humans to be scientific.

In the twentieth century, Freud (d. 1939) equated myth with dreams that symbolically expressed unconscious wishes that are predominantly sexual in nature. All religious ideas have a psychical origin because 'they are illusions, fulfilments of the oldest, strongest and most urgent wishes of mankind'.[19] In place of religious ideas, Freud's mythical deity became science. In contrast to the psychological reductionism of Freud, Carl Jung (d. 1961) connected myths, dreams and neurotic fantasies. Myths and dreams revealed a collective unconscious which manifested archetypes: 'In the individual, the archetypes occur as involuntary manifestations of unconscious processes whose existence and meaning can only be inferred, whereas the myth deals with traditional forms of incalculable age.'[20] Myths, original revelations of the preconscious psyche, are not invented; they are experienced as meaningful. Psychology was not the only scholarly discipline concerned with myth in the twentieth century.

Within the discipline of anthropology, Clyde Kluckhohn (d. 1960) found, by analyzing Navaho myths, that myths embodied anxiety about health and life and expressed supernatural dangers, although they also provided protection along with ritual for humans.[21] The functionalist anthropology of Malinowski (d. 1942) understood myth as an active force that maintained society itself. The pragmatic nature of myth helped to codify social beliefs, safeguarded and enforced morality, and attested to the efficacy of ritual. 'Myth is thus a vital ingredient of human civilization; it is not an idle tale, but hard-worked active force; it is not an intellectual explanation or an artistic imagery, but a pragmatic charter of primitive faith and moral wisdom.'[22] In contrast, the structuralism of Lévi-Strauss attempted to examine all the variants of a given myth in order to discern its structure or constant element. The overall purpose of myth was to provide a logical model that was capable of overcoming contradictions.[23] Therefore, myth – a type of binary thinking – functions to resolve human problems that are raised to the logical status of a contradiction. This is the same binary thought-process used in scientific and philosophical thinking, although the application of this thought-process is different in mythic thinking.

Beside the disciplines of psychology and anthropology, contributions to the study of myth have been made by those working in the history of religions. Van der Leeuw (d. 1950), for instance, sought to elucidate the inner structure of myth. Not only was the telling of myth significant, its reiteration was a presentation of some event replete with power.[24] On the other hand, Rafaele Pettazzoni (d. 1959) wanted to emphasize the historical nature of myth, which he understood as a true history because it represented a sacred history. Myth was not a truth of reason, it was rather a truth of faith.[25] This brief survey of the modern study of myth is not totally exhaustive, but many of the major attitudes have been reviewed. It was this scholarly examination of myth that Eliade inherited during his career.

In Chapter 3 it was observed that the context for hermeneutics was symbol and myth, basic components of a primary religious language. Since the context for the interpretation of the sacred is the study of the language of symbol and myth, we can complement the chapter on Eliade's hermeneutics by reviewing his theory of symbol and myth. We will discover that myth is more than an entertaining story because Eliade conceives of it as having a mimetic and soteriological function for *homo religiosus* and secularized beings. By considering the soteriological aspect of myth for Eliade, further light will be shed on his theological position. We want to pursue this path by comparing Eliade's work with that of three post-modernist thinkers: Kristeva, Derrida and Eric Gould, a deconstructionist literary critic. This will enable us to view aspects of Eliade's theory of myth that we might not have considered without the comparative perspective.

SIGN AND SYMBOL

Taking a debatable historical approach to the subject, Kristeva argues that the later half of the Middle Ages (from the thirteenth to the fifteenth century) represented a transition period from thought based on the symbol to that founded on the sign, which she finds in the narrative structure of the novel that reveals the ideologeme, an intersection of a given textual arrangement providing its historical and social coordinates, of the sign. The basic distinction between a symbol and a sign can be conceived in terms of the diachronic and synchronic classification.

This means that a symbol exerts a vertical dimension by indicating universals, which Kristeva interprets as restrictive in relation to that which it symbolizes.[26] This suggests that symbolized universals are irreducible to the symbolizer, two separate and non-communicative spaces. Even though a symbol does resemble that which it symbolizes, it is a cosmogonic semiotic practice which precedes symbolic discourse. Kristeva explains: 'the course of semiotic development is a circle where the end is programmed, given in embryo, from the beginning (whose end *is* the beginning), since the function of the symbol (its ideologeme) exists prior to the actual symbolic statement'.[27] From either a logical or chronological perspective, Kristeva wants to emphasize that the semiotic, pre-Oedipal drives deriving from contact with a mother's body, precedes even the advent of the symbolic and its object. From a diachronic dimension, a symbol functions to free itself from paradox, being by nature horizontally anti-paradoxical.[28]

In contrast, Eliade is opposed to a search for the origins of religious phenomena or behaviour because these quests have proven to be valueless in the past, although he does think that symbols and symbolic thinking are more primary than language and reason: 'Symbolic thinking is not the exclusive privilege of the child, of the poet or the unbalanced mind: it is consubstantial with human existence, it comes before language and discursive reason.'[29] If symbols precede language and discursive reason, Eliade implies that symbols are spontaneously formed, and are not an illusory product of someone's imagination. Unlike ordinary means of knowledge that do not reveal the deepest aspects of reality, symbols do reveal these deeper layers of reality. *Homo religiosus* is also *homo symbolicus* because all one's activities involve symbolism. For Eliade, not only do all religious phenomena have a symbolic character, every religious act and object aims at a meta-empirical reality.[30] Symbols respond to a basic human need of manifesting the most hidden modalities of being to our purview, even though symbols are not an exact replica of objective reality.[31] From Derrida's perspective, a symbol is a supplement of the thing itself, which implies that it is exterior to that to which it is added. A symbol is also alien 'to that which, in order to be replaced by it, must be other than it'.[32] As a supplement, a symbol adds to a thing and thereby replaces it. On the other hand, Eliade suggests that symbols can reveal hidden aspects of being because of their primitive nature, which represents an ontological approach in direct conflict with the psychological and linguistic approach of Kristeva.

Eliade also disagrees with Kristeva's claim that a symbol is anti-paradoxical. Eliade thinks that an important function of a religious symbol 'is its capacity for expressing paradoxical situations or certain patterns of ultimate reality that can be expressed in no other way'.[33] An example of this aspect of a religious symbol is the *coincidentia oppositorum* which reveals more profoundly than any rational experience ever could the actual structure of divinity.

We have noted that Kristeva thinks that the symbol is restrictive. What does she mean by the term restrictive? If a symbol functions to point beyond itself to a universal, it is restrictive in the sense that it does not refer to a single unique reality, which suggests that it is not arbitrary. Thus a symbol is restrictive in a relational sense because it is limited in respect to its symbolized universal. For Eliade, symbols are not restrictive except in a very limited contextual or historical sense. Eliade finds symbols to be multivalent, which means that they have a capacity to express several meanings simultaneously and whose unity is not apparent on the plane of immediate experience.[34] The symbolism of the moon, for instance, reveals a connatural unity between the lunar rhythms, temporal becoming, the waters, the growth of plants, women, death and resurrection and so forth. Thus the symbolism of the moon reveals a correspondence of a mystical order between the various levels of cosmic reality and certain modalities of human existence, which does not become manifest by immediate experience nor by critical reflection; it is a result of a certain mode of viewing the world. It would be misleading to refer to a symbol as restrictive.

According to Eliade, a consequence of a religious symbol's tendency to reveal several coherent meanings is that the symbol is 'capable of revealing a perspective in which diverse realities can be fitted together or even integrated into a system'.[35] This consistent and systematic nature of symbols is its logic.[36] Besides allowing one to discover a certain unity of the world, a religious symbol enables one to become aware of one's own destiny as an integral part of the world. The symbolism of night and darkness, for example, manifests a structural unity between the pre-cosmogonic and pre-natal darkness, on the one hand, and death, rebirth and initiation on the other. As this symbolism is used in initiatory rites, one can intuit a certain mode of being, the place of this being in the constitution of the world and the human condition. *Homo religiosus* is able to discern what existed prior to oneself and the world and to understand how things came into existence, which are impossible from the viewpoints of Kristeva and Derrida.

Using Derrida's conceptual framework, we can refer to a symbol as a mark, which means that a symbol refers to the totality of objects that function as marks grounded in a differential system where it acquires its identity to refer to something else other than itself. Its identity hinges, however, on its relation to another mark, which makes it possible in the first place. By referring to that which makes it possible, a symbol, as a mark, is always in advance a remark, a doubling of the mark.[37] By remarking itself, a symbol effaces itself and produces the illusion of a referent. Thus a symbol, according to Derrida's line of thinking, is a form of repetition and duplication, whereas Eliade stresses its referential nature.

When Kristeva asserts that the function of a symbol exists prior to a genuine symbolic statement she seems to neglect the historical dimension of a symbol. Kristeva is insensitive to the fact that the creation of a symbol may depend on a certain historical situation. Consequently, a given symbol could not have existed before a certain historical moment. The spade, for instance, could not have been assimilated to the phallus before the discovery of agriculture. According to Eliade, to afffirm that a symbol possesses a history also means that the symbol spread from a precise cultural centre. This means that one must not consider a symbol to be spontaneously rediscovered in all the other cultures in which it is found.[38] Thus archaic symbols relating to death or sexuality, for example, are modified or replaced by similar symbols due to migrations of higher cultures. Although old symbols are found in a new culture, they are formed in the same manner because they are the result of existential tensions and total apprehensions of the world.[39]

Although Kristeva and Eliade disagree to a considerable extent about the nature and functions of a symbol, they do agree that a symbol possesses a cosmic aspect. According to Eliade, the world speaks and reveals itself through symbols. There are several depths to this revelation because symbols are capable of expressing a modality of the real or a condition of the world which is inaccessible to human experience.[40] Water symbolism, for instance, is capable of revealing the pre-formal, the potential and the chaotic. Another example is the cosmic tree which reveals the world as a living totality with the ability to periodically regenerate itself, which symbolizes the world as continually fertile, rich and inexhaustible. These examples are not a matter of rational cognition but of an immediate comprehension of the cipher. Since the world speaks through a medium like the cosmic tree, it reveals a deeper and more mysterious life in comparison to that grasped by everyday experience.

The gap of agreement widens even more between Kristeva and Eliade, if we compare their definition of a sign. According to Kristeva, a sign shares many of the characteristics of a symbol because it is irreducible, dualistic, hierarchical and arbitrary. By irreducibility, Kristeva means that a sign cannot be reduced from a referent to a signifier or from a signified to the signifier. By dualistic and hierarchical, Kristeva suggests that a sign, within its vertical function different from that of a symbol, indicates more objective things like reified universals that have become objects.[41] Because it is connected with a profuse number of linked images and ideas that are expressive, the arbitrary nature of a sign is due to its not referring to a single reality and tendency to distance itself from any transcendental support. In contrast, Eliade agrees that a sign is arbitrary, but it is arbitrary in the sense that a sign can be consciously invented and replaced by other signs. On the other hand, a sign is much less arbitrary when it terminates relativity or confusion by introducing the absolute into a situation.[42] Eliade also agrees with Kristeva that a sign manifests a more objective nature and represents a lower dimension of reality than a symbol. If one views the horizontal function of the sign for Kristeva, it is different from a symbol because it becomes expressed as a metonymic sequence that continually creates metaphors.[43] According to Kristeva, a sign can also be distinguished from a symbol by means of the way that they resolve contradictions: non-disjunction by a sign and by disjunction or non-conjunction by a symbol.[44] This feature of a sign can be explained by its correlative aspect due to its being a part of a web of meaning, a result of an interaction with other signs. Moreover, a sign is transformative because it is forever generating and transforming new structures.[45] From Eliade's perspective, a sign is freer to generate new structures because it does not participate in the reality and power to which it points, whereas a symbol does participate in the meaning and power of that to which it points.

POSTCARD AND MYTH

While reading a thirteenth-century book on fortune-telling by Matthew of Paris at the Oxford University library, Jacques Derrida sees a drawing that he calls an apocalyptic revelation because it depicts a seated Socrates writing at a desk in front of a more diminutive, standing figure of Plato, who appears to be dictating to his teacher.[46] This is, of course, a reversal of their traditional roles which assumed that Plato did the writing that captured in textual form the dialogues of Socrates. This drawing in the form of a postcard suggests to Derrida something about the messages of the Western literary, philosophical and theological traditions because these messages are more complicated then the tradition admits and some have been altered, garbled, and even lost. The plethora of messages, or what Derrida refers to as *envois* (packets, parcels, things sent), reflects the many voices of the senders. It is not always possible to determine who is speaking and to whom a message is directed. According to Derrida, successful communication depends upon writing, whereas Eliade recognizes the importance, accuracy, and validity of an oral tradition.

If we take Derrida's postcard and change the figures to a mythmaker seated at a writing desk with members of the community whispering in his/her ear, we get a very different view of the transmission of a mythical tradition. In other words, the mythmaker preserves and transmits the tradition by following the dictates of the community from the position of Derrida. Thus the community speaks through the mythmaker, an effect of the society, who sends forth its message. Just as Plato creates Socrates, the community creates the mythmaker. There is, of course, no guarantee that the oral message of the community, patched together by the mythmaker, will arrive at its destination. Like a postcard, the message that a myth conveys can get lost, although it is potentially recoverable by a community. And unlike a patched-together postcard that is indeterminate, a myth is something indeterminate because it tells a mysterious, uncertain, and dubious story of what occurred at the beginning of time.

By playing with Derrida's notion of the postcard and its possible implications for myth from a deconstructionist perspective, we can comprehend the wide differences between Derrida or most postmodernists and Eliade. For the latter, a person living in a culture in which myths are a vital part of living finds that the world speaks to him/her through myths, the language of the sacred. The world reveals itself as language: 'It speaks to man through its own mode of being, through its structures and its rhythms.'[47] In order to know what the world is saying one must understand the symbols and myths. Eliade is suggesting that myths are not private fictions created in isolation by an individual, but are rather socially and culturally important. When myths are an integral and living part of a given culture they are characterized by social consensus.[48] But from Derrida's viewpoint, the mythmaker constructs from a *bricolage*, a haphazard collection of miscellaneous materials and signifying structures, a world-view that is very remote from that of postmodern individuals.[49] What the mythmaker is doing from the purview of Derrida is building a world from the debris of social discourse.

There is nothing arbitrary about the nature of myth for Eliade because it relates a primordial event that took place at the beginning of time; it thus relates a sacred history which is equivalent to revealing a mystery. 'The myth, then, is the history of what took place *in illo tempore*, the recital of what the gods or the semidivine beings did at the beginning of time. To tell a myth is to proclaim what happened *ab origine*.'[50] Thus myth relates a new cosmic situation or primordial event, making the creation myth primary for Eliade. Since myths narrate origin stories, they explain why the world, events and humans are as they are because the primordial events constitute human existence and the world.[51] Thus human life is a direct result of the original mythical events. By providing a narration of origins, myths do not inform one about trivial events or the idiosyncrasies of a culture. Myths relate issues of importance and substance for an entire society because its stories reveal the shape of a culture and inform one about how a culture understands itself. According to Derrida, any question of origin embodies a metaphysics of presence. If one views a creation myth, which is a primary story for Eliade, as a trace, there is no simple origin.[52] More than a disappearance of origin, a trace implies that an origin never disappears because it was never constituted except reciprocally by a non-origin. In a sense, a trace is an origin of origin.[53] Moreover, if an origin is absent, it is replaced by a supplement, an addition and vicarious substitution.

From the postmodernist perspective of Eric Gould that is shaped by the philosophy of Derrida, myths are characterized by absence in two senses: lack of meaning and author. Eliade would agree that myths are anonymous; he would not agree with Gould that myth, a metaphorical language constructed from a lack, directly confronts non-being like no other form of language.[54] And the absence associated with myth cannot be associated with the death of the ego which is symbolized by writing for Derrida. Since myth tells how something was accomplished or came to be for Eliade, it is connected with ontology, embodies meaning, and speaks only of realities. If myth represents the language of the sacred, and if the sacred is equivalent to the real, then the realities conveyed by myth are sacred realities and enable myth to participate in being. In contrast, a myth possesses no single or final meaning for Derrida because it carries no extratextual referent by which its referring function can come to an end. Moreover, a myth also possesses no meaning because it does not refer to something outside its system of referentiality. Yet there may be a myth on the condition that it does not exist, which implies that for a myth to be present it must be devoid of all essence. Thus a myth is there only if it lacks presence. If one concludes that Derrida is contradicting himself, one is mistaken because 'to exist' and 'to be there' are not synonymous for him. They should be construed rather as two heterogeneous models of description. According to Eliade, those activities accomplished or done according to the mythical model, primordial actions of the gods or ancestors of a religious culture, belong to the sphere of the sacred and being.[55] On the other hand, those activities that are done without the mythical model belong to the realm of the profane. The profane acts are initiated by humans and thus remain illusory and unreal.

If we take a chronological view of three thousand years of religious history and combine that with a cross-cultural perspective, it is easy to acknowledge the universality of myth. From his deconstructionist purview, Gould attributes the universality of myth to the repetition of the signified and not the continual recurrence of the signifier. What he means is that a mythic signified repeatedly becomes the signifier of the next myth by incessantly following the archetype.[56] This suggests that one myth, being somewhat the same and somewhat different, relieves another myth by replacing it. By adding one myth to another, the older myth supplements the newer rendition, and the newer myth repeats the narrative of the older story. Along this line of argument, Derrida can claim that a myth is a supplement of a symbol, making myth a supplement of a supplement. Derrida elaborates, 'It is the strange essence of the supplement not to have essentiality: it may always not have taken place.'[57] From a deconstructionist viewpoint, the repetitive aspect of myth suggests its identifiability, clarity and stability. If myth is, however, a supplement of a symbol, it adds itself and forms a surplus of a symbol and itself.[58]

Even though a myth is repetitive by nature, this does not mean that it lacks structure and intention, representing inseparable features, from the deconstructive perspective of Gould. This means that myth is not simply anecdotal; its intention is to confront the unanswerable and to convey a universal message made vital by the logic of its story that enables one to authenticate oneself.[59] The logical intention of myth is associated with filling in its gaps with signs. For Gould, this means that myth explains its own origin in its own terminology and to reconcile its origin with the present.[60] This suggests reconciling its terminology with its meaning. From Eliade's perspective, Gould appears to be saying that myth is about itself. In contrast, Eliade asserts that myth informs *homo religiosus* about the creative activities of the gods because it reveals absolute sacrality and describes the irruption of the sacred into the world: 'It is the irruption of the sacred into the world, an irruption narrated in the myths, that establishes the world as a reality.'[61] This implies that the sacred is the ultimate cause of all real existence.

Because myth relates the actions of the supernatural beings, it is an exemplary model for all significant and meaningful human activity for Eliade. In contrast, Gould understands the mythic model as a repetitive metaphor that provides an ideal model for the imagination, possesses its own self-contained systems, and gives a necessary explanation to difficult questions.[62] Comparatively, when Eliade conceives of myth as functioning as an exemplary model he means it in a more ontological sense. This means that, by serving as a prototype for human actions, myths determine every-day actions because of their normative character for human behaviour. In this way, myths are social and personal heuristic devices and provide members of a society with knowledge of their identity. In contrast to Eliade's view, myth cannot be an exemplary model for all human behaviour for Derrida because it makes no sense to imitate the divine archetypes: 'For imitation affirms and sharpens its essence in effacing itself. Its essence is its nonessence.'[63]

According to Gould, when myth serves as a model for human behaviour, as Eliade claims, it is not a universal sign but rather a metaphorical event without a fixed reality.[64] In comparison, Eliade thinks that myths have a universal message, serve as a universal sign, and represent a fixed reality. This possesses important consequences for Eliade because to know the myths enables individuals of archaic societies to repeat in rites what happened *ab origine*. Archaic persons are thus able to reenact and to repeat what the gods or ancestral heroes did in the beginning of time, if they model their behaviour on that provided by the divine prototypes. Eliade explains further:

> This faithful imitation of divine models has a twofold consequence: on the one hand, by imitating the gods, man remains within the sacred and therefore within the confines of reality; on the other, the world is sanctified by the uninterrupted reactualization of divine, exemplary gestures. The religious conduct of man contributes to the maintenance of the world's holiness.[65]

Knowing and repeating the myths not only possesses an existential and cosmic significance, it also means that by knowing the myths one learns the secret origin of things.[66] And to know the origin of something implies having power. One does not only know how things came into existence, but one also knows where to discover them and how to make them reappear. By knowing the myth, one possesses an esoteric knowledge not only because it is secret and conveyed during the course of an initiation ceremony but also because the knowledge is accompanied by a magico-religious power. Thus to know the origin of something is equivalent to acquiring a magical power by which one can control, manipulate or reproduce it. This is not an abstract form of knowledge; it is rather a knowledge that one experiences ritually, either by ceremonially recounting the myth or by performing the ritual for which it is the justification.

The myths that members of a given society learn are without an author in the sense that no one signs his or her name to a myth. According to Derrida's theory of signature, an author signs his/her name both inside and outside the text. This continual process of signing one's name implies

signing one's name to the title page and signing one's name by means of
what one writes in the interior of the text. Since the signature is both inside
and outside the text, any distinction between author and text dissolves due
to the unconscious and unintentional nature of the act. By inserting a
signature unto a text, it becomes an objective monument or tomb that causes
the author to lose his/her identity or ownership of the text.[67] In response to
Derrida's theory of signature and its implications for a theory of myth, it is
possible to fabricate what Eliade might reply. Due to the anonymous nature
of the mythmaker and the original oral character of myths in religious
traditions, myth is free from the constraints of texuality and signature
because its texuality is never really finalized due to additions being made to
a given myth and other parts being deleted over a course of time, and there
is no title page to sign because a myth is often a living, vital, oral tradition.
As a symbolic narrative, myth cannot be reduced to a mere sign. Moreover,
because Eliade indicates that myth precedes empirical space and time, it
gives these elements a coherent meaning.

   In archaic religious cultures that tend to be non-literate, myth is kept
alive by the speech of the group. In fact, there is a close relationship
between speech and knowledge for Eliade because one can display how
well one knows a myth by reciting it: 'He who recites or performs the origin
myth is thereby steeped in the sacred atmosphere in which these miraculous
events took place.'[68] In contrast, writing takes precedence for Derrida because it represents a radical originality and creativity. When Derrida refers
to writing as arche-writing he wants to emphasize that nothing precedes it,
nothing establishes it, and nothing controls it. By means of its movement,
writing isolates and effaces itself in the process of writing itself because in
itself it does not exist.[69] In other words, writing is not an entity and can
never become an object. In contrast, Eliade approaches this problem from
a different angle by asserting that neither the existence nor creativity of
myth disappears with writing, but it continues to exist within writing.[70]

   For Eliade, the transmitter, by telling the myth to others is passing along
the traditional wisdom of a culture and keeping alive cultural traditions. In
a sense one becomes contemporary with the mythical events, or one lives in
the presence of the gods or heroes. Thus one lives in the myth in the sense
that one is seized by the sacred. By living in the myth, one emerges from
profane time and enters a sacred time which is primordial and indefinitely
recoverable. By ceasing to exist in the everyday world, one is a witness to
the creative deeds of the gods. By its ability to transport one to the beginning of time, myths 'act as sacraments of imagination'.[71] The verbal recitation of myths helps members of a society to remember and overcome
their fallen character of forgetfulness, whereas writing signifies forgetful-

ness for Derrida and provides a spontaneous memory.[72] From the philosophical perspective of the deconstructionists, Eliade's assertion that
one can become contemporary with the time of origins as embodied in
creation myths is nothing more than a nostalgia for presence. Therefore,
Eliade is a creator of a logocentric myth that includes a craving for origins,
presence, truth, and meaning. From Derrida's viewpoint, Eliade's fundamental error is to think that the basic categories of reality can be directly
present to consciousness.

MYTH AS SOTERIOLOGY

For Eliade, myth is much more than a primordial event that explains how
things originated, more than a description of an irruption of the sacred into
the world, more than a sacred history, and more than an exemplary model
of human behaviour. Myth possesses this surplus for Eliade because it also
functions in a soteriological way, whereas Derrida grasps myth as a metaphysics of absence. In a sense, Eliade agrees with Derrida because he
perceives an absence of myth in contemporary culture, but the former
wants to bring myth back into presence, which is where he parts company
with the deconstructionist. In the late twentieth century, Eliade thinks
that the saving power of myth is needed for the survival of modern
beings because of a twofold process: desacralization of the religious universe
and demystification.

By desacralization, Eliade is referring to the process of secularization
in which human life and the world are expunged of religious content.
Eliade calls this a triumph of *logos* over *mythos*, by which he means a vic-
tory of the book over oral tradition or the static over the dynamic. Eliade
traces the origin of desacralization in Western culture to the early Judeo-
Christian tradition which emptied the cosmos of the sacred. Since the
cosmos before the advent of the Judeo-Christian tradition acted as a recep-
tacle of hierophanies and theophanies, it was neutralized and banalized by
being desacralized. This process rendered possible the development of
modern science and the objective scientific study of nature.[73] Demystification
is actually part of the same process of desacralization which empties the
cosmos of the sacred, although demystification tends to refer more to the
denuding of mythology. Eliade connects demystification with the
reductionism of Marxists and Freudians, who can understand culture only
by reducing it to some common denominator. Eliade interprets this as a
neurotic attitude: 'The neuropath demystifies life, culture, the spiritual

life.'[74] What is needed is a demystification in reverse in order to discover the sacred elements camouflaged in Western culture.[75]

Eliade implies that the processes of desacralization and demystification are not complete or totally successful because the sacred survives hidden in culture. Myth, for instance, never completely disappears. We can find survivals in the biological Aryan myth of Nazi Germany, the eschatological myths of Marxist Communism, comic-book figures like Superman and the modern art of Chagall, which uses biblical motifs and messianic nostalgia in the forms of the eye of God, angels, and the ass, a messianic animal. Although modern individuals may desire to be areligious on the level of ordinary consciousness, one continues to participate in the sacred by means of one's imagination and dreams.[76] In the exterior world the sacred lies camouflaged and in one's interior world the sacred lies forgotten, although it survives either beneath the objective surface or buried in one's unconscious. Therefore, the sacred embodied in religious symbols and myths never completely disappears.[77] They are rather disguised and hidden within the world and human unconsciousness.

Since modern individuals have forgotten the sacred, this implies that they are adrift, not at home in the world, and without a meaningful centre to their existence. According to Eliade, this dim portrait of modern beings is not without hope, because of the soteriological nature of myth. By considering the soteriological aspect of myth for Eliade, we will be able to view its creative, transformative and liberating nature.

Not only are myths creative, they can help one overcome doubts. The sacrosanct models that myths provide stimulate one rather than paralyze human initiative and creativity by stimulating one to create based on an encounter with the new perspectives provided by myths. Since myths provide models to imitate, they help us to overcome our doubts because we have the implicit assurance that the undertaking has already been done by others.[78] This gives one stimulus and confidence to proceed with one's actions.

Myth possesses the ability to transform us to the extent that we understand a myth; it changes and modifies us to the extent that we can take 'a step forward in the process of self-liberation'.[79] If we correctly understand the myth, it demonstrates a cathartic function by liberating us from our inhibitions and benightedness.[80] Thus myth can liberate us by helping us to find our true centre within the labyrinth of human existence and making us feel free of anguish and secure in the world.

The liberating function of myth is wonderfully illustrated by Eliade's novella entitled *Mântuleasa Street*, and published in English as *The Old Man and the Bureaucrats*. An old man named Zaharia Farama possesses an extensive repertoire of fantastic, myth-like stories. With his extraordinary memory, he is able to recall the smallest details. In the sixth chapter of the novella, Farama tells the story, for instance, of Oana, who is a beautiful, seven foot and nine inches tall, earth goddess. Oana goes to the mountains to seek her husband whom the earth spirit said would come riding on two horses. After being raped by a farmer and other men, she continues to have sexual intercourse with them, tires the men out, and agriculture begins to wane. This scenario represents a return to chaos, a frequent theme in Eliade's literary and scholarly works. The old man, a former headmaster of a primary school on Mântuleasa Street, raises the suspicions of the authorities when he visits Major Vasile I. Borza, Minister of Internal Affairs, who denies to Farama that he ever attended the old man's school. The major symbolizes lies and loss of memory. The other bureaucrats who interrogate the old retired teacher are impressed by his stories and are almost captured by them during the Stalinist era of the early 1950s in Rumania. The various bureaucrats represent untruth, reality, history, logic, unreligious, and un-imaginative schemers. The bureaucrats are unable to live in the stories, whereas the old man lives in them and is sustained by them. The old man, symbolizing truth in the novella, is saved by his stories and his faith in myth from the anti-mythical world of a suspicious and secular political power.[81] Eliade's novella represents the colliding of two antagonistic worlds: the historical bureaucratic realm and the world of myth. In the novella these two worlds tend to gradually impinge and merge into each other in the fantastic stories of the old man.

The soteriological nature of myth possesses wider implications for the work of Eliade because the disciplines of phenomenology and history of religions are spiritual techniques.[82] Although Eliade may be taking his methodological approach unwisely beyond its limits, what he means is that the hermeneutical effort by a historian of religions can enrich one's consciousness by deciphering the meaning of what one encounters in the symbols and myths. Eliade writes more emphatically in his journal:

> The history of religions, as I understand it, is a 'saving' discipline. Hermeneutics could become the only valid justification of history. A historical event will justify its appearance *when it is understood*.[83]

Thus the soteriological nature of myth is part of a wider liberating aspect of the history of religions and reflects Eliade's theological concerns. In this sense, Eliade can be understood as a prophetic figure calling contemporary, secular, areligious individuals out of the wasteland of the profane world.

If myth possesses this soteriological function for Eliade, is there anything comparable for the postmodernist thinker that has been discussed in this chapter? Any potentiality that myth might have to serve a saving function for the postmodernist must lie in the possibilities of language. If we consider the philosophy of Derrida and use him as the spokesperson for the postmodernist position, we find that he claims that language possesses intrinsic limits because we cannot speak about it in any profound sense. If we try to speak about it or name something, we distinguish that which we name and it becomes separate or other. As Derrida shifts from spoken language to the importance of writing, even though writing does not know where it is going, language is erased and exposed to its limits. As writing itself shifts to arche-writing, that which is like writing but even more like actual writing, the movement of arche-writing allows for a presence–absence relation.[84] This line of thinking leads us to think that for Derrida myth could only become a metaphysics of absence without any soteriological potential, whereas writing could serve as a saving mechanism in order to save him from a total effacement. We find a suggestion of this when Derrida discusses how writing estranges itself from the truth; he writes, 'It inscribes in the space of silence and in the silence of space the living time of voice.'[85] In other words, the writings of Derrida save him from being totally silent.

There is even less of a chance that myth will have a soteriological role in the philosophy of Kristeva because for her myth is a symbolic device made possible by the thetic, a break that produces signification.[86] Kristeva connects myth, symbolism in action, with what she calls *jouissance*, an all-encompassing joy or ecstasy, to emphasize two aspects of the thetic function: a prohibition of *jouissance* by language and an introduction of it into language. She argues that religion prohibits by seizing the initial function of the thetic, whereas art accepts the second function.[87] The introduction of *jouissance* appears to allow for a possibility of soteriology in some sense. What Kristeva offers instead is a Dionysian festival that dissolves 'in a dancing, singing, and poetic animality'.[88] This chaotic bacchanalian orgy of revolutionary poetry is combined with an apocalypse without God in which laughter prevails over the death of hope and the process of rejection decentres the self.[89] Kristeva leaves us to struggle with the powers of rejection and the process of abjection. The latter is a narcissistic crisis, but ironically there is no self to be found because it is continually separating itself from others and itself. In fact, what Kristeva offers us is a radical nihilism in which the self is finally sacrificed after being sadistically tortured without any reason.

CONCLUDING REMARKS

We have seen that for Eliade myth represents truth and meaning. If signs are incomplete, if symbols are arbitrary, and if language is a realm of play for some of our postmodernists, any complete meaning is impossible. For Derrida, we are left with a system of differences: 'Within a language, within the *system* of language, there are only differences.'[90] If play is limitless, infinite and indefinite, and if the play of differences represents the source of meaning, it follows that meaning possesses the same characteristics as play. This implies that meaning cannot be present to us because it is postponed to an indefinite future, whereas Eliade finds a real and meaningful world revealed with the discovery of the sacred embodied in myth.

This does not imply that Derrida, for instance, wants to do away with something like myth, but he does, however, want to subvert, expose, undo, transgress, or demystify it. Once the concept of myth is subverted, it is then retained in order to focus on the act of subversion itself. Why not just leave behind outmoded views about the nature of something like myth? Derrida finds it expedient not to allow outdated views to die or be replaced. It is more playful to focus on them occasionally in order to be able to continually debunk them. This procedure seems somewhat like beating a proverbial dead horse. This repetitive process suggests that Derrida is a captive of the repetitive nature of his own conception of language.

If we reflect more critically on Eliade's theory of myth as a whole, we can see that it recognizes the polyfunctionality of myth. He does not appear, however, to acknowledge that myth may alter its meaning at different times in a culture's development, the personal growth of an individual member of a given culture, or that it might mean different things to several members of a culture.[91] If we view myths in a cross-cultural perspective, this does not mean that all myths will have the same functions, a danger that Eliade attempts to avoid but without complete success. It is also a mistake to interpret and criticize Eliade's general theory of myth, as Strenski does,[92] as an example of his right-wing political thinking. It is not sufficient to argue that someone is guilty of right-wing scholarship, philosophy, or theology by simply stating that one held conservative political beliefs and associated with members of right-wing political groups at one time. A writer must be able to specifically demonstrate concrete instances of right-wing political thinking that influenced Eliade's theory of myth.

From a positive perspective, Eliade's concern with myth tends to bring language into the centre of the focus of the history of religions. From a more critical perspective, there is a lack of sensitivity and appreciation in Eliade's conception of myth, of the tradition of mythology within a given culture, when he uses morphological classification. By standing within a mytho-logical tradition, an interpreter can begin to grasp its religious world and understand its people. A deconstructionist view of myth presents major difficulties for any historian of religions because one cannot get inside a myth in order to interpret it. From a deconstructionist viewpoint, myth hides itself from any interpreter.[93] If a myth is forever imperceptible, an interpreter can never enter the myth in order to understand it, a position which is anathema to the hermeneutical position of Eliade.

We can also reflect critically on Eliade's theory of myth by focusing on the performative nature of myth, an aspect that he tends to neglect in his work. This procedure is important because myth comes alive when it is related orally to other members of a society and frees it from mere repre-sentation. By the performative action of telling a myth, the mythical storyteller is engaged in a form of play. If play is comprehended as a to-and-fro-movement between participants, it is ontologically central because it provides a clue to the character of being by indicating the way things and consciousness come to be in certain ways.[94] Myth not only comes to be by the recitation of its narrative story, it also comes to be by presentation, an internal aspect of play. The presentation of a myth – its bringing forth – is the dramatic aspect of the mimetic movement. Not only is the myth itself presented by the storyteller, there is also a self-presentation of the performative aspect. In other words, the being of the myth resides in its being told, heard, and reenacted dramatically in rites. By its transformation into a dramatic per-formance, myth represents a leap into truth because the ontology of myth becomes a public reality and is raised to an ideality beyond momentary performance. As a dynamic back-and-forth movement, the playful nature of myth involves not only a storyteller but also an audience. By means of this mutually participatory event, myth is a bringing forth of truth and a self-presentation of understanding. Since myth is a mimetic event, it is a per-formance in which storyteller and audience are gathered together in an unfolding of an event of truth, an unconcluded occurrence. Eliade seems to suggest that the truth of myth appears at the beginning that it narrates, whereas it is wiser to conceive its truth as unfolding in the interim, or in the process of recitation. When a myth is imitated in a rite it is recognized as something else because it becomes something extra to what it was prior to just being a story. By becoming more than it was, it becomes more fully itself and is more accessible to everyone.

Both the telling of a myth and the hearing of it involve interpretation. By its very nature, myth opens itself to interpretation. By being open to inter-pretation and by the very process of being interpreted, the myth exists. In other words, the being of myth is the multiple possibilities of its interpretation. Paul Ricoeur is affirming something along the same lines when he states that the Adamic myth is hermeneutical because it is already an interpretation of the primordial symbols. According to Ricoeur, the Adamic myth represents a first-degree hermeneutics, whereas original sin is a second-degree hermeneutics.[95]

By reciting a myth, hearing it, or interpreting it, one is not only interpreting the myth, but one is also being interpreted oneself because one is captured by the continuing life of the myth. Since myth comes alive when it is recited, its existence and any accompanying interpretation are advents of being. Thus the narrator of a myth presents it and also presents him- or herself in the retelling. This double mimesis of myth and narrator implies that we cannot differentiate between what the narrator relates and the myth itself.[96] A genuine interpretation is not just true to the myth; it is also an interpretation of the truth of myth.

Even though a myth unfolds the truth by its own becoming and returns the storyteller and audience to a time contemporary with divine happenings, myth is, by means of its becoming and returning nature, radically temporal because it comes to be by being repeated, recited and heard. This radical temporality of myth approximates a type of eternal permanence within which anything is possible. The radical temporality of myth must not be construed as a limitation because the realm of myth is an arena of great potential. Whether representing the unity of life or something else, myth is the realm in which the impossible becomes possible.

A corollary of the radical temporality of myths is that they are culturally bound. The culturally specific nature of myth means that a particular myth is not universal, since all myths are culturally bound and relative. Yet, myths are absolute within their cultural milieu. In other words, myths are absolute within their particular cultures, but are relative in relation to other religious cultures. This reflects the paradoxical nature of myth – its relative absoluteness. Thus the absolute meaning of a given myth is manifested in a relative way because a myth is true for those living in the myth and yet is only relatively true cross-culturally. In a sense, a particular creation myth, for instance, manifests the absolute for a certain religious culture and is definitive for that culture. A particular creation myth represents only a single manifestation of the absolutely true, whereas a cross-cultural comparison of a given myth renders it relative. This assertion does not necessarily invalidate a particular myth because the relativity and absoluteness of a myth can coexist in praxis. This position does not undermine the absoluteness of a particular myth and its meaning for a given culture; it rather takes seriously the plurality of mythic messages and is consistent with the radical temporal nature of myth.

7 Ontology and the Sacred

While on his quest for the Holy Grail, the heroic Parsifal comes to a castle and asks a single question which turns out to be the right question. According to Eliade, this episode is instructive about the human condition because human beings have a choice: either to refuse the right question or to ask it. An overwhelming number of humans refuse to ask the correct question because they are lost in the labyrinth of history wandering without direction and purpose. Eliade explains:

> This episode from Parsifal illustrates excellently the fact that even *before a satisfactory answer is found*, the 'right question' regenerates and fertilizes – not only man's being, but also the whole Cosmos. Nothing reflects more precisely the failure of man who refuses to ask about the meaning of his existence than this picture of the whole of nature suffering in anticipation of a question. It seems to us that we are wandering all alone, one by one, because we refuse to ask, 'Where is the way, the truth, and the life?' We believe that our salvation or shipwreck is our concern, and ours alone.[1]

Eliade asserts that the right question is about the nature of being, an ontological question. The question is primary because it is intertwined with the cosmos and meaning. To begin to find one's way out of the labyrinth of existence involves asking the ontological question. Eliade also suggests that the spiritual destinies of human beings are tied together and form a single union of humans in solidarity with each other. In other words, human beings share the same existential condition and the same destiny.

Prior to Eliade and exerting an influence upon him, Martin Heidegger, the German phenomenologist, asked: 'Why are there existents rather than nothing?'[2] In other words, why is there something rather than nothing? What does it mean to say that something 'is'? There is nothing that can be found that is prior to the question of being. When someone asks the ontological question there is a preconceived notion of being, the most fundamental thing that all sentient entities have in common.

Even if it is agreed that the ontological question is philosophically primary, what makes ontology so important to Eliade? For Eliade, religion is ontology: 'Every religion, even the most elementary, is an ontology: it reveals the *being* of the sacred things and the divine figures, it shows forth *that which really is*, and in doing so establishes a world . . .'.[3] Thus the historian of religions must unravel, relive, and interpret a multitude of ontologies in order to hermeneutically grasp religious modes of existing in the world. By being concerned with the fundamental ontological question, Eliade comprehends this part of his work as philosophy. He compares his meditation and philosophizing to the work of Nietzsche and Rhode on Greek mythology as the hidden meaning of his own work. Eliade comprehends this aspect of his work as a mission to assist Western culture to rediscover all modes of being: 'My duty is to show the grandeur, sometimes naive, sometimes monstrous and tragic, of archaic modes of being.'[4]

In this chapter we will be concerned to elucidate the ontology found in Eliade's phenomenology of religion. It is important to make clear that Eliade is concerned with an archaic ontology that is revealed by *homo religiosus* of traditional cultures. This chapter will focus on what Eliade understands to be the two basic modes of being, the ontology of religious language, the place of ontology in patterns of initiation, and the relationship between being and non-being. We will also attempt to develop covert implications of Eliade's description of archaic ontology for his understanding of the sacred mode of being and language of the sacred. Considering the criticisms levelled at his ontology by some scholars mentioned in Chapter 1, a question that must be asked is the following: is Eliade imposing his own ontology upon his material or is this ontology derived from the religious phenomena that he investigates? In order to answer this question, we will use the insights of other scholars working primarily on African and American Indian religions. We will also include a comparison of Eliade's archaic ontology with Derrida's deconstruction of ontology.

TWO MODES OF BEING

According to Eliade, there are two modes of being in the world – sacred and profane. The former represents the real, structure, order and the significant. In contrast, profane being is the exact opposite of the sacred mode of being: amorphous, relative and homogeneous.[5] By asserting that the sacred is real, Eliade certainly suggests an identity that would be unacceptable to Derrida because any sameness between the sacred and real is referred to as *différance* for the deconstructionist thinker, which does not involve identity. *Différance* is without essence, which also implies that it cannot be equated with Being, truth, or reality.[6] Derrida is convinced that ontology conceals rather than reveals anything.[7] Not only does the sacred form of being reveal reality for Eliade, it also possesses orientation because the holy reveals a fixed point or centre for it. Thus *homo religiosus* is at home in the world because he/she possesses a fixed orientation, otherwise impossible in the profane mode of being that is symbolized by chaos. If no true orientation is possible for the profane mode of being, it suggests no unique ontological status because everything is relative and homogeneous.[8] To have orientation or a fixed point not only provides one with a centre to one's being, it also enables one to act, to make things and to be creative.

Eliade seems to suggest that, by its very nature, the sacred is more primordial than the profane, even though the letter must be transformed from the chaos it represents by a hierophany into something with order and sacredness. Based on his position, Derrida would assert that both the sacred and profane are secondary and neither can be all-encompassing because *différance*, which can never become either a sacred or a profane object, is the condition that makes it possible for both the sacred and profane to exist. At the same time, there is no sacred object that is wholly sacred or none that is totally profane because *différance* exists within the structure of either entity as such.

In a spatial sense for Eliade, the profane mode of being involves no definite directionality, whereas the sacred mode is both horizontal and vertical. The latter form of directional orientation is primary because a sacred mode of being is impossible without an opening to the transcendent, revealing eternity, infinitude, power, and holiness. For Derrida, there can be no absolute horizontal, vertical, inside, outside, or centre, once we recognize it as an interval and an openness upon the outside. 'Space is "in" time; it is time's pure leaving-itself; it is the outside-itself as the self-relation of time.'[9] This temporalization process is called 'spacing' by Derrida. From the intersection of the vertical and horizontal for Eliade in contrast, *homo religiosus* centres one's world, a realm of sacredness, order and structure opposed to the chaos of the profane. *Homo religiosus* can only live meaningfully in a sacred world because it is only in such a place that one can participate in being. This need to live near a sacred centre, near the divine beings, or near the source of the holy suggests that this is the only way for *homo religiosus* to enjoy real existence. Anything else would be unreal. This basic need of *homo religiosus* is instructive because, 'This religious need expresses an unquenchable ontological thirst.'[10] Thus *homo religiosus* thirsts for being – the real and sacred. This ontological thirst manifests itself, for instance, by the need of *homo religiosus* to be at the centre of the cosmos, a place of original orientation and realm of communication with higher beings. If one lacks the sacred mode of being, one's ontological obsession can become a nostalgia for being, a wish to recapture and reintegrate the time of the origin of the world.[11]

In contrast to the fixed orientation provided by a sacred centre, 'Derrida asserts that the concept of the centre is contradictory: 'The center is at the center of the totality, and yet, since the center does not belong to the totality (is not part of the totality), the totality *has its center elsewhere*. The center is not the center.'[12] Moreover, Derrida wants to affirm that all concepts, groups of predicates clustered around primary predicates, are paradoxical because the primary predicates are conditioned by other predicates, constituted by their differences from other concepts, relations to a plurality of other concepts, and include within themselves traces of those things to which they are opposed.

Before proceeding with our discussion of archaic ontology, it is important to make a brief detour. There are some remarkable similarities between Eliade's distinction between the sacred and profane and Nietzsche's contrast of Apollonian and Dionysian opposition. Like the sacred examined by Eliade, the Apollonian is a symbol of form-giving force, light, reason, order, limitation and the perfection of dreamland. The Dionysian element is like the profane in Eliade's conception of it in the sense that the former can become a destructive force, rules over the more chaotic realm of music, symbolizes fantasy, disorder, limitlessness and drunkenness.[13] Nietzsche's interpretation of the opposition between the Apollonian and Dionysian is unlike Eliade's contrast of the sacred and profane in the sense that the Apollonian symbolizes illusion and protection from the harsh realities of existence, whereas the Dionysian symbolizes the annihilation of illusion and an opening to a direct experience of reality.

According to Eliade, being is not simply confined to, strictly speaking, human creatures; ontology also applies to the world. The cosmos is alive and communicates with human beings. As a creative work of the gods, the world exists for creatures to see and contemplate it. Since the cosmos is a real, sacred, living organism, it is the place where ontophany (manifestation of being) and hierophany (manifestation of the sacred) meet because it reveals simultaneously the various modalities of being and the sacred.[14] Because the cosmos reveals that which is meaningful, it is incumbent upon *homo religiosus* to be open to what the world reveals. This openness does not demand a blind and total immersion in nature by human beings. To be open to the world means to be prepared to receive its sacred message. By being open to the world, *homo religiosus* gains knowledge not only of the world but also of him- or herself.[15] This knowledge is both religious and ontological.

By means of knowledge conveyed by the world, *homo religiosus* conceives of him- or herself as a microcosm, forming a part of the whole of creation. The microcosmic individual mirrors on a smaller scale the whole cosmic ontology. Hence the discovery by *homo religiosus* of being part of the sanctity that characterizes the cosmos.[16] Eliade's conception of ontology is all-encompassing because it includes humans and the world. With its transhuman structure and its human and cosmic aspects, life is called an open existence by Eliade, since it is not strictly confined to the mode of being of *homo religiosus*.[17]

Unlike the ontology of Sartre where existence precedes essence, the archaic ontology examined by Eliade finds that 'the essential precedes existence'.[18] What does this mean? It means that *homo religiosus* is what one is precisely because of primal events at the beginning of time. An individual's particular mode of being is constituted in the present moment at the origin of the cosmos and one's acceptance of these formative events and their consequences. According to Derrida, *différance* is older and more primordial than the ontological difference or Being itself. In fact, the movement of *différance* renders possible the difference between Being and beings. This represents the play of traces: 'It is a trace that no longer belongs to the horizon of Being but one whose sense of Being is borne and bound by this play; it is a play of traces or *différance* that has no sense and is not, a play that does not belong.'[19] By presenting itself, this does not suggest that the trace, a minimal structure needed for the existence of any difference, presents itself as such but rather when presenting itself effaces itself. For Eliade, the existential decision to accept these paradigmatic events possesses important consequences that they do not have for Derrida. Since authentic existence begins with a primordial history in the form of a creation myth, *homo religiosus* must consciously repeat the archetypal actions of the cultural gods and ancestors. But why is this procedure necessary? Any object or act is real only by imitating or repeating an archetype: 'Thus, reality is acquired solely through repetition or participation; everything which lacks an exemplary model is "meaningless," i.e., it lacks reality.'[20] To repeat the archetype gives one's own actions meaning and allows one to participate in real being. By repeating periodically the cosmogonic acts, *homo religiosus* is ontologically reborn and remains near the centre of existence. According to Eliade, the repetition of archetypes is paradoxical because *homo religiosus* is real only to the extent that one ceases to be oneself by imitating and repeating the divine archetypes.[21] If one imitates the gestures of other beings, one ceases to be oneself and yet perceives oneself to be a real being with purpose and meaning.

The diverse religious phenomena that combine for Eliade to constitute an archetype possesses no relationship to meaning for Derrida. Within a chain of signification, meaning represents the space between terms, their relations and interrelations. If we focus on the terms as such, we will miss their relations to one another and their differences wherein their meanings, non-self-originating products, reside. Meaning is not something that can be grounded; there is nothing that precedes it, and nothing ultimately controls it. In fact, meaning is a function of play which itself is meaningless.[22]

How can one characterize the archaic ontology expounded by Eliade? The ontology of *homo religiosus* is prominently relational. The individual is a being related personally to other beings in so far as one imitates and repeats the impersonal, divine archetypes. If to understand Being is 'to let be' for Derrida, any grasp of Being involves the alterity of the other, which suggests that one can only let be what one is not. 'If Being is always to be let be, and if to think is to let Being be, then Being is indeed the other of thought.'[23] Even if one lets Being be, thought and other, their sameness does not imply that they are identical. In other words, the thinking of Being does not mean, for instance, that the other becomes a part of the genre of Being, if we recall that Being is not a category. The other is not reducible to my ego because the other can assert ego just as you do: 'The other, for me is an ego which I know to be in relation to me as to an other.'[24] Therefore, one's relationship to oneself is always already within a system of inter-relationships with others. For Eliade, *homo religiosus* is also meaningfully related to the world because it communicates the nature of Being. This aspect of archaic ontology suggests that Being is a unity in the sense that the world is the union of beings. This implies that Being cannot be made into a unity; it is given with the creation of the world. What are the implications for saying that Being is a given? Since Being just is, it is not derivable from something else and is not reducible to anything else. Consequently, the sacred mode of being for *homo religiosus* cannot be denied, since it forms the basis of that which exists. The certain, non-derivable and non-reducible character of Being suggests that it cannot be created by consciousness, forming a mode of reality prior to the rise of consciousness.

There is, however, a sense in which Being is contingent. Eliade suggests that the profane mode of being is radically contingent. The sacred mode of being is non-contingent or, more strictly speaking, less contingent because it adheres to eternal archetypes and by repeating the paradigm it can continually renew itself, which implies that it is not totally non-contingent. There is a sense in Eliade's description of archaic ontology in which Being is both something static and dynamic. On the one hand, the being of *homo religiosus* is dynamic in the sense that it is an inner power to be. On the other hand, since *homo religiosus* must model his/her behaviour on the divine archetypes in order to maintain the sacred mode of existence, Being tends to be static overall rather than a dynamic drive to reach one's ontological potential. Because archetypes are static once they are established, one's mode of existence and actions are real only to the extent that one faithfully imitates the divine, unchanging paradigms. Eliade does insist, however, that archaic religious individuals did allow for innovations because their religious society is not absolutely closed.[25] If Eliade's description of archaic ontology represents Being as both static and dynamic, and if archaic ontology depends on unchanging archetypes and represents a power within *homo religiosus*, his observations about archaic ontology tend to oscillate between a rational structure and an organic vitality, a power within oneself.

When Eliade asserts that Being is, he suggests that it is present. In other words, something is because it presents itself to a subject as the present object of perceptual experience. On the other hand, Derrida argues that we cannot presuppose Being as presence. By calling into question the presence of Being, Derrida does this from the standpoint of *différance*. What makes such a question even possible is the difference between Being and beings. 'The first consequence of this is that *différance* is not. It is not a being-present, however, excellent, unique, principal, or transcendent one makes it.'[26] *Différance* never presents itself as present because it does not exist, does not belong to any kind of being-present, nor a category of being.[27] Because of the movement of *différance*, presence, usually a determination and an effect in a philosophical system, cannot have a privileged place in Derrida's philosophy. In response to Derrida, Eliade might argue that it appears that trace exists, that is, comes to presence. To clarify his position, Derrida asserts that 'The trace is not a presence but is rather the simulacrum of a presence that dislocates, displaces, and refers beyond itself.'[28] Moreover, the trace does not exist in and of itself.[29] The trace can neither exist itself nor become present because it is always overtaken by effacement which makes the trace disappear.

Although Eliade makes numerous insightful comments about the nature and relationship of the sacred and profane, his theory is not completely helpful because it is too simplistic and misleading when one applies it to the actual world-views of Native American Indians and Africans. Even though he is referring to Durkheim's distinction between the sacred and profane, the three major criticisms directed against this theory by Evans-Pritchard can also be applied to Eliade's theory of the sacred/profane dichotomy. Evans-Pritchard criticizes the sacred/profane distinction because on the level of religious experience they are not distinct but 'are so closely inter-mingled as to be inseparable'.[30] What is considered sacred in one religious context or occasion might not be considered so in another context or on another occasion. Moreover, even though the distinction plays an important role in some tribal religions, it is not universally valid.[31] By reviewing other evidence from an African tribe and a Native American Indian tribe, we can validate Evans-Pritchard's three major criticisms.

Within the context of an African tribe, Robin Horton discusses the complexity of the world-view of the Kalabari of the eastern Niger Delta. The Kalabari world-view involves four levels of reality: the world of humans, various spirits, *tamuno* and *so*, and *tamuno* and *so* considered as unities. There are three categories of free spirits that work in relation to each other. On the third level, the *tamuno* is a personal creator of each person, and a *so* refers to one's destiny. The fourth category refers to *tamuno* as the creator of the entire world, whereas *so* represents the closely related sky and the collective destiny of tribal members.[32] Due to the complex inter-relationship and interdependence of the four levels of the Kalabari world-view, the sacred/profane dichotomy cannot be applied and is thus not universally valid.

Among Native American Indians, a study of the Tewa Pueblo by Ortiz, for instance, indicates that there is no simple opposition between sacred and profane in their spatial scheme. The Tewa world-view is more complex than that offered by the sacred/profane polarity; it is a duality expressed in terms of the following distinctions: winter–summer, material/natural, and spiritual/supernatural. The Tewa unify and mediate this basic duality by classifying all human and spiritual existence into a hierarchy of six categories, three human and three spiritual. The spiritual categories are also associated with specific geographical points in the Tewa world. The six levels of being are linked into three pairs. By means of bridging the material–spiritual duality, the spiritual categories represent counterparts of the human categories because at death the souls of each human category become spirits of its linked spiritual category.[33] Unlike the static tendency of the sacred/profane polarity, Native American Indian views of reality are more dynamic because they incorporate non-static and conflicting elements; that is, distinctions between inside and outside space, beginning time and historical time, order and disorder are interdependent. Referring to Navajo religion, Gill observes, 'Navajo life can be portrayed as a path way out of the sacred domain into history, into the profane world. But it also provides a way in which even disorder and the threatening aspects of life may be seen as meaningful, real, and necessary.'[34] Lienhardt suggests a similar type of interdependence among opposites within the world-view of the Dinka of Africa.[35]

By means of the symbolic cross, circle or world-tree, Native American Indians express their identity to a cosmic totality that includes nature. Because Indians are both a part of nature and apart from it, it cannot be affirmed that they exist in harmony with nature, as Eliade claims for *homo religiosus.* On the one hand, Indians think that they are alienated from nature because they have to exploit it in order to survive. On the other hand, nature is the Indian's spiritual source of life.[36] Thus Indians hold an ambivalent attitude towards nature: feelings of friendliness because of the bounty that it gives and feelings of fear because of its terrible power and potential wrath. This ambivalent attitude toward nature leads to an ethical dilemma: a tension between exploiting and loving nature. Moreover, the love of nature is not conceived in universal terms because Indians love particular locations.[37] This specific type of veneration of nature is called geopiety by Hultkrantz. The original ambivalent attitude toward nature is reflected in the Indian's practical attitude toward it because nature is a means of subsistence and Indians also experience it as a realm of mystery because the divine manifests its being through it.

As a part of nature, Native American Indians and some African tribes do not draw a sharp distinction between themselves and animals. Hallowell discovers that the Ojibwa comprehend everything in their world to be invested with life and their conception of personhood is very broad.[38] Thus there is no clear distinction between human and non-human: persons and animals are capable of metamorphosis, although there is less chance of humans undergoing metamorphosis. Among African tribes, the Dinka also do not draw a sharp distinction between human and animal life. In fact, an individual Dinka's self-esteem, identity, and social standing are intimately connected to cattle. Men imitate cattle because these animals are intimately connected with human personality.[39] Moreover, the Dinka believe that one can change outwardly from human to animal form, although the essential nature of such a person does not change.[40] Eliade's sacred/profane polarity does not easily account for the lack of clear distinctions between human beings, nature and animals within some tribal religions. Thus the sacred–profane distinction is not universally helpful nor applicable to all tribal religions because of the often complex nature of their worldviews.

ONTOLOGY AND LANGUAGE

As we noted in the previous chapter, the language of the sacred is symbol and myth. According to Eliade, sacred language implies an ontology because, assuming that one knows their meaning, myths and symbols reveal Being. By pointing to something real, a cosmic or a paradigmatic gesture, religious symbols manifest Being or that which is significant, powerful and alive.

To assert that an archaic person is *homo religiosus* implies that he/she is also *homo symbolicus*. If one is a creator of symbols, one is in contact with a pre-systematic ontology that is manifested by symbols.[41] By a pre-systematic ontology, Eliade refers to an expression of thought from a period prior to the constitution of conceptual vocabularies. The cosmic rhythms of lunar symbolism, for instance, express the passage of time, birth, death and rebirth. These manifestations of becoming are embedded at the pre-conceptual levels of archaic culture by symbols of the spiral, light and weaving. The fact that symbols can express such events as becoming suggests their existential value, an ability to indicate a positive or negative situation about human existence.[42] Thus symbols reveal secrets about the human situation and the world and are significant for human existence. Many of the deep secrets of human and cosmic existence manifested by symbols are often expressed simultaneously, a reflection of the multivalent nature of symbols. The secret depths revealed by symbols and their multivalent nature are aspects related to their ability to reveal levels of ontology (e.g. the cosmological, anthropocosmic and anthropological levels). These three levels of being are interdependent and form a single structure.[43] Thus symbols can open several levels of being and manifest different perspectives on human existence, suggesting an interdependence between human existence and the larger cosmos. If *homo religiosus* can make, live, and correctly decipher the multiple messages of a symbol, one can gain access to the universal or become open to the spirit.[44]

Whereas Eliade suggests that the language of the sacred – myth and symbol – possesses a universal quality, even though there is a plethora of such languages, Derrida maintains that language is a finite totality by which is implied a particular, determinate and natural language. 'But it ceases to be such as soon as it posits itself as such . . .'.[45] Once natural language relieves itself of its limits by overflowing itself toward the universality of concepts, 'Language then is immediately universal language that destroys within itself natural language.'[46]

If symbols can reveal deep mysteries about human existence and manifest the significance of several levels of being, can symbols reveal something about the pre-ontological? Eliade's answer is affirmative because water symbolism, for instance, reveals all the possibilities of existence. Since the cosmic waters precede form and order and support every creation, it indicates potentiality for being in various modes. The pre-formal is also suggested   by immersion in water, a regression to an undifferentiated form of pre-existence in which all forms are dissolved.[47] Even though immersion in water is a regression to a pre-ontological condition, it embodies future significance for the cosmological and anthropological levels of being: 'But both on the cosmological and the anthropological planes immersion in the water is equivalent not to a final extinction but to a temporary re-incorporation into the indistinct, followed by a new creation, a new life, or a "new man," according to whether the moment involved is cosmic, bio-logical, or soteriological.'[48] The examples of water symbolism and immer-sion in water enable one to perceive the radical nature of symbols.

As noted in the previous chapter, myth is a narrative form of symbol, which is also instructive about ontology. Myth, especially the cosmogonic type, is directly connected with ontology:

> When the cosmogonic myth tells us how the world was created, it is also revealing the emergence of that totality of the real which is the Cosmos, and its ontological laws: it shows in what sense the world is. Cosmogony is also ontophany, the plenary manifestation of Being.[49]

The cosmogonic myth tells *homo religiosus* how things and events came to be. In this sense, myth is a revelation of Being and of truth. By revealing Being, myth projects it forth from concealment and allows *homo religiosus* to take possession of it. According to Derrida, by reason of its own internal structure, language destroys itself as it develops. From a system of natural signs, it raises itself to the level of a concept and then denies that it was a system of natural signs. It thus relieves itself with each part of the structure relieving its related part as in the following example: 'The concept relieves the sign that relieves the thing. The signified relieves the signifier that relieves the referent.'[50]

Once *homo religiosus* possesses myth for Eliade, he/she can repeat its sacred events, imitate its paradigmatic gestures, and retell its marvellous deeds. By following any or all of these actions, one discloses the ontological message contained within the myth. Thus human beings not only reside in the revealing light of myth, a coming to luminosity of Being, but they also guard the Being revealed in the myth of being in the service of myth. Consequently, it is not entirely true to say that *homo religiosus* possesses myth; it is more accurate to assert that myth possesses him/her. In other words, *homo religiosus* belongs to myth and dwells in it. This is similar to what Heidegger means by saying that we live in language as in a house of Being.[51]

According to Eliade, myth unveils a mystery.[52] It does so by naming things and bringing them into being. The archaic cosmogonic myth teaches us a lesson: 'It is a matter, naturally, of ontophany, for cosmogony means this: *Being which comes into being*.'[53] Eliade suggests that Being is the ground of myth which the narrative symbol brings to light. It is to this revelation of Being that *homo religiosus* stands as a responder and guardian.

According to Derrida's mode of thinking, it is impossible for myth to reveal Being because it is without stability and cannot signify or refer to anything outside itself. If there is no referentiality outside its own system of reference, there can be no final meaning of a myth, and it certainly cannot reveal Being in any way. Since the ontological message of mythical language is so powerful for Eliade, in sharp contrast to Derrida, ordinary human language is subordinate to it. The message of myth is neither particular, private nor personal because of its own mode of being.[54] Eliade suggests that the ontological message of myth is universal because it tells the truth about the origin of things and events. Preceding the encounter of *homo religiosus* with myth, the sacred language of myth and symbol forms the horizon of Being. Eliade's position implies an important philosophical insight: language and being are equivalent. This position possesses significant implications for hermeneutics because, if existence is partially transparent, what can be stated can be understood. At the same time, Eliade wants to maintain that there is a mysterious depth to human existence that is not fully transparent and is not fully reflected in language, which is exemplified in his literary works.

Eliade's use of dreams and fantasies in his literary works resembles mythical narratives that have the ability to reveal something mysterious. In his novella 'With the Gipsy Girls', the main character loses twelve years of his life and at the end of the story encounters a former lover who says that everyone is dreaming. The main character, a piano teacher, wants to be an artist in order to create. Within his dream-state, he attains freedom, transcendence, temporal dislocation and is able to create by means of his dreams. The biological regeneration of Dominic Matei after being struck by a bolt of lightning in 'Youth Without Youth' is a good example of Eliade's use of the fantastic motif to convey the phenomena of death and rebirth, the search for paradise, eternal return, anamnesis, and *coincidentia oppositorum* (e.g. old age and youth; sacred and profane; real and unreal; ordinary and fantastic; time and eternity). In the 'Nineteen Roses' Eliade tells the story of Pandele and his quest for the meaning of one crucial moment in his life obscured by amnesia. The distinction between reality and unreality is a major theme of this work. While visiting a forester's home, Pandele sees at the window the face of a beautiful woman that suddenly vanishes. Subsequently, he tells his female companion Eurydice, and she admits to staging the entire episode. He replies to her that he thought that he was dreaming and he could not recall when the dream began. With three other people, Pandele takes a sled-ride into a forest that was destroyed 25 years earlier. The road into the forest symbolizes freedom from history and a path to a mythical realm, an imaginative, non-existent forest.

Turning away from Eliade's literary works, it can be stated that the paradigmatic function of myth asserted by Eliade is not totally affirmed by evidence from tribal religions. According to Hultkrantz, Indian beliefs tend to be 'transformed into active ritual behavior, but the *myths* are not'.[55] Hultkrantz finds that myth often operates at variance with religious beliefs and sometimes myth contradicts tribal beliefs. Since mythology represents an older world-view, it does not necessarily reflect everyday religious reality, creating a gap between mythology and everyday religion. Among the Shoshoni, this gap between mythology and everyday religion results in a tension that can lead to conflicting views on a common topic.[56] Along similar lines, Gill notes that Native American Indian world-views are not simply reenactments of sacred prototypes of primordial events because Indian world-views 'are open to history, to change, to threats from both within and outside the culture'.[57] To cite a final example, Ortiz asserts that myth does not provide an explanation for all Tewa social and ritual behaviour. Myth provides more of an outline for the Tewa Pueblo and details are given by various types of symbolic action of which ritual prayers are a good example.[58]

By means of Eliade's methodological insistence upon morphological classification, myths are taken out of their social, historical and religious context in order for their meaning to be interpreted. Some scholars of tribal religions insist that myths and symbols cannot be isolated from their context and decoded to discern their meaning. As Gill makes clear, symbols are inseparable from the performance of which they are a part.[59] Gill cites the example of dancing, a symbolic process, among the Hopi, which defines the structure and patterns of the culture: 'Through the symbolic movement of dance, culture and its underlying religious principles are effected and brought into being.'[60] Scholars of African tribal religions also indicate the importance of context when attempting to grasp the significance of a symbol. Turner thinks that symbols must not only be examined within each ritualistic performance, but they must also be viewed within the context of the total system of a tribe.[61] If rain is called God, a cucumber is an ox, or a crocodile is referred to as a spirit and the converse of each assertion cannot be made, then these statements are not items of identity. Evans-Pritchard explains, 'They are statements not that something is other than it is but that in a certain sense and in particular contexts something has some extra quality which does not belong to it in its own nature; and this quality is not contrary to, or incompatible with, its nature but something added to it which does not alter what it was but makes it something more, in respect to this quality, than it was.'[62] Thus these scholars of tribal religions perceive the necessity of examining symbols and myths within their given contexts.

Eliade's distinction between the sacred time that is recorded by myth and the profane time of history is also not a totally accurate observation of tribal religions. According to Ray, there is little speculation about the origin of the cosmos in most African religions. In fact, myth and history tend to overlap and shade into one another: 'Myth blends into history as cosmic and archetypal events bear upon local situations, and history blends into myth as local and human events become ritualized and infused with cosmic and archetypal meaning.'[63] The concept of time is also more complicated among the Tewa Pueblo, whose society is divided into winter and summer moieties. Each season is ruled by a chief, and activities appropriate to each time period are performed, like planting and harvesting corn in the summer and hunting during the winter. Although the Tewa society is divided into these two time frames, it is also united because there is a temporal overlap and the six levels of existence provide social unity.[64] Because the two systems of time operate concurrently, they serve to erase the temporary asymmetry which exists at any given time between the summer and winter moieties. Thus Eliade's distinction between sacred and profane time cannot be universally applied to all tribal religions.

ONTOLOGY AND INITIATORY PATTERNS

Birth, initiation, marriage and death are examples that human life is a continual series of changes in one's status. Since these periods of change are considered dangerous by *homo religiosus*, rites are essential to ensure one's safe passage from one stage of life to another. If we concentrate on the phenomenon of initiation, it is possible for an individual to experience a number of initiation rites in a single life. A Catholic priest, for instance, is baptized, confirmed and ordained into the priesthood during the course of his life.

As Arnold van Gennap makes clear in his classic work on the subject that is accepted by Eliade, initiation rites manifest a threefold structure: rites of separation, transition and incorporation.[65] The initial type of rite entails being separated from one's former condition, whereas transition rites involve a movement from one position to another; for instance, from infancy to childhood, from adolescent to adult, or from unmarried to married. Incorporation rites mean the adoption into one's society. Thus initiation is a rite of passage.

Since initiation denotes a body of rites and oral teachings, it is the purpose of these rites and teachings to produce a radical modification in the religious and social status of the individual to be initiated. Initiation is equivalent to a basic change in one's existential condition.[66] The initiate emerges from his/her ordeal endowed with a totally different being from that which he/she possesses before the initiation. The transition aspect of the rite symbolizes the death of the novice and the achievement of a new ontological status. The bodily operations, like knocking-out of teeth, tattooing, scarring, amputating fingers or circumcising, that are performed on the novices are initiatory ordeals symbolizing death, a temporary return to chaos. The end of one's former mode of being is a prelude to a new form of being: 'Initiatory death signifies the end at once of childhood, of ignorance, and of the profane condition.'[67] This change in ontological status involves both an existential and a social transformation of the individual. At least one anthropological critic of Eliade contends that there is no data to support Eliade's claim that the initiation experience existentially transforms the novice.[68] Nonetheless, the overall structure of a rite of passage, its ordeals and the liminal nature of the transition aspect of the rite enable one to agree with Eliade that an ontological change does in fact occur for the novice, even if it is not articulated by the initiate.

The scenario of death and ontological rebirth is also found by Eliade in shamanism and mysticism. Before a shaman can become a master of ecstasy, he/she must experience an initiatory death and be ontologically transformed. The dismemberment of the body and scraping away of flesh until the body is reduced to a skeleton are examples of initiatory ordeals symbolic of death. The shaman is transformed into his/her vocation by the substitution of internal organs and viscera and the renewal of one's blood. By descending to the underworld, the future shaman is taught by the souls of dead shamans and demons. Afterwards, the shaman ascends to heaven to be consecrated by the divine.[69] The shaman's new ontological status enables him/her to communicate with the souls of the dead, cure the sick, reveal hidden things, lead ceremonies and rites, control nature and protect the community.

The initiatory symbolism of death and rebirth into a new mode of being is also found in various forms of mysticism. The attempt by the mystic to liberate him- or herself is equivalent to gaining another mode of being transcending the human condition.[70] The path of a yogi, for instance, is similar to an initiation pattern of death to one's former condition and rebirth to a totally different mode of existence. When interpreting the meaning of *samādhi* (absorption, union) in Yoga philosophy, Eliade notes that it is a paradoxical state – a coincidence of opposites: 'Through *samādhi*, the yogin transcends opposites and, in a unique experience, unites emptiness and superabundance, life and death, Being and nonbeing.'[71] Rather than a symbolic coincidence of opposites, *samādhi* is a concrete, experiential paradox. While practising and advancing along the mystical path, some mystics have an experience of light that radically changes their ontological condition.[72] The mystic's ontological transformation suggests his/her liberation and transcendence of his/her former, limited, temporal condition and freedom from the world.

The way Eliade perceives the initiatory symbolism of death and rebirth would be unacceptable to Derrida. Death, an end to all life, represents the principle of repetition for Derrida in the sense that, on the one hand, humans cannot repeat, reproduce or represent anything. On the other hand, they always repeat, reproduce and represent. By repetition, Derrida means repeatability or the repetitions of repetition, whose potentiality depends on the possibility of an absence of the repeated. And repetition itself is the possibility of self-duplication.[73]

The theme of rebirth plays an important role in several literary works of Eliade. In his novella 'With the Gipsy Girls', Gaurilescu, a piano teacher with the soul of an artist, goes with three young, beautiful, gipsy girls to a house where he is led through a maze and falls asleep. He awakens to find himself naked, thinner, wrapped in a curtain, and returns to society to discover that he has lost twelve years of his life, a pattern similar to death and rebirth. In another novella entitled 'Youth Without Youth', Dominic Matei, a 70-year old teacher experiencing a rapid loss of memory, travels to town to commit suicide on Easter night, carrying a few milligrams of strychnine in a blue envelope. While standing in the rain on a street corner, Matei is hit by a bolt of lightning and turned into a mass of charred flesh that the doctors do not expect to live. Defying all the laws of biology, he begins to regenerate himself as his old teeth fall out and new ones take their place, his muscles become strong, he gains a new personality, his skin becomes soft, elastic and tight, and he recovers his memory to the extent of knowing the Chinese language. Thus Matei's symbolic death occurs on Easter, and his actual physical death occurs in the month of December, which coincides in a reverse way with the life of Christ.

Although scholars of tribal religions tend to disagree with Eliade about the ontological implications of the distinction between the sacred and profane with regard to world-views, symbols, and myths and concepts of time, they tend to support Eliade's claim, at least indirectly, that a novice experiences an ontological change during an initiation rite. Among the Tewa Pueblo, initiation is called 'finishing', and boys and girls are told that they will become respectively men and women.[74] Evans-Pritchard states that the initiation rite of the Nuer marks a change in young boys.[75] And Turner's discussion of liminal beings tends to support Eliade's theory.[76] Moreover, Turner notes the change from childhood to adulthood effected by initiation among the Ndembu.[77] Writing on African tribal customs, Zahan notes, 'Initiation is meant to be a sort of sacrament with the ability to grant the initiate resurrection and a new life after he has been symbolically put to death.'[78] By offering one's body and soul to Wakan Tanka (the great Spirit) at the Sun Dance, a Sioux tribal member gives up the ignorance symbolized by flesh, suffers on behalf of the tribe, and gains a new existential status of enlightenment. The painful ordeal of wooden skewers breaking through the flesh of one's breasts and any accompanying visions of the divine while dancing represent the death and rebirth of the dancer. Besides the death and rebirth symbolism associated with the rite, the dancer's new ontological status is confirmed by eligibility for leadership roles within the tribe.[79] The Sioux equate the dancer with the moon,[80] a symbol of death and new life, which represents the dancer's new status and successful completion of the rite.

NON-BEING AND NOSTALGIA

At the joint annual meeting of the American Academy of Religion and the Society of Biblical Literature in November of 1973 at the Palmer House in Chicago, Eliade gave one of the plenary lectures on the topic of death in the history of religions. In this address he discusses non-being in archaic religion at some length. Since I have not been able to locate a written copy of this lecture, I have made use of an audio-tape of this address in my possession. Although the use of this taped lecture may be somewhat unorthodox, it is, nonetheless, similar to the reconstruction of someone's lectures by using the notes taken by students. What follows will not be a complete reconstruction of Eliade's lecture, but rather a concentration on what he says about non-being and nostalgia.

According to a cross-cultural study of mythology by Eliade, death is unknown to the first humans, who eventually experience death because of something that happens in the beginning of time. The Judeo-Christian mythic explanation that death is the result of a transgression by the first humans of a divine law is an exception in the history of religions. Death is more commonly attributed to a cruel and arbitrary act of a demonic being, an adversary of the creator-figure. Sometimes, death is attributed to an accident, like the message that fails in some African tribes. In one version, god sends a chameleon with a message that humans will be immortal. A little later, a lizard is sent by god with an exact opposite message. Because the chameleon stops along the way, the lizard arrives first with its message that humans must die. This tragic accident results in human mortality.

Because the passage from being to non-being is so absurd, only an absurd story makes sense to *homo religiosus*. This is evident in a Melanesian origin myth, which tells that originally humans could rejuvenate themselves when they grow old by sloughing off their skin. Having sloughed off her skin, a woman is unrecognized by her child when she returns home. In order to pacify the child, she put on her old skin, and her act stops the effectiveness of the process. A Micronesian myth tells the tale of a wrong choice made by cultural ancestors in the story of the stone and the banana. In the beginning the sky was very near to the earth, and the creator used to let down his gate to humans by sending down a rope, a form of communication between the earth and the sky. One day, the creator sent down a stone tied to the rope. The ancestors did not want the stone because they did not know what to do with it. They called upon the creator to send something else, and god complies with their request by sending a banana tied to the end of the rope, which they accept joyfully. Then, the ancestors hear a voice from heaven: 'Because you have chosen the banana, so shall your life be. When the tree gives birth to offspring, the parent's stem dies and its place is taken by the young stems. So shall you die. If you had chosen the stone, your life would have been like the stone – changeless and immortal.'

According to Eliade, this last origin-myth of death illustrates the dialectic of life and death. The stone symbolizes indestructibility, inviolability, changelessness, opacity, immobility and inertness. On the other hand, life is characterized by activity, creativity and freedom. Although death becomes part of the human condition, it is not a totally negative event because death renders intelligible the meaning of the spiritual and spiritual being. In contrast to Eliade, Derrida connects death, a radical absence of both subject and object, with *différance*: 'Death is the movement of *différance* to the extent that that movement is necessarily finite. This means that *différance* makes the opposition of presence and absence possible.'[81]

According to Eliade, death is not a natural occurrence for an archaic individual. It is incongruous to an archaic individual to believe that death is a natural event. The change from being to non-being is a product of accident, magic or something absurd. When death does occur it changes one's ontological status by transforming one into a ghost or spirit. Thus death represents a second birth, a non-biological one that must be ritually created by other living members of the deceased's culture. By being transformed into a ghost or spirit, the deceased gains a new and more powerful life. Therefore, the act of dying is the beginning of a new mode of existence. Since being and non-being are dialectically related, death is inconceivable if it is not related to a new form of being, e.g. resurrection of the body, rebirth, immortality or some other form of post-existence.

For Derrida, death is an abyss because it is radically unknowable and intrinsically unnameable. Thus death cannot be formalized in any way. Because death is represented by the abyss, there is a possibility for repetition, a process that kills both the repeater and the repeated, which indicates the paradoxical way in which death is both non-representable and a condition for all representation.

According to Eliade, it would have been better if the Micronesian ancestors had chosen the stone and the banana. Eliade's reason for choosing both is that neither can meet paradoxical nostalgia of *homo religiosus*: that is, the wish to be fully immersed in life and also to partake of immortality. Due to this paradoxical nostalgia, to choose either the stone or the banana would not be a satisfactory solution. Human beings want to nostalgically live in time and eternity.

For Derrida, human beings never aim at death, even though it is the end of life. They also never directly face death, but approach it circuitously through the detour of historical time and space. Human beings certainly anticipate death. And it is at this point that Derrida connects death with imagination because it belongs to the same chain of significations as the anticipation of death. 'Imagination is at bottom the relationship with death. The image is death.'[82] Due to this relationship, imagination shares with death its characteristics of being representative and supplementary.

Citing the work *Sein und Zeit* by Martin Heidegger, Eliade quotes the German philosopher in effect by stating that death is the shrine of non-being that hides within itself the presence of being. Eliade agrees with Heidegger that one can encounter being in the very act of dying. Eliade approvingly claims that Heidegger proves the co-existence of death and life, of being and non-being. Thus death is at the very core of life. Death unifies in a different way for Derrida. As a person encounters his/her own death, such a person therein constitutes his/her own subjectivity.[83] This suggests that death is not an isolating factor in life, but is rather a unifying factor. Derrida states that death destroys singularity.[84]

If we turn from comparing Eliade and Derrida on death to comparing the former with some scholars of tribal religions, we find that some tribal-religion scholars would disagree with Eliade's claim that death is unnatural in archaic religion. The common causes of death in African religions include magic, sorcery, witchcraft, curses, the living dead, spirits and god, which seems on the surface to support Eliade's claim about the unnatural nature of death. However, Mbiti writes, 'Man has since accepted death as part of the natural rhythm of life; and yet, paradoxically every human death is thought to have external causes, making it both natural and unnatural.'[85] What Eliade fails to grasp is the paradoxical nature of death among African tribes. Many Native American Indian tribes perceive death as a natural passage from life to another form of existence. The Pueblo, for instance, comprehend the goal of life in terms of living a healthy life culminating with death in old age. 'Hence death in old age is often not an imbalance in cosmic forces or the final failure of efforts to ward off ill health but a passage that has been prepared for throughout the journey along life's road.'[86] Although a premature death is a serious concern for Pueblos, they perceive it as a natural end to life.

CONCLUDING REMARKS

According to Eliade, by living the sacred mode of existence, *homo religiosus* of archaic cultures finds him- or herself secure in the world, with his or her own self and social milieu. *Homo religiosus* is self-assured and safe because close to the centre of Being. Located at the intersection of the vertical and horizontal lines of reference, *homo religiosus* is able to communicate with the divine and with other beings within a realm of meaning. By living within the sacred and real, *homo religiosus* is able to satisfy his/her ontological thirst. This ontological thirst is also nurtured by the constant ontological revelation of the cosmos itself, revealing knowledge about oneself and the world. *Homo religiosus* can continue to participate in Being by repeating and imitating the divine archetypes that give reality and meaning to one's life. Eliade's exposition of archaic ontology suggests several unspecified implications: it is relational, non-derivable, non-reducible, non-contingent, dynamic and static.

Symbols and myths reveal Being. Symbols can manifest secrets about the human condition and the world on several levels. Thereby, symbols can reveal the interconnectedness, complexity and mysterious nature of Being and give one many perspectives on human existence. Symbols can also exhibit the pre-ontological realm of pure potentiality. On the other hand, cosmogonic myths inform one how things came into existence. Within the revealing light of myths, *homo religiosus* witnesses the coming forth of Being and serves as its guardian. *Homo religiosus* belongs to myth, is possessed by it and dwells in its sacredness. Myth tells the universal truth about the emergence of Being and forms the horizon of Being. Within this horizon, there is a co-existence of being and non-being. And it is only with the co-existence of being and non-being that *homo religiosus* can satisfy one's nostalgia for living in time and eternity.

Eliade and Derrida are like two scholars that pass each other in the night and have little to say to one another because they seem to have so little common ground, although they do share some common philosophical concerns like language and ontology. They differ about the reality of the sacred itself and the revelatory powers of being. Eliade's fundamental distinction between the sacred and profane is questioned and undermined by Derrida's position on the role of *différance* because neither can be primary and nothing can be wholly sacred or profane, if what Derrida says about *différance* is accurate. Not only does *différance* make possible the distinction between the sacred and the profane, it also renders possible the distinction between Being and beings for Derrida. From Derrida's perspective, Eliade's works on religious phenomena represent the play of traces and a hopeless quest to find religious meaning, a function of play itself. A fundamental error of ontologists like Eliade, for instance, is to assume that Being implies presence, an unacceptable assumption for Derrida. Whereas Eliade finds a universal quality within the nature of language, Derrida asserts its finite nature. Finally, there is no centre of existence for Derrida in sharp contrast to Eliade. For the former, there is only erring.[87]

By recalling the hermeneutical differences between tribal religion scholars and Eliade, it can be concluded that Eliade takes the distinction between the sacred and profane, a basic binary opposition to use Lévi-Strauss's terminology, and makes it a primary opposition for all archaic religions. As we have noted, this is much too simplistic and does not do full justice to the material from tribal cultures. Eliade's hermeneutical straitjacket tends to distort the variety of religious expressions found in tribal religions. Thus his sacred/profane polarity is only helpful to a limited degree. More insightful interpretations can be made by viewing a particular religious phenomenon within its specific cultural context. The diverse and pluralistic nature of archaic religions makes grand, universalistic theories difficult to execute with total validity. Eliade's theory seems to suggest that he is more concerned with similarities and tends to neglect the importance of difference.

If we try to answer the question proposed at the beginning of this chapter concerning the possibility of Eliade imposing an ontology upon his material, the answer must be affirmative. Although the archaic ontology espoused by Eliade may be derived from some tribal cultures, it does not do full justice to many tribes. The non-contextual nature of the archaic ontology expressed by Eliade makes it appear that it is imposed by him upon his subject.

8 The Phenomenon of Power

The concept of power is ubiquitous in the history of religions. In Edward B. Tylor's *Primitive Culture* (1871), power is associated with *animism*, a belief in a spiritual soul animating nature. By 1909, R. R. Marett's work entitled *The Threshold of Religion*, borrowing insights from the work of R. H. Codrington, rejected Tylor's rationalistic scheme and advocated that *mana*, a power believed to be inherent in all things by the Melanesians, was an earlier stage of religion. Other anthropologists discovered power in the tribal religions of North American Indians: *manitou* among the Algonquian, *orenda* among the Iroquois, and *wakan* among the Sioux. Due to the vague nature of these terms, it is not certain to what extent they specifically designate power. As Hultkrantz observes, *manitou* and *wakan* are best rendered supernatural, whereas *orenda* means supernatural power.[1]

In the major monotheistic religions of Judaism, Christianity and Islam, God is the source of power and is considered omnipotent. The Quran, for instance, states that Allah is all-powerful and possesses power over everything (6.17). The Arabic term *barakh*, which means blessing, is a kind of mysterious power possessed to the utmost by the prophet Muhammad and to a lesser degree by Muslim saints that is used to perform miracles by the grace of God.

Religious and philosophical concepts suggesting power are also to be discovered in China and Japan. The notion of *kami*, shadowy spiritual forces, is vaguely associated in Japan with various types of natural and supernatural powers, which makes it an elusive concept. Even more elusive are the concepts of Tao and Te in Chinese Taoism. The Tao, mother and ancestor of all, is a mysterious power because it is invisible, inaudible and subtle.[2] The all-pervading, all-embracing Tao is being and non-being, respectively its function and essence.[3] The empty, nameless, unmarked Tao brings all things into existence and governs them. If Tao is what is common to all things, Te (virtue, power) is the force within things, a function of Tao, that differentiates one thing from another.[4] In other words, Tao is the underlying cosmic order of everything and Te is its power. To live one's life according to Te is to return to one's original condition and reach complete harmony.[5]

In ancient India, the governing principle of the universe is called *ṛta*, a cosmic law similar to *asha* in ancient Iran, *ma'at* in ancient Egypt and *dike* in Greece. *Ṛta*, 'the course of things', represents the law, unity or rightness underlying the orderliness of the universe. This rhythm and structure of the universe is more fundamental than the gods and goddesses. Not only did *ṛta* give to a thing or event its own structure and nature, it also directs the emergence, dissolution and re-emergence of existence. Thus without *ṛta* there would be chaos instead of cosmos, and, on the social level, there would be immorality and disorder instead of community. This cosmic power enables the sacrifice to work. If one follows the course established by *ṛta*, one becomes fixed in truth (*satya*) and achieves a fuller and more harmonious existence.

A fundamental part of the Vedic Indian structure of reality is *tapas* (heat), a natural power. In the Rig Veda (10.190.1) creation hymn, *ṛta* (cosmic order) and *satya* (truth) are born from *tapas*, a natural heat of the sun or fire. By means of this natural heat associated with biological conception, embryonic maturation and birth,[6] one could gain certain powers: invincibility and ability to reach the higher point in the cosmos (RV. 10.154.2); poetical inspiration (RV. 8.59.6); a gain in strength and the ability to conquer death (RV. 10.183.1). By extracting oneself from the human condition, one could gain secret wisdom and contact with the gods.[7] From a natural heat in the Vedic hymns, *tapas* became in the Upaniṣads the non-natural heat of asceticism connected to spiritual rebirth. By kindling an inner fire of illumination, an ascetic is purified and, according to the *Mundaka Upaniṣad* (1.2.11), achieves immortality.

Due to the ubiquitous nature of power in numerous world religions and the often vague nature of the concept in a particular religion, historians of religions have been impelled to describe how it works and discern what it means. And it is certainly true of the scholarship of Gerardus van der Leeuw (1890–1950) and of Eliade (1907–1986). This chapter will attempt to review their contributions to this important topic, to contrast some of their findings, and to offer some further reflections on the nature of power. Although he is not a historian of religions, we will also include a review of Michel Foucault's view of power because of its importance for the postmodern era. A comparison of the positions of these three scholars on the concept of power, will help us to grasp the peculiarities of each of them.

THE NATURE OF POWER

In contrast to the profane, the sacred is, for Eliade, strong, efficacious, durable, real, powerful and wholly other. The sacred is not only saturated with being; it is equivalent to a power.[8] By logical and ontological necessity, sacred power is equivalent to reality. A sacred stone, for instance, manifests power due to its ruggedness, hardness and permanence. By transcending the precarious human mode of being, the sacred stone manifests an enduring mode of being.[9]

According to Eliade, *homo religiosus* desires to be near the source of power, to participate in power and to be soaked with it. If one desires to be near it, to participate in it, and to be saturated with power, these bodily postures suggest that *homo religiosus* wants to be in very close proximity to that which will sustain one's existence and will allow one to use it for one's own benefit and the welfare of others. Since power is equivalent to reality or what comes to be, it is creative like the *shakti* (feminine power) that continually creates the world in Hinduism.

When encountering the structure of a hierophany, or act of manifestation of the sacred, one confronts a mysterious action because what is manifested is wholly other (*das ganz Andere*), a reality not of this world; it is yet manifested in things of this profane world.[10] This is the dialectical nature of the sacred. To recall the example of a sacred stone, it can be affirmed that the power of the stone does not originate in itself. A sacred stone is holy because it shares in a higher principle that betrays a heavenly origin. In other words, a thing possesses power because it receives it from a superior force or because it participates mystically in the sacred.[11] Thus a sacred stone is a sign of something greater beyond itself, and contains the sacred power of the hierophany for which it is an instrument.[12] The sacred quality of iron is another good example. Whatever its origin in the remote past, iron, a sign of the beyond, was believed to be charged with power which tended to evoke feelings of awe, reverence and respect for a strange object.[13] Although a hierophany shows forth the sacred or wholly other, it contains a mysterious aspect because it manifests the sacred, and by coming forth into the profane realm, the sacred limits itself.[14] It should also be noted that not all manifestations of sacred power possess the same degree or frequency of occurrence. Some manifestations of sacred power are mediate because they are effected by sharing in or becoming part of a larger symbolic system.[15]

For Eliade, every hierophany, a manifestation of the sacred, is a kratophany, a manifestation of force or power.[16] They indicate some sort of choice.[17] That which is chosen is strong, efficacious, fertile, creative, dynamic or perfect. Or the chosen can be dreaded, awe-inspiring or fearful. Hierophanies and kratophanies also form a system which is always greater than individual manifestations of the sacred and its power.[18] Thus the particular instances of the sacred and power are part of a total system.

As already implied, kratophanies are ambivalent because humans can venerate or fear them. By attracting and/or repelling beings, power is psychologically ambivalent, and by being both holy and defiled, power reveals an ambivalent order of values.[19] Thus power can provide attraction and/or withdrawal by human beings due to its uncertain, paradoxical and dangerous nature. A kratophany of something unusual, disastrous or mysterious is set apart from ordinary experience. 'This setting apart sometimes has positive effects; it does not merely isolate, it elevates.'[20]

For van der Leeuw, power reveals itself as a potency in an unexpected manner. The person or thing in which power is revealed is set apart and distinguished from everyone or everything else around it.[21] This distinguishing indicates that the powerful person or thing is dangerous and thus taboo, a warning that the powerless one should maintain his/her distance and secure protection.[22] Therefore, the potent is dangerous. When power is revealed in a person or thing it is being authenticated.[23] Power can become a collective or thesaurus. The actions, thoughts and principles of human beings can represent a collection of power, even though it may be independent of its bearer.[24] The accumulation of power constitutes an effective potency, which can benefit an individual or group in an impersonal or personal way. In the final analysis, power is the essence of things and human beings.[25] Due to its dynamic nature, it tends to expand and deepen into a universal force. This universality of power leads van der Leeuw to discover power often at the base of religion, giving it its potency and life.[26]

To the dangerous potency of power, human beings, according to van der Leeuw, react with awe, amazement and fear.[27] If the powerful inspires awe, one must maintain a distance from it and respect it. Awe is, for instance, ambivalent because one is repelled by power and attracted to it.[28] Although one's initial reaction to power may be to avoid it, one is drawn to it because one also seeks it. Regardless of one's reaction to power, it makes an absolute demand upon one, although pure power itself possesses no moral value.[29] Even though seized with dread, one loves the dread. Thus, once awe becomes one's established reaction, it develops into observance in the form of worship.[30] It must be made clear that one does not worship a natural object or physical being, one adores the power revealed within and behind a thing or person.[31] Foucault agrees with van der Leeuw and Eliade that power possesses a mechanism of attraction, but he does not seem concerned with the human reaction to power as are the latter thinkers.[32]

When an individual understands power one experiences a will according to van der Leeuw. In order to delimit one's experience from other similar experiences, one assigns the will a name: 'The names of things subsist before they acquire a "personality"; and the name of God is there even before "God" exists.[33] The encounter with will, a collision with power, is a formless and structureless numinous experience.[34] To assign a name to a will is, according to van der Leeuw, to authenticate power, to give it form and unity. By giving power and will a form, one makes it concrete. To call a formless power 'God' is to name a personal experience of power.[35] Therefore, there is a unity of will, form and name which is power, the absolutely one in the universe. Nonetheless, power itself, a universal energy, is never personal. Power can develop in two directions: psychologically, it becomes a superpersonal soul, or cosmologically, it becomes a divine agency activating the universe and uniting it into a world order conforming to universal laws.[36] Therefore, van der Leeuw conceives of an evolutionary dynamic from pure power to God.

In contrast, Foucault argues that power is without essence, is not an attribute of something, is not a form of something, is not essentially repression, is not subjugation nor domination of one group over another, is not a structure, is not acquired, and is not something that can be, for instance, isolated in the apparatus of a state; it is rather a relation between forces.[37] Force is not singular because it always exists in relation to other forces and possesses no other object or subject than itself. Foucault suggests that power is something that circulates in a large, net-like manner. If power is diffuse and forms a complex web of interconnections, power relations are not binary opposites like the sacred and profane of Eliade. Power is more like an air-conditioning system that circulates cool air over a wide area. Since power circulates over a broad area, it is never localized in a particular place nor in the possession of any single person.[38] Power is also multi-directional because it operates both from the top down and from the bottom up, although Foucault informs us that he wants to conduct an ascending analysis of power.[39]

Even though power might be integrated into the structure of a society for Foucault, it only exists when it is put into action. To exercise power does not necessarily imply that it occurs between one person and another individual or between a person and a group. The exercise of power, a form of action, is rather a way that certain actions modify other actions.[40] By not acting directly or immediately upon others, power, an action acting upon an action, is able to impact upon present or future actions. This does not mean that violence and/or consensus, instruments or results of power, are part of the basic nature of power: 'In itself the exercise of power is not violence; nor is it consent which, implicitly, is renewable.'[41] Foucault seeks to define it in an non-confrontational and non-adversarial way. Yet he still recognizes that a power relationship involves potentially a strategy of struggle.

According to van der Leeuw, phenomenology describes how the religious person conducts him- or herself in relation to power. By orientating oneself to power, one's life is touched by it.[42] The phenomenological method for Eliade is intended to elicit the specific dimensions of religious experience that manifest the differences between the profane experience of the world and the religious experience.[43] The methodological starting-point for the former is power and, for the latter, the distinction between sacred and profane, whereas Foucault wants to begin from the bottom of the social network of power relations. For Eliade, power is an essential element of the sacred; it is an attribute of the sacred. For van der Leeuw, though the sacred is equivalent to power, it is, strictly speaking, more of an attribute of power, whereas Foucault emphasizes the relational character of power. The three thinkers appear to agree that power is ambivalent because it can be creative and destructive and attracts and repels. Eliade and van der Leeuw agree that power is mysterious, dangerous, possesses degrees of potency, and is something set apart from everything else in the world. Both acknowledge that humans seek power, and they are also concerned with the human reaction of awe, fear, reverence and respect for power. Foucault's understanding of power is considerably different at this point, which can probably be attributed to the fact that he is writing from outside the field of religion. Foucault emphasizes the familiar nature of power that is embedded within the social fabric and institutions of a society. Although power is not something mysterious nor necessarily sought by human beings, we need not fear it because its network of relations is something within which we are apt to find ourselves. Eliade does not share van der Leeuw's nor Foucault's convictions about the universality of power, although Foucault does not agree with van der Leeuw the idea that power is the essence of religion nor does he think that power is a product of individual or collective wills as van der Leeuw does.[44] All three thinkers suggest that there is an intimate, if not identical, relationship between power and truth. In comparison to the scholars of religion, Foucault tends to stress the material and corporal nature of the exercise of power.[45] If power only exists when it is put into action for Foucault, this position seems to contradict what he states about its ubiquitous and ever-present nature. On the one hand, Eliade represents a dualistic understanding of power because the sacred is powerful and the profane is powerless. On the other hand, van der Leeuw represents a monistic position because power is the all; it is to be discovered within all religious phenomena and actions. Foucault represents a third position because power is all-pervasive, but it cannot be equated with the single principle of the cosmos.

POWER, SPACE AND TIME

The qualitative distinction between sacred and profane shapes Eliade's interpretation of space and time. On the one hand, profane space is neutral, homogeneous, without structure or consistency. This amorphous mass is relative and lacks orientation, which is experienced by an individual as chaos. On the other hand, sacred space entails a hierophany, which implies that a hierophany consecrates profane space, thereby rendering it sacred and ensuring that it will continue to be such. Thus sacred space marks a radical break in the homogeneity of undifferentiated profane space, providing a point of spatial orientation that implies the acquisition of a fixed point.[46] To acquire orientation means to establish a world in the sense of fixing its limits and establishing order. This ordering is accomplished by following a paradigmatic model – creation myth – of the activity of the divine beings *in illo tempore* (at the beginning of time). By repeating the paradigmatic work of the divine beings, *homo religiosus* transforms the chaos of profane space into cosmos, a transformation that occurs along a horizontal point of reference and a vertical axis of communication, an *axis mundi* or centre of the cosmos.[47] Thus around the cosmic axis lies the world in contrast to the uninhabited, unknown, chaotic mass of space.

Homo religiosus does not choose a sacred place; rather, he/she discovers it. What one discovers is not simply a sacred place; one also finds the place where power manifests itself to be transformed from profane to sacred.[48] In order to develop what we stated in the preceding paragraph, this process of transformation involves repetition of the primeval hierophany which consecrates a particular place. Eliade elaborates:

> The hierophany therefore does not merely sanctify profane space; it goes so far as to ensure that sacredness will continue there. There, in that place, the hierophany repeats itself. In this way the place becomes an inexhaustible source of power and sacredness and enables man, simply by entering it, to have a share in the power, to hold communion with the sacredness.[49]

Coming to *homo religiosus* from without, the sacred power expresses itself according to its own inner dialectic. Eliade's statement also implies that there is a continuity of sacred and powerful places, which suggests the autonomy of hierophanies. Since any contact with a sacred power is dangerous to an individual, it is presupposed that one must be prepared to encounter it by prophylactic gestures of approach. Otherwise, it is possible for one to be overwhelmed or destroyed by power. Rather than power coming from outside the world from a higher source as suggested by Eliade, Foucault wants to suggest that power possesses an existence of its own and is self-reproducing. It is, for instance, able to dictate its own rule to sex, which places sex in a binary – licit and illicit – system, and prescribes an order for it.[50]

In general, van der Leeuw tends to agree with Eliade that the sacred is power and the profane is relatively powerless. Enclosed within boundaries, the power of the sacred creates a place for it.[51] From another perspective, sacred space is a locality created by power repeating itself or being repeated by human beings.[52] According to Foucault, power could never be enclosed within margins because power is not located in any single place: 'It seems to me that power is "always already there," that one is never "outside" it, that there are no "margins" for those who break with the system to gambol in.'[53]

In contrast to sacred time, profane time is, for Eliade, ordinary, irreversible, temporal duration that is measured in hours, days and years, whereas sacred time is reversible, repeatable and recoverable.[54] Sacred time repeats and regenerates itself in religious festivals, a sacred event that took place in primordial mythical time. By returning to the time of origins, a religious festival reactualizes a mythical event, coinciding with the *illud tempus* or time when the world initially came into existence.[55] For Eliade, sacred time is an eternal present, a timeless sort of time. The acute distinction between sacred and profane time is made lucid by Eliade:

> Periodic recurrence, repetition, the eternal present: these three marks of magico-religious time taken together explain what I mean by saying that this time of kratophany and hierophany is not homogeneous with profane time.[56]

By returning to the time of origins, profane time is abolished. This possesses an important implication for power 'for all powers, even the divine, become weakened and lost if exercised in profane time'.[57] Van der Leeuw agrees to a certain extent with Eliade's position because power manifests itself in the sacred time of festivals.[58]

For Eliade, ritual activity possesses a power to enable *homo religiosus* to become contemporary with the original creative actions of the divine beings and to repeat their acts. By returning to primordial time, one is symbolically reborn and gains power. According to van der Leeuw, the powerfulness of life would stagnate without festivals.[59] If *homo religiosus* embodies the extrahuman models in his/her own actions, Eliade asserts that he/she will participate in its power and become powerful. The human need to live close to the gods or sources of power is called an ontological obsession by Eliade, which implies a thirst for the sacred, a desire for power and a nostalgia for being.[60]

There is no need for an ontological thirst, according to Foucault, because the relations of power are immanent in many kinds of relations (e.g. economic, social and sexual). By not being exterior to these relations, power conditions these other relations and is also conditioned itself by other relations.[61] Foucault wants to emphasize that power is not simply related to itself, but is interwoven with a variety of other relations. Power relations are also both intentional and non-subjective, which means that the exercise of power involves a series of aims and objectives.[62] By studying the interconnections of power relations and their relationships to other forms of relations, one can come to grasp the conditions of domination within a social body.

A rite, for van der Leeuw, is a drama and a game governed by rules with the intention of gaining control over the vicissitudes of life and to draw power from it. Since one's goal is the acquisition of power, one's behaviour must be directed towards that end.[63] Sacrifice, for instance, preserves the cycle of power by strengthening the power of the community and binding its members firmly together into a more powerful group.[64] By means of ritual action, *homo religiosus* is able to harness natural powers for personal and communal benefits.[65] This gives *homo religiosus* the ability to dominate the world by ritual actions by utilizing the potency inherent within natural powers, which demonstrates the failure by humans to accept life as it is given and to change it by seeking its source of power. This implies that ritual action develops power.[66] Religious rites, which are creative and regulative, can endow human life with power because power is given with life and rites guarantee one access to power.[67] This suggests that human existence is not fixed, but is a dynamic possibility that becomes real by the acquisition of power through ritual.

For van der Leeuw, sacred action also serves power: 'Power is served by being actualized; it is represented by being brought into the present.'[68] The agent of power in this case, like the Christian eucharist celebration or sacred dance, is not the individual or community but the divine being or beings representing the sacred power. Thus power can be conjured up by *homo religiosus*, or it can renew itself. This is an example of *homo religiosus* mobilizing power rather than actually controlling it. Although both scholars acknowledge that *homo religiosus* submits to power, Eliade tends to emphasize the accommodation of *homo religiosus* to power by conforming to the sacred archetypes, whereas van der Leeuw tends to stress the more aggressive role of the religious individual and Foucault emphasizes its relational nature.

POWER, SYMBOL AND MYTH

A kratophany or a manifestation of power can become a symbol according to Eliade.[69] This possibility enables power to communicate with us and to convey a message. For instance, sky symbolism reveals transcendence, holiness, changelessness and an epiphany of power.[70] The sky gods of polytheistic religions include the element of sovereignty, a new expression of power.[71] Sky symbolism indicates the nature of a symbol to participate in the reality, meaning and power of that to which it points.

A religious symbol is multivalent, according to Eliade, because it can express simultaneously several meanings. The symbolism of the moon, for instance, embodies a lunar metaphysics that includes: (1) fertility, the recurrence of creation and the inexhaustibility of life; (2) periodic regeneration and growth; (3) time and destiny are indicated by the measuring, weaving and binding together of diverse cosmic levels – humankind, animals, rain, and vegetation – and heterogeneous realities by the moon; (4) change is marked by the opposition of light and darkness.[72] Therefore, the symbolism of the moon manifests the powers of fertility, growth, regeneration, unity, lunar rhythms, death and immortality. Symbols are also able to express a modality of the real that is inaccessible to ordinary human experience. Knots possess, for instance, the power to bind: 'Knots, nets, laces, cords, strings are among the vivid images that express the magico-religious power necessary to command, govern, punish, paralyze, strike dead; in short, 'subtle' expressions, paradoxically delicate of a terrible, inordinate supernatural power.'[73]

If a kratophany can reveal itself in a symbol, it can also manifest itself in a myth, a narrative form of a symbol. Since a myth relates a primordial event that took place at the beginning of time, it conveys a sacred history about how things came to be and what really happened.[74] The sacred realities and divine activities revealed by myth form models for meaningful human behaviour that possess important implications for power. By learning the origin myth, *homo religiosus* is able to know, according to Eliade, the origin of things and hence can control and manipulate the various cosmic realities.[75] To acquire a knowledge of the origin of something is equivalent to having a magico-religious power over it. The knowledge of the creation myth enables the archaic individual to repeat in rites what happened *ab origine* and to re-enact the creative activities of the divine beings. Thus it enables *homo religiosus* to be creative and powerful. The ability to recall and recite a myth also suggests the power of memory, which is even greater than that of knowledge: 'He who can *recollect* possesses an even more precious magico-religious power than he who *knows* the origin of things.'[76] Eliade arrives at this conclusion because memory frees one from time.

Just like Eliade, Foucault also finds an important link between power and knowledge. They are integrated with one another and create each other. Foucault makes their relationship clear: 'It is not possible for power to be exercised without knowledge, it is impossible for knowledge not to engender power.'[77] Moreover, power produces knowledge rather than preventing its advent. Although power and knowledge are not identical, Foucault wants to indicate the specificity and materiality of their interconnections in order to emphasize the intimacy of their relation.

If there is a connection between knowing a myth and power, Eliade can state that the cosmogonic myth itself possesses a power because it contains the rudiments of the sacred actions connected with creation.[78] The power contained in the cosmogonic myth can be recited to cure illness or correct certain imperfections. Since myth provides the exemplary model for all meaningful activities of *homo religiosus*, an individual not only embodies these extrahuman paradigms, but can also participate in their power. By participating in the power of the cosmogonic myth, *homo religiosus* gains power and ensures personal success in his/her endeavours.

From Foucault's position, Eliade's explication of power is indicative of its productive aspect. To describe the effects of power in negative terminology like repression, exclusion, censorship, and concealment is to miss its productive aspect: 'In fact, power produces; it produces reality; it produces domains of objects and rituals of truth.'[79] In what to some might seem to be an audacious assertion, Foucault states that sexuality, a notion that gives rise to and is historically superior to sex, is produced by power.[80] Power is also productive in the sense that it can produce knowledge, discourse and pleasure. Thus it is best to think of power as a productive network that circulates through the entire social body but not as a commodity, position or plot.[81]

A different type of productive power comes to the mind of van der Leeuw when he discusses the ancient smith, who wields a power embodied in his tools which he may understand, but of which he is not the master. Since tools embody a power superior to the craftsman, they are always made on the same model. If a craftsman deviated from the archetype, the potency might be injured and become a source of danger to its user.[82] Thus great care must be taken to assure adherence to the original model.

For van der Leeuw, to utter a word is to exercise power because utterance awakens a dangerous or beneficial power by setting it in motion.[83] A curse, vow or oath would be relevant examples. The word itself is myth, a representation of an event replete with power. Not only does myth possess power, its power is stimulated by reciting and repeating its narrative message.[84] The dynamic quality of myth-telling can be controlled by writing down the story. Since *homo religiosus* can use the written word according to his/her own will, he/she attains power over the myth by giving it a more permanent form.[85] *Homo religiosus* can also use symbols to control the world. By means of the power inherent within symbols and myths, one seeks to use it to one's own advantage. This practice is a manifestation of the human tendency not to accept the given world, 'but to manipulate it until it has been adjusted to one's own life'.[86]

According to van der Leeuw, there are two ways of creatively dominating the world: the magical attitude and the mythical form-conferring attitude. These two ways are to be distinguished: if one manifests the magical attitude one absorbs the world into oneself and the other evokes events as myths and ejects the world from oneself.[87] The latter endows the world powers with form in order to control them more effectively, whereas the former absorbs the world in order to manipulate it.

Eliade and van der Leeuw agree that myths have a creative power. The knowledge of a cosmogonic myth, for instance, gives one power over the whole cosmos. They disagree, however, on the extent to which *homo religiosus* can manipulate the symbols and myths to gain control over the world. Foucault would agree with them that language possesses a creative and productive power.

POSSESSORS OF POWER

Various types of religious figures possess power and manifest it in their lives. According to a basic presupposition of van der Leeuw's position, an individual does not accept life as it is given to one because one is basically dissatisfied with what is offered by life. Thus one seeks power in life for oneself.[88] By demanding, seeking and finding power, one discovers meaning in life. Power can be elusive because it cannot only be difficult to gain but can also be lost.

Shamans, masters of ecstasy for Eliade, exhibit several powers: healing, curing disease, descending to the underworld, ascending or flying. By assuming a bird form or a normal human shape, shamans can fly through the air to retrieve souls. This is an indication of their spirit condition.[89] Furthermore, shamans manifest a mastery of fire because 'they can also incarnate the spirit of fire to the point where, during séances, they emit flames from their mouths, their noses and their whole bodies'.[90] Mastery over fire enables a shaman to swallow burning coal, handle red-hot iron and walk on fire, which indicates an access to an ecstatic state or an unconditioned realm of freedom.[91] The ability to see spirits in dreams or awake is a determining aspect of the shamanic vocation, which is another sign of one's spiritual condition and transcendence of the profane situation of the remainder of humanity.[92] The origin of shamanistic powers can be celestial or natural.[93] In the latter case, tutelary animals help the transformation of the shaman into an animal or bird, or physical pains can be a source of power. In the former category, power is bestowed by the soul of ancestral shamans and by divine and semi-divine beings.[94] By gaining the power to know the language of animals granted by an animal spirit, the shaman is able to prophesy and to know the secrets of nature.[95] The celestial source of shamanist powers grants other types of extraordinary powers.

Like a shaman, a yogin also exhibits similar powers: the ability to fly, to know the language of animals, to know the mental states of others, to be aware of the moment of one's death, intimately know subtle things, the ability to become invisible, and extraordinary physical power. On the path to liberation, the yogin's physiology is modified by the practice of *tapas* (asceticism or literally heat) and this awakens the magico-religious powers (*siddhas*) inherent to the ascetic. The acquisition of powers enables the yogin to satisfy his 'thirst for the unconditioned, for freedom, for "power" – in a word, for one of the countless modalities of the sacred.'[96] Although the various powers attained by a true yogin are not his ultimate goal, they allow the yogin to gain autonomy of the spirit.[97] Escape from the body, freedom from space and time, and gaining a divine condition are all powerful by-products of the practice of *tapas*, a creative and potentially dangerous warmth. By surpassing the profane human condition, the yogin becomes an embodiment of the sacred power.

To be able to cure the sick, defend the community against black magic, fly, travel underground, disappear and reappear, and discover those responsible for premature deaths are all powers exhibited by medicine-men in the tribal religions of Australia. Being called to his profession by superior beings or medicine-men of his tribe, the medicine-man's ability to surpass the human condition is made possible by the supernatural beings.[98] The medicine-man is transformed physically and spiritually by supernatural beings during his initiation that consists of an ecstatic experience and replacement of bodily parts.[99] Functioning as an intermediary between his tribe and mythical ancestors, the medicine man is given his powers to help his tribe. By transgressing a religious principle, neglecting one's duty, or offending the supernatural beings that granted his powers, the medicine man can lose them.

For van der Leeuw, when power reveals itself in a person, such an individual receives a specific, self-sufficient character that sets that person apart.[100] Besides the bearers of power mentioned by Eliade, van der Leeuw refers to the spontaneously revealed power of the medicine-man, the power inherent in the life of a priest, a prophet as a tool of power, saints generating power by means of their relics and the ability of martyrs to produce power. The divine nature of kings, a living, active and change-able power, can heal and bestow cosmic events like rain and sun. Although the regal power of a king is confined within a human form, the king is revered as an embodiment of power, not as a man.[101] In a similar fashion, angels are soul-beings that embody potencies from a higher power. Thus angels are not independent forms of power, but they emanate from a central power greater than themselves.[102] Moreover, strength, keen senses of sight and smell, ability to fly or run with terrific speed, are all examples of the superiority of animals over human beings. The non-human attributes of animals force humans to regard them as bearers of power.[103] Thus animals must be treated with respect and awe because of their superior powers.

Rather than something to possess, power is a force to be exercised by its possessor for Foucault. The productive exercise of power can take the form of a ritual. A good example of this from Foucault's work is his discussion of the Panopticon originally designed for a prison by the Utilitarian philosopher Jeremy Bentham. The design of the Panopticon includes a central observation tower surrounded by prison cells in a circular manner. Since a prisoner could not tell when he/she was being watched, the incarcerated individual felt visible before an invisible power 'that assures the automatic functioning of power'.[104] If discipline is a type of power, the Panopticon is a good example of the technology and asymmetry of power. By the asymmetry of power, Foucault means the ubiquitous panopticism of power that enables it to operate beyond fixed limits in a surreptitious way that tends to undermine the limits traced by the legal system.[105] The Panopticon is an informative example of the micro-physics of power that is integrated into the macro-physics of the web of power. Foucault also wants to emphasize that power cannot only be made automatic, but it can also become deindividualized, which elucidates its widespread distribution beyond any single possessor.

By reviewing the religious bearers of power and recalling the previous sections of this book, we can more readily comprehend that power is the central organizing principle for van der Leeuw, whereas the basic organizing principle for Eliade is the distinction between the sacred and profane. For van der Leeuw, power is the key to understanding a wide variety of religious phenomena. Thus power functions as a heuristic device for van der Leeuw by giving insight into the nature of religion. Although the sacred is equivalent to power for Eliade, it does not play the same central role in his theory of religion as it does for van der Leeuw in his. Eliade and van der Leeuw concur with Foucault that the individual can be a vehicle of power. Foucault explains: 'The individual, that is, is not the *vis-à-vis* of power; it is, I believe, and at the same time, or precisely to the extent to which it is that effect, it is the element of its articulation. The individual which power has constituted is at the same time its vehicle.'[106] Even though an individual can dispose of power and can act as a vehicle for transmitting it, power passes through a number of channels as it is exercised and can become more ambiguous for Foucault.

CONCLUDING REFLECTIONS

Since the positions of Eliade, van der Leeuw and Foucault on the nature of power have already been compared at the end of the various sections of this chapter, I do not want to simply conclude with a summary of their positions. I rather propose to offer some random reflections on religious power that these thinkers suggest for further development and to add some other thoughts of my own influenced by other sources.

If this chapter implies any message, it communicates the following fact: power *is*. In other words, power is equivalent to being. Within the religious way of life, power conquers non-being and makes life possible. Assuming that it does not become impotent, power renders possible the being of things – animate and inanimate – and determines the structure of things. Although we may begin by presupposing the existence of power, it is only real to the extent that it actualizes itself. As we have seen, *homo religiosus* can participate in power and share it with others. Thus power helps *homo religiosus* to affirm life by overcoming the threat of non-power, of non-life, of negation.

Although power may be impersonal, it is meaningful and gives meaning to life. In a sense, power, whatever form it may take, challenges us to find meaning. It challenges us to find concomitantly our centre of being. This is significant because the more centred one is, the more one can control one's world, one's individual situation and oneself. To be more centred suggests being self-related and more interrelated with others, although it does not necessarily imply being simply egocentric. Thus one is more self-aware and further aware of others. Of course, power can also set an individual bearer of it apart from others, an unavoidable possibility in some cases. Self-centredness also suggests being in control or being powerful. At the same time, to possess power is to be possessed by it. By possessing power and discovering meaning, we find that power provides us space in which to live.

According to Aristotle, everything in the world possesses the power to operate in a distinctive way depending on what kind of thing it is. Thus everything possesses a drive, impulse or tendency, which Aristotle calls *hormē*. A *hormē* is implanted into each thing for it to realize its potential. What is the *hormē* of power? The drive of power is to empower, which suggests that power gives itself, increases itself and enhances itself. As power generates itself, it increases itself and takes command over the previous stage of power. To pause or to rest at any stage of empowering suggests the commencement of impotence.

Religious beings are drawn towards power and are repelled by it. Our ontological experience informs us that power is ambivalent: creative and destructive. Due to the ambivalent character of power, when we draw it into ourselves we can either be strengthened or weakened by it. An encounter with power demands care, if we are not to be overwhelmed and overawed by it.

As a force within the universe, power suggests strength or potency. It affects things to some degree and suggests degrees within itself when it manifests itself in the world. Since there appear to be degrees of power, how can we measure it? We can only measure power when we encounter it. In other words, when power manifests itself we can measure it, although we can never be absolutely certain in our final calculations because power always remains ultimately mysterious and elusive.

Power affects things by forcing them to move or behave in a certain manner. Aristotle refers to the capacity to do something as *dynamis* and the putting of power to work or the working of force as *energia*. As a dynamic, energetic force, power possesses a compulsive aspect because it can coerce certain actions and even prohibit other actions. When power actualizes itself its compulsive nature is manifested, and *homo religiosus* is compelled by it to react in a certain way. In short, power is the exercise of force. By itself, power presupposes something over which it exerts force. This fundamental presupposition of power suggests that power is never isolated because it must necessarily, by its own inner dynamic, exert force over something. By its force of compulsion, it coerces that which it encounters and controls it. As we have noted, *homo religiosus* seeks to be near power, to participate in it, to share in it, and to gain it for him- or herself because power offers one control over oneself and other things. In a religious sense, power gives one control over oneself, other entities and the cosmos. In the final analysis, power gives one control over being and becoming. To gain control is an instance of power extending beyond itself. In summary, power suggests ontological, psychological, social, and cosmological implications.

9 Time and Nostalgia

The ancient Hebrews believed that God intervened at the beginning of time to create the world and its first human couple, whose descendants were to live in the realm of history, a record of God and His creatures. At crucial times God rendered special assistance to His chosen people and saved them from despair. The failure to attain political stability for their civilization appeared, however, to the Hebrews to be so irreconcilable a misfortune that they envisaged God's final triumph specifically in terms of theocratic nationalism. Since the course of history had begun by a special act of God, history would end by God restoring the kingdom to Israel. This new regime would be presided over by God Himself or by one especially anointed by God.[1] The Hebrews understood their history as a unity, which prompted Bultmann to write, 'Its unity is constituted by its meaning, the guidance or education of the people of God.'[2] But what is the significance of the Hebrew understanding of history? For the first time in the history of the world, we find affirmed the idea that historical events have a value in themselves, in so far as they are determined by the will of God. The classical concept of eternal recurrence is rejected, and time is now understood as moving forward. Commenting on the uniqueness of the Hebrew achievement, Eliade writes, 'It may, then, he said with truth that the Hebrews were the first to discover the meaning of history as the epiphany of God, and this conception, as we should expect, was taken up and amplified by Christianity.'[3]

As inheritors of the Hebrew concept of history, early Christians computed their interpretation of history from a central event, a moment where time was fulfilled. With regard to this central event, time was reckoned forward as well as backward.[4] The Christian understanding of history is delineated as a history of salvation progressing from promise to fulfilment and focused on Jesus Christ. 'In Christ the whole meaning of history is unveiled and the redemptive activity of God finds its consummation; nothing that men can desire or hope for can be found apart from Him.'[5] Another unique feature of Christianity was that history was no longer concerned just with a chosen people. As evident in the letters of Paul, it was altered to include the history of humankind.[6] In comparison to the Hebrew view of history, the Christian comprehension was much more cosmopolitan. It was this Judeo-Christian tradition that was inherited by Augustine in the fifth century, Hegel in the nineteenth century, and Eliade and Foucault in the twentieth century. Each of these figures was to reinterpret this tradition in terms of his own experiences and philosophical insights.

The problem of time and history is a phenomenon that concerned Eliade throughout his career as a historian of religions, a novelist and even as a youngster. When he was five years old (Eliade informs us in his auto-biography) he was holding his grandfather's hand while walking one evening. The youthful Eliade spied a young girl of his age holding her own grand-father's hand. As their paths crossed, they gazed deeply into each other's eyes. After she passed him, Eliade turned his head to catch another glimpse of her and discovered that she had turned to look at him. Eliade confesses that, 'For years the image of the girl on Strada Mare was a kind of secret talisman for me, because it allowed me to take refuge instantly in the fragment of incomparable time.'[7] By visualizing the image of the little girl, Eliade was able to slip into a prolonged state of bliss beyond ordinary time and to feel free from the bonds of time.

This chapter will try to comprehend Eliade's reflections on time in his role as an historian of religions and a literary figure because a common theme runs through both types of his work. We will investigate the terror of history, or why history is problematic for him, and we will also look at his solution to the problem that history presents to modern individuals caught in its grip. In order to enhance our understanding of Eliade's position, we will also include a discussion of Augustine (an ancient Christian figure), Hegel (a modern thinker) and Foucault, a postmodernist. The major reason for including these figures is to compare aspects of their understanding of time with Eliade and to bring forth some of the peculiarities of Eliade's position.

TWO KINDS OF TIME

According to Augustine and his contextually unique, philosophical contri-bution to the subject, time is created by God.[8] Compared to the eternal Absolute, time is changeable, mutable and impermanent with a beginning and end. Time, a tendency toward non-being, consists of a succession of indivisible instants, which have nothing to do with past nor future: 'For the past is not now, and the future is not yet.'[9] If a thing exists only in the present, one cannot say that the present is long or short because any selected unit, such as a day or an hour, is subject to continuous abridgement. Since the present is not spatial, one cannot divide it. By stating that the present just is, one expresses how one experiences it.[10] Can time be measured?

Augustine answers, 'When, therefore, time is passing, it can be perceived and measured; but when it has passed, it cannot, since it is not.'[11] It can be inferred from this statement that one can only measure the absence of the present.

Augustine is caught in a paradox because, while no part of time is, we yet measure it. Augustine attempts to solve this paradox by contending that time is present in and measured by the mind.[12] Since time is not the motion of bodies, it can only be discerned in the mind.[13] The past and future are not unreal because, 'Wheresoever, therefore, they are, whatsoever, they are, they are only so as present.'[14] Thus it is best to refer to three modes of present time that correspond to acts of the mind. The past corresponds to memory, the present to sight, and the future to expectation.[15] These three modes of time coincide, although the present is the only real time. The mind can measure time because it is fixed and retains the impressions that time makes on it. Moreover, time is a distension of the soul which enables the future and the past to exist together in the present. This enables one to perceive duration and to measure it.[16]

According to Hegel's interpretation of Greek mythology, Chronos (Time) was the first ruler, but Zeus limited the devouring agency of time. Zeus and his race are, however, themselves swallowed by the very power that produced them: 'For them is the concept itself, which is there and which represents itself to the consciousness as an empty intuition; because of this, spirit necessarily appears in time, and it appears in time as long as it does not grasp its pure concept – that is, as long as time is not annulled by it.'[17] By its essence, Spirit necessarily appears in time and is actualized historically in time, a succession of nows that are either no-longer or not-yet. Time is intuited being which means that it is primarily understood in terms of the 'now'. Hegel's concept of time is not actual human time but time in terms of thought; it is something to be thought and not lived.[18]

In contrast to the positions of Augustine and Hegel, Eliade conceives of two basic kinds of time: sacred and profane. The latter type of time is ordinary temporal duration; it is time measured by clocks in seconds, minutes and hours. On the other hand, sacred time is the period of religious festivals, a succession of eternities. The essential difference between these two types of time is that sacred time is reversible, an eternal return or cyclical structure of time. 'No event is irreversible and no transformation is final.'[19] A religious festival, for instance, repeats a sacred event that took place in primordial mythical time (*in illo tempore*), which is recoverable and indefinitely repeatable.[20] 'This eternal return reveals an ontology uncontaminated by time and becoming.'[21] In contrast, profane time represents an irreversible duration.

There is an intimate connection between the world and sacred or cosmic time. If the cosmos is conceived as a living unity, it is born, matures and dies on the final day of the year and is reborn on New Year's Day. North American Indian languages express this by equating the term 'world' with 'year'. On the first day of the new year, the cosmos is reborn because time begins anew.[22] The intimate connection between the cosmos and time is related to the fact that they are created by the gods. Just as the cosmogony is the archetype for all creation, cosmic time is the paradigmatic model for all other times. Eliade asserts that the archetypes constitute a history for the archaic individual in the sense that the gestures, acts and decrees originated in time. Thus the archaic being knows a primordial history, a mythical time outside of concrete duration.[23]

Homo religiosus becomes contemporary with the *illud tempus* (time of origin) by participating ritually in the end and recreation of the world. In other words, *homo religiosus* is magically projected back into the beginning of the world, returning to the original time by which one is symbolically reborn.[24] This implies that life cannot be repaired, but can only be recreated through symbolic repetition of the cosmogony.[25] To be projected back to the beginning of time also means to become contemporary with the gods to repeat their creative act. The reproducing of the paradigmatic acts of the gods by *homo religiosus* points to the need to live close to the gods, the sacred, the course of existence and the centre of life.

Eliade's distinction between sacred and profane time involves a fundamental difference between *homo religiosus* of traditional cultures and modern beings. On the one hand, *homo religiosus* attributes no value to an historical event because it is not a significant part of one's existence, whereas modern individuals give value to historical events.[26] From the spontaneity, dangers and unpredictability of history, an archaic individual takes prophylactic measures against the dangers presented by history by periodically abolishing time through repetition of the cosmogony and finding a periodic metahistorical meaning.[27] The ahistorical position and defence against the onslaught of history by *homo religiosus* of archaic cultures is opposed to the acceptance of time as real and meaningful by Western religious individuals. Whereas the individual of traditional societies seeks to abolish concrete time through the repetition of an archetypal, religious act, a modern being finds value in the past, present and future and accepts him- or herself as an historical being. The overall attitudes and rites of *homo religiosus* of archaic cultures devalue time. The only significant time is a continual present.[28]

In Eliade's novel *The Forbidden Forest*, a dialogue occurs between Anisie, the non-historical man, and the hero Stefan, historic man. Anisie summarizes the distinction between them:

> And for historic man, for that man who wants to be and declares himself to be exclusively a creator of history, the prospect of an almost total annihilation of his historic creations is undoubtedly catastrophic. But there exists another kind of humanity besides the humanity that creates history. There exists, for instance, the humanity that has inhabited the ahistoric paradises: the primitive world, if you wish, or the world of prehistoric times. This is the world that we encounter at the beginning of any cycle, the world which creates myths.[29]

In the novel Anisie hopes for an annihilation of his civilization in order to escape from concrete time. Rather than demanding what he perceives as a high price for the realization of Anisie's dream, Stefan tells his friend:

> Human existence would seem vain to me if it were reduced solely to mythical categories. Even that ahistoric paradise of which you speak would be hard for me to endure if it didn't have the hell of history accompanying it. I believe – I even hope – that an exit from time is possible even in our historic world. Eternity is always accessible to us. The Kingdom of God is realizable at any time on earth. . . .[30]

Stefan's comments summarize the fundamental difference between the Judeo-Christian concept of time and the cyclical concept of time of traditional societies.

In his work *The Archaeology of Knowledge*, Foucault writes about history aspiring to the condition of archaeology. Traditional historical research is considered inadequate because its themes of convergence, culmination and the possibility of creating totalities are unable to account for discontinuity. 'The notion of discontinuity is a paradoxical one: because it is both an instrument and an object of research; because it divides up the field of which it is the effect; because it enables the historian to individualize different domains but can be established only by comparing those domains.'[31] Within the realm of archaeology, an intrinsically descriptive method, the notion of discontinuity is no longer an obstacle, but it rather becomes the focus of one's attention and is integrated into the discourse of the historian. With the transfer of discontinuity from an obstacle to a central focus of concentration, the possibility of conceptualizing a total history starts to disappear.[32] From Foucault's perspective, the traditional approach of historical research does not deal adequately with temporal ruptures and factual gaps, and seeks to overcome differences that are encountered. In sharp contrast, archaeology seeks to untie the tidy knots of the historian, to analyze differences, to compare, to divide and increase diversity of discourses, and to blur lines of established communication by distinguishing several possible levels of events within discourse.[33] By decontextualizing history, Foucault is not creating a horizon of intelligibility and thereby does away with meaning.

In his later works Foucault turns away from archaeology and the attempt to develop a theory of discourse and adopts Nietzsche's concept of genealogy in order to find an adequate method for his purposes. The earlier archaeological method is not rejected, but tends to serve genealogy as they work to complement each other. If the archaeologist plays a descriptive role, the genealogist is a diagnostician who focuses on the interrelations of power, knowledge and the human body. In his *Discipline and Punish* Foucault executes a genealogy of the body in relation to punishment by which he finds three modes of punishment: (1) body is publicly tortured because crime is considered an act of war in the sense that it is a violent attack on the body of the king; (2) with the humanist reform, the most ideal form of bodily punishment becomes public work; (3) the hiding of the body by incarceration. Genealogy is interested in the technology, tactics and strategy of the penal system. In the initial volume of his history of sexuality, Foucault informs his reader that his genealogical approach is concerned with what was said and what was left unsaid. In order to discern the 'said and unsaid', genealogy focuses on a heterogeneous ensemble consisting of institutions, architectural forms, discourses, laws, administrative decisions, scientific statements and philosophical and moral propositions.[34] Without going into great depth, it can be stated that Foucault is interested in the punctuating gaps of history, how power–knowledge relations replace each other, and how things or events descend, and not their origin. When the genealogist concentrates on power relations he/she sees these relations unfolding in particular historical events or movements.[35] In order to perceive the power relations, the genealogist must be situated within the web of power in the present moment. This implies that the genealogist is not arbitrarily located and also suggests that genealogy does not provide a standpoint outside the web of power relations.[36] Following the lead of Nietzsche, Foucault agrees that genealogy can become an effective history (*wirkliche Historie*), severed from metaphysics and recognizing no absolutes, that records historical justifications of power. '"Effective" history differs from traditional history in being without constants.'[37] Without hiding behind a facade of objectivity, effective history would not make any truth claims and would acknowledge that all knowledge is relative.[38]

When making such claims about truth and knowledge, the genealogist is located in a 'non-place' between conflicting forces from whence the emergence of new ideas and values is discovered.[39] From this non-point, the genealogist can study the dispersions of descent rather than the origins of accidental events or phenomena and interesting beginnings. Why should one be concerned to study descent? Since genealogy is the disclosure of differences, the study of descent reveals differences, discontinuities and divisions within history and culture. Genealogy is also concerned with the study of the recurrence of events by isolating 'the different scenes where they engaged in different roles'.[40]

With their linear conception of time and history, Augustine and Hegel conceive of historical events as irreversible and autonomous. Although history does not repeat itself, it does conform to the plans of providence. By its repeatability, nature stands opposed to history for Hegel. According to Eliade's interpretation of archaic concepts of time, the Augustinian and Hegelian concepts of time are profane because they lack the cyclical nature of sacred time. There is no connection between profane time and the cosmic rhythms. Profane time cannot recapture and relive the past; it is without value for archaic individuals.

When we compare these figures with the position of Foucault the differences are especially striking. The genealogy approach of Foucault rejects the subject, a product of power–knowledge relations, as the possible creator of history and the bearer of the continuity of history. Foucault is also opposed to Hegel's position because history is not the progress of universal reason, but is rather the play of relations of power.[41] He is also opposed to the suprahistorical perspective of Augustine and Hegel because history can never be totalized in any way, and one cannot find a normative framework with which to make judgements about the exercise of power from a standpoint outside the analysis. The individual's problems are compounded because within history there are no facts. There are only interpretations, although not in the sense of uncovering hidden meaning. 'If interpretation is a never-ending task, it is simply because there is nothing to interpret. There is nothing absolutely primary to interpret because when all is said and done, underneath it all everything is already interpretation.'[42]

TERROR OF HISTORY

According to Augustine, the biblical story of paradise is pre-history, whereas actual history begins with the expulsion from paradise. Similar to the murder of Remus by his brother Romulus in Roman history, Cain murders Abel to initiate the first act of history in the biblical account: 'Thus the founder of the earthly city was a fratricide. Overcome with envy, he slew his own brother, a citizen of the eternal city, and a sojourner on earth.'[43] This first act sets the theme of conflict and sinfulness that is to characterize history.

From the story of Cain and Abel, one can discern that there are two communities of human beings. Cain, the first-born, belongs to the city of man, and Abel is a member of the City of God:

> Accordingly, two cities have been formed by two loves: the earthly by the love of self, even to the contempt of God; the heavenly by the love of God, even to the contempt of self. The former, in a word, glories in itself, the latter in the Lord. For one seeks glory from men; but the greatest glory of the other is God, the witness of conscience.[44]

The city of man is ruled by expediency, pride and ambition, whereas the City of God is governed by self-sacrifice, obedience and humility. 'The one is *vanitas*, the other *veritas*.'[45] Augustine understands Cain as a child of flesh who builds a city to protect and promote his carnal desires. On the other hand, Abel is a child of promise and looks toward the future to the City of God, the eternal and immortal compared to the temporal and mortal city of man. Moreover, the temporal city is predestined to suffer eternal punishment, whereas the City of God will reign eternally with its Maker.[46] It can be easily inferred from the characteristics of these two cities that they are in opposition and conflict with each other. 'Cain and Abel', writes Augustine, 'illustrated the hatred that subsists between the two cities, that of God and that of men. The wicked war with the wicked; the good also war with the wicked.'[47] This conflict is the substance of human history.[48]

In his work on the philosophy of history, Hegel argues that world history is a process whereby Spirit (*Geist*) comes to actual consciousness of itself as freedom. The philosopher of history who discerns that there are many levels of spirituality and freedom within history, realizes that progress in the consciousness of freedom is attained only in and through the human mind. Since history shows how human spirituality develops and how Spirit emerges by stages out of nature, we find a progressive achievement of human freedom by reflectively investigating the facts of history.[49] If this potentiality for freedom (or the progressive consciousness of freedom) is the aim of history, what does the principle of freedom use for its realization? The goal is achieved by means of human will, although not in a deliberate sense. Even though virtuous actions are performed by historical persons, they are as insignificant as individual spiritual development, which is not normally the aim of historical individuals. It is rather the passions and interests of human beings that 'are the sole springs of actions'.[50] Since there does not appear to be a rational purposive process working within history, the passions of humans serve as the unconscious efficient agent. Thus we can regard 'History as the slaughter-bench at which the happiness of peoples, the wisdom of states, and the virtue of individuals have been victimized . . .'.[51] Although indubitably there has been monstrous suffering recorded throughout history, these sufferings have not been altogether in vain, because they helped to accomplish a new stage in the movement of history. According to Hegel, it is the cunning of reason that sets the passions to work for itself and moves humans toward a rational goal.[52]

Within the realm of history for Foucault, there are not eternal essences, no metaphysical truths, no fundamental laws and no depths to ponder because history possesses no interior, no origin, no end and no meaning. Although history possesses no meaning, this does imply that it is absurd or incoherent. History is concerned with relations of power and not relations of meaning.[53] Assuming that what Foucault says about the nature of history is true, it is best to look at the discontinuities, recurrent events, and small details of history, an arena without conscious intention, which makes genealogy the most appropriate method of studying it. Actually, Foucault is not concerned with objectively studying the events of history, but is more interested in using it for his own political purposes. Foucault writes about historical events not to preserve the past but to revolutionize history and to destroy the present. His revolutionary Communist sympathies are evident when he discusses, for instance, the development of the penal system and insane asylum in Europe. With regard to the former, Foucault states that the bourgeoisie imposed on the proletariat certain moral categories that further created a barrier between the two groups by means of penal legislation and prison construction.[54] In seventeenth-century France the Hôpital Général was developed with the purpose of establishing order by the monarchy and bourgeois.[55] Being a committed Maoist, Foucault seems to be convinced that it is necessary for historical study to be an active part of the political struggle. Therefore, Foucault's methodology can be characterized as anti-historical, and his historical works can be classified as fictions and not an attempt to depict events of the past as they occurred.[56] Like a loyal revolutionary Maoist, Foucault wants to destroy bourgeois civilization and his works are evidence of his contributions to the struggle. His contributions exposing the evils of bourgeois society are an excellent example of the intrinsically political nature of, at least, some forms of hermeneutics.[57]

Foucault's perception of the need for historical revolutionary struggle, Augustine's understanding of history as a realm of conflict, and the Hegelian perception of history as a slaughter-bench and a realm of suffering in which one's fondest hopes are crushed are partly shared by Eliade who discusses it in terms of the terror of history. In Eliade's novel *The Forbidden Forest*, the hero Stefan experiences many forms of suffering: the entrance of Rumania into the Second World War; the bombing of London; the revolution of the Iron Guard in Rumania; the earthquake of 1940; the bombing of Bucharest in 1944; mistaken incarceration in a detention camp; the death of his wife Ioana and his son in the bombardment of Bucharest; the entrance of the Russians into Rumania; the torture and death of Biris, the professor of philosophy, by the Communist police; and the fatal car-crash of Stefan and Illeana. It is history that condemns human beings to suffer. If we grant with Eliade that there are prodigious amounts of suffering in history, what makes history so terrifying?

In contrast to *homo religiosus* of archaic societies, who lives in the security provided by the myths of his/her culture, history represents a different mode of existing, although not mutually exclusive of the mythical mode of being, in the face of risk and danger. In sharp contrast to Hegel, Eliade perceives the irrational lurking within history.[58] And Eliade does not see Divine providence working within history as does Augustine. Within twentieth-century history, transcendent values are absent, and human existence is meaningless without a transcendent reference: 'The horror is multiplied, and the collective slaughter is also rendered "useless," by the fact that it no longer has any meaning. That is why such a hell is a true hell: its cruelty is a pure and absurd cruelty.'[59] The demonic element reigns and decrees crimes, cruelty and absurdity. Since historical sufferings are devoid of any transhistorical significance, they have ceased to be meaningful trials inflicted upon a people or an individual by a caring deity. Unable to find ultimate meaning in the drama of history, contemporary beings are condemned to hopelessness. The meaningless flux of time confronts us as the terror of history, and contemporary beings are paralyzed before the overwhelming onslaught of this demonic force.

The terror of history is often represented as the awesome spectre of death that ominously looms before modern beings as their instantaneous destiny, grinding to ashes any hope of future personal achievement or spiritual fulfilment within time or beyond it. In *The Forbidden Forest*, Stefan speaks to his lover about escaping from time:

> I don't want to grow old to turn into a mineral spiritually, and then one day to die. I want to live eternally young, as in our folk tale 'Youth with

Age and Life without Death'. I believe I have this right: to ask for my share of immortality. . . .[60]

Stefan's belief betrays a nostalgia for paradise, a place beyond the grip of time. It would be absurd to ask history for one's just rewards because it possesses no conscience, no justice, no law of compensation, and no hope. In the novel, Stefan's secret room functions symbolically like a womb, a safe, warm, extra-historical, atemporal place. When he leaves the confines of his secret room he becomes lost in historical time. Thus his historical journey is conceived as a labyrinth from which he must find the exit.

Lost within the labyrinth of history, Stefan laments his existential quandary:

I seem to wake up and realize that since then my life has lost its meaning. It's as though it's no longer my life. I don't know how to explain it to you. Since then everything has been false and artificial. My life has not been lived by me, but by events. I've only been carried along by a life that wasn't mine. . . .[61]

Out of control, carried along by the flow of events and lost in the maze of suffering, Stefan makes another tragic discovery: history destroys one's memory. History works gradually upon the memory by modifying it, according new – negative or positive – values to it and finally annulling it.[62] Therefore, modern beings cannot even recall the sacred revelations that have occurred in history.

Stefan is Eliade's spokesman in the novel against the position of historicism and the tendency to ascribe too great an importance to history. Stefan says, 'Life for the people of the modern world, for us, wouldn't be worth living if it were reduced only to the *history* that we make. History takes place exclusively in Time, but man by means of all his higher powers opposes Time.'[63] Biris, the professor of philosophy in the novel, criticizes what he calls Stefan's phobia of history and his nostalgia for a childhood paradise. Biris, the archetypal person living in history and defined by it, insists that Stefan should look at him because the professor is reconciled with history and nothing ever happens to him. Later in the novel Biris is tortured to death by his interrogators – another victim of rapacious history.

Although Biris is reconciled to history, it is curious to read in the novel that it is he who tells Stefan the story of the ascetic Narada and Vishnu from Hindu literature. According to this story, the deity Vishnu granted Narada a desire because of his saintliness, and the ascetic wants to know about the god's power of *māyā*. After following Vishnu for a while, the god asks

Narada to go to a village for some water to drink where the ascetic meets a beautiful girl and forgets his task. After marrying the girl, Narada spends twelve years as a farmer, fathers three children, and assumes leadership of the household upon the death of his father-in-law. During the twelfth year, torrential rains flood the area and the former ascetic loses his herds, house and family. While crying, he hears the voice of Vishnu who says that he had been waiting for half an hour. Not seeing the destructive waters but rather fields gleaming under the sun, Narada is asked by Vishnu if he understands what *māyā* is. Vishnu teaches Narada that time is illusion and that existence in time is without significance and unreal. The myth also conveys the message that an individual cannot make history because one is not in control of one's destiny. With its cycle of twelve years ending in death, this myth parallels the life of Stefan in the novel. The labyrinth that Stefan attempts to escape is characterized by *māyā*. To be free one must break out of its grip. Thus we need to turn next to a consideration of the proper response to the terror of history.

ABOLITION OF TIME

A basic presupposition of Eliade's position on time and his solution to the terror of history is his conviction that the growth of history increases alienation from any transhistorical model. Thus historicism, an Augustinian theology of history, an Hegelian philosophy of history or Foucauldian genealogy, does not provide an adequate answer to the terror of history because it is dubious that a modern being can make history. 'For history either makes itself . . . or it tends to be made by an increasingly smaller number of men who not only prohibit the mass of their contemporaries from directly or indirectly intervening in the history they are making . . . but in addition have at their disposal means sufficient to force each individual to endure . . . the consequences of this history, that is, to live immediately and continuously in dread of history.'[64] If one's freedom to make history is a false dream, modern beings have two apparent options: to oppose the small minority that is creating history or to seek refuge in a subhuman way of life. The latter is a form of fleeing from the dread of history, an inauthentic mode of being for Heidegger and Eliade. To decide for either choice does not seem to be adequate for Eliade, who appears to call for two paths that are interconnected: a re-evaluation of Christianity and an abolition of time. By following his suggestion, we will gain a religious interpretation of the terror of history.[65]

From one perspective, the call to abolish time appears to be an impossible illusion or another example of the romantic strain in Eliade's work. There are, however, precedents in history. Ancient alchemists, for instance, tried to master time, a success finally achieved by means of organic chemistry and its production of synthetic products at the present time.[66] Dreams enable an individual to conquer time: 'It is always in dreams that historical time is abolished and the mythical time regained . . .'.[67] The individual rediscovers an ahistoric existence in dreams. Poetic and literary creation imply an abolition of time because such creative artists try to recreate ordinary language and substitute a private and personal language that 'tends towards the recovery of the paradisiac, primordial situation; of days when one could *create spontaneously*, when the *past* did not exist because there was no consciousness of time, no memory of temporal duration'.[68] The poet is like the individual of archaic society who wants periodically to remake the world and view it as if time did not exist. This abolition of time and nostalgia for the myth of eternal repetition are evident in the contemporary literary works of T. S. Eliot and James Joyce, according to Eliade.

Eliade's more traditional answers to the terror of history is to re-evaluate Christianity. He calls for a philosophy of freedom that does not exclude God.[69] The Judeo-Christian tradition replaced the horizon of archetypes and repetition with faith, which implies that everything is possible.[70] Referring to a passage in the Gospel of Mark (11:22–4), Eliade comments: 'Faith, in this context, as in many others, means absolute emancipation from any kind of natural "law" and hence the highest freedom that man can imagine: freedom to intervene even in the ontological constitution of the universe.'[71] With its source in God and supported by the highest Being, this creative freedom, engendered by faith, is one's defence against the onslaught of the terror of history. Unlike the individual of archaic society with myths and periodic rites, modern individuals need God because of the threat presented by history. Rather than being led to despair, one gains autonomy by means of one's freedom grounded in faith and a certainty that the tragedies of life have a transhistorical meaning by presupposing the idea of God.[72] By revolting against the irreversibility of time, one can recreate one's world and free oneself from the threat of time.[73] If one can abolish time, one can always begin one's life anew.

Augustine would argue that Eliade's nostalgia for eternal recurrence is a pagan concept of time that must be rejected. For Augustine, the world demonstrates the mark of the creative work of God, but compared to God the order and beauty of the world are nothing.[74] The world, created out of nothing by God, is created simultaneously with time.[75] The pagan belief that the world, with its ever-recurrent motion, is eternal is a strange deception due to impiety and not a lack of intelligence, because the pagans attribute to the world only what can be said of God, a being infinitely distinct from the world. In his more moral argument against the pagan concept of time, Augustine asserts that a real future cannot exist because past and future are equal phases within the cyclic conception of time. Therefore, the cyclic view of time is hopeless because hope and faith are essentially related to the future and true happiness is excluded.[76] Augustine would also reply to Eliade that his solution to the terror of history is non-scriptural.

Although Hegel would agree with Eliade that history is a realm of suffering, a nostalgic return to an archaic form of eternal recurrence is not a viable solution, because Hegel understands history as developing toward a definite goal. Hegel conceives of development in the following way: 'This formal conception finds actual existence in Spirit; which has the History of the World for its theatre, its possession and the sphere of its realization.'[77] Hegel's notion of development is rather ambiguous; however, he thinks that what occurs in all development is a transition from the imperfect to the perfect, from the abstract to the concrete. This notion of historical development is absent to any great degree from Eliade's concept of historical dynamic. The development that occupies Hegel's interest is that of freedom, and history represents its story. By investigating world history, the philosopher can see that 'the Eastern nations knew only that one is free; the Greek and Roman world only that some are free; while we know that all men absolutely (man as man) are free . . .'.[78] This development represents a rational process, which can be viewed in the manner that its goal is achieved and displayed by the order demonstrated by the successive stages of the process. Hegel would agree with Eliade that there is abundant irrationality in history. But unlike Eliade, Hegel affirms that history exhibits a logical progression and order called 'dialectical'.[79] Hegel's view of historical progress is teleological, even though any notion of infinite progress is the embodiment of a contradiction. The notion of progress is meaningless unless history is orientated towards a definite goal. Thus Hegel comprehends history as the development of Spirit in time, just as Nature is the development of the Idea in space.[80]

Foucault's shattering of traditional cultural distinctions among categories prefigures his answer to Eliade about the terror of history. The only real solution to the suffering and injustice experienced in history is a Maoist revolution. In short, the answer is power. Foucault is opposed to institutionalized power that enhances centralization and unification and develops instruments of discipline to coerce compliance by people because it is too bourgeois. By reducing justice to power, Foucault is led to a form of nihilism in which there is an inversion and not a transvaluation of values as in Nietzsche's philosophy. Foucault's type of nihilism possesses a central hermeneutic component because it seeks to explain away any apparently meaningful interpretation that deludes people into believing that there is meaning.[81] Foucault wants to demonstrate that meaning and its assumed efficacy is illusory.[82]

TIME AND NOSTALGIA

Chapter 4 called attention to the nostalgic elements in the theological reflections of Eliade. Within the context of this chapter, his call for an abolition of time could be characterized as an unrealistic fantasy conjured by a dreamer of archetypes. It is more useful to envision his call for the abolition of time as a nostalgic wish for a return to what he calls cosmic Christianity. Thus the following remarks will complement Chapter 4.

In Eliade's novel *The Forbidden Forest*, Biris is tortured by Communist police to reveal something about an alleged conspiracy against the communist rulers of Rumania. His sublime message is a recitation of the popular Rumanian poem 'Mioritza' (Little Lamb) published by the poet Vasile Alecsandri in 1850. The poem tells the story of a young shepherd who is warned by a lamb about his impending death by jealous companions. The shepherd does not decide to defend himself, but tells the lamb of his final wishes. Eliade summarizes his final requests:

He asks it to say that he is to be buried in his own fold, so that he will be near to his sheep and can hear his dogs. He also asks it to put three shepherd's pipes at the head of his grave. When the wind blows it will play on them, and his sheep will gather around and weep tears of blood. But above all he asks it to say nothing of his murder; it must say that he has married, and that at the wedding a shooting star fell, that the moon and sun held his wedding crown, that the great mountains were his priests and the beech trees his witnesses. But if it sees an old mother in tears, looking for a 'proud shepherd,' it must tell her only that he has married 'the peerless queen, the bride of the world, in a beautiful country, a corner of paradise;' but it must not tell of the falling star or the sun and moon holding his crown or the great mountains or the beech trees.[83]

This summary allows one to grasp the shepherd's acceptance of his fate, his wish for continued life in another mode of existence, and his betrothal to the cosmos. By reciting the folk poem to his tormentors, Biris vicariously identifies himself with the young shepherd. The message of the poem is capable of breaking the grip of time and death.[84] The threat of time and death is transformed for Biris into a marriage ceremony with the cosmos, a sacred place, and continued post-existence beyond the terrors of history. Eliade understands the shepherd's situation as a triumph over his fate by imposing a meaning on his absurd condition as a sacramental mystery.[85] Thus the absurdity of Biris's torment and the fate of the shepherd receive value and meaning.

Other characters in *The Forbidden Forest* nostalgically seek to escape from time. Stefan tells Biris, for instance, about emerging from time:

> Once when I was little, I rode home in a wagon full of hay. This happened at our vineyard near Ramnicul Sarat. I had gone to sleep and suddenly I woke up alone in the wagonload of hay, and there above me were only the stars. Only the stars. And it seemed as though everything had stopped there, in its place. It seemed as though time no longer flowed.[86]

When one unites with the cosmos time ceases to flow, whereas identity with historical time makes one a slave and humiliates one. The exemplar of cosmic Christianity is Anisie in the novel. It is he who gains awareness of how time passes and how to prevent it from flowing. Anisie, a symbol of eternal peasant wisdom, is not a slave of time measured by a clock because what matters to him is the rhythm of the cosmos – the fluctuations of day and night, the waxing and waning of the moon and the change of seasons, that is, the eternal flow of the cosmos. The cosmos is the bearer of value and meaning; it contains metaphysical truths and answers to such mysteries as death and resurrection.[87] Thus Anisie serves as Eliade's representative for cosmic Christianity in the novel.

If the cosmos can teach us the answers to the mysteries of life and free us from the bondage of historical time, as Anisie believes in the novel, the death of Stefan should be instructive. On the Night of St John, Stefan meets Illeana, his beloved, in the mysterious forest of Banesasa in which a car disappears at midnight. On the same summer evening twelve years later, symbolically representing a perfect cycle, the former lovers are reunited in a forest. Illeana is driving the car that formed Stefan's obsession throughout the novel. The car becomes Stefan's way out of the labyrinth of his existence by becoming his, as well as his beloved one's, coffin. Illeana reveals herself as the angel of death, and she helps Stefan to end his search, a quest for death.[88] Although Stefan's twelve-year nostalgic quest forms a cycle and would seem to suggest a final return to the cosmos of Anisie, the novel consistently portrays him as a victim of history. Stefan's twelve-year infatuation with Illeana and nostalgic obsession with the car drive him to his historical fate – a tragic and fatal car crash.

By nostalgically trying to recapture a magical night in 1936, Stefan is a representative of modern beings who are neither free nor creators of history. Throughout the novel, he is a witness to and victim of historical forces. On the contrary, a member of cosmic Christianity is free and creative. Such a person can cope with the terror of history because of one's ability periodically to abolish time and regenerate oneself and one's world. Therefore, the cosmic Christian can transcend time and live in eternity.

CONCLUDING REMARKS

Augustine does not offer a true philosophy of history, a view based on inductions from observable trends in history, but his work is similar to a theology of history.[89] Augustine is not concerned with world history or with finding patterns in history to discern general laws. History is not a scientific discipline; it is rather providential, a play written by God. According to Augustine, time and history are redeemed because of the Christ-event that gives history its meaning. Time is no longer cyclical and reversible because Christ lived, died and was resurrected only once.

According to Hegel, the World-Spirit (*Weltgeist*) is the operative force in world history, a process whereby Spirit comes to actual consciousness of itself as freedom. This consciousness is attained in and through the human mind. In order to attain its end, the Spirit works through world-historical individuals. The individual is a bearer of the *Weltgeist* by participating in the more limited totality referred to as *Volksgeist* (spirit of a people) or State, a cultural complex integrating the art, religion, politics and technology of a people into a unified self-consciousness.[90] Thus the state or culture is the ultimate bearer of history, and the individual is significant only as a moment in the movement of universal freedom. The meaning and progress of history perceived by Hegel and Augustine is not shared by Eliade.

Foucault's inverted nihilism leaves no place for either meaning or a centre where a seeker might find the truth. His corpus of writings can be viewed as an attempt to decentre Western culture and leaves no privilege to any centre. In Foucault's radical scheme there is no room for origins, transcendence or self. Since there is a plurality of differences and not a reductive single system of them, this implies that Foucault's method of genealogy dissociates itself from identity and synthesis.[91] Although the other three thinkers discussed in this chapter accord a place to memory in some sense, Foucault's genealogy severs history from any connection to memory 'and constructs a counter-memory – a transformation of history into a totally different form of time'.[92] Foucault also does not seek atemporal structures but historical conditions of possibility.[93]

As stated in Chapter 4, Eliade asserts that modern individuals have fallen into history, a living hell, where they are threatened by the terror of history. To have fallen into the dark hole of history implies the loss of one's centre of meaning. The character Stefan in *The Forbidden Forest*, for instance, represents the bulk of humanity wandering in a labyrinth of absurdity searching for a centre, meaning and escape. Eliade tries to provide a religious answer to this ominous threat of history by calling for a revaluation of Christianity and the abolition of time. With his advocacy of cosmic Christianity and the abolition of time by an eternal recurrence to a primordial history embodied in myth, the strong nostalgic strain reappears in Eliade's work, a trend discussed in Chapter 4. Eliade's solution to the terror of history does not, however, account for progress and meaning.

The growth of the sophistication of human tools, the development of technology, the advance in knowledge, and the rise of consciousness point to historical progress, which emphatically suggests an improvement of the human situation and a value to history. A better alternative for modern beings would be to strive to integrate history and nature. Due to the ambiguity and mysterious nature of history, meaning remains an object of courageous faith, a means of transcending the apparent ambiguity and disconnectedness of secular history. As Augustine indicates in his works, history is not a source of fear and despair to the believing Christian. Even though the meaning of history is hidden and one is never able to grasp its mystery in any total sense, one must have courage grounded in faith to believe in the significance of history. What Edith Wyschogrod states about Hegel's contention that evil in history is overcome in the life of the Absolute can also be applied to Eliade, that is that the atrocities of the twentieth century belie both thinkers.[94] Thus neither thinker provides a way to cope with a horror like the Holocaust. Rather than trying to escape from history, it is better to take one's stance within it. Unless we take our stand within history and reject any attempt to escape it, we can never solve the problem of suffering, and we can never reject political fanaticism and other forms of absurdity.

10 Seeking the Centre

The Pima and Papago tribes of southern Arizona on the North American continent conceptualize life as a road that is difficult, painful, sorrowful, confusing and full of conflicts. They envision the road of life as a labyrinth that is symbolically expressed in the following way: 'It consists of a circle, in the center of which a small circle represents the earth. Beginning a short distance from the earth in the center, four lines radiate in each direction, but they encircle the center in a fashion that concludes with the ends of these lines enclosed within the pattern formed by the other lines.'[1] The objective is to find one's way safely through the labyrinth and secure the centre, the place to which life is originally directed. The complexity of the road of life depicted by these Native American Indian tribes partially resembles Eliade's view of life. Although Eliade did not conceive of human life as an intricate labyrinth, the unity of Eliade's life and work suggests that he spent his creative career searching for the centre of his own existence. And this quest for a meaningful centre of existence is a theme that runs throughout his scholarly and literary publications and is the reason for making it the concluding theme of this work. This final chapter, then, is an attempt to tie together the threads of his quest for a centre. In order to accomplish this task, we need to examine Eliade's conception of life and to see what he discovers at the centre of human existence. We will also compare Eliade's position with that of the a/theology of Mark C. Taylor that we began to discuss in Chapter 4; we did not really conclude that discussion, because we concentrated on his deconstruction of the Western theological tradition and did not examine his deconstructive a/theology in any depth. This final chapter and comparison is not a repeat of Chapter 4, but is intended as a supplement to that chapter and an attempt to understand how Eliade's literary and scholarly work in the history of religions were part of his quest for personal meaning.

The a/theology of Taylor is characterized by its playful nature, an unbounded play of erring, and its vision of the end of traditional theology. This playful a/theology must not be taken too seriously or practised for some exalted purpose. Without any goal, reward, purpose, meaning, or result, play is totally useless.[2] Taylor claims that it is a ceaseless game that performs a drama depicting the death of God, the disappearance of the self, the termination of history, and the end of scripture. This entire dramatic game is a play of differences, a divine milieu, in which the transience of things becomes evident. This game is played while the end of theology

157

approaches and includes an end that is not the end of difference, an alternative and that opens the a/theological imagination. The end of theology involves a new kind of thinking that entails thinking beyond the end of theology. How is this possible? It is necessary to think what has been left unthought by going beyond immanence and transcendence to an end that is untheological.[3]

THE FALLENNESS OF LIFE

From Eliade's scholarly and personal perspective, the search for the centre is a dangerous journey because one is constantly threatened by the loss of one's sanity, physical well-being, and direction. What makes the quest for the centre of existence so difficult is its disjointed nature, whose mysterious, beguiling and dangerous characteristics are embodied in the given human situation. In Chapter 4, a review of Eliade's comprehension of the basic human condition expresses this situation as human fallenness, the death of God, and the fall into history. To fall from original paradise involves a loss of primordial perfection that is characterized by dissatisfaction, forgetfulness of a timeless, paradisaical condition, and separation from that which is holy. Thus fallenness represents a state of disunity that Eliade calls a 'sonorous hell in which we are condemned to live'.[4] With the death of God, human beings have lost the possibility of experiencing the sacred at the conscious level of existence, although the unconscious remains religious. The fall into history or time recognizes that one is conditioned and victimized by forces beyond one's control. As an area of human despair, the drama of history is devoid of meaning and value.

The implications of the death of God for human beings contain different possibilities for Taylor because it marks a loss of a stable centre that provides the foundation for an authentic, unique, transcendent self. This decentred self does not simply disintegrate, but rather finds itself situated within the flux of a multitude of ever-changing relations. This decentred, fluctuating, presentless condition of the self leads Taylor to conclude: 'The lack of an absolute center is tantamount to the absence of an absolute subject or original self.'[5] Adrift in a hostile world, the self is lost, nameless, and anonymous and experiences a continual kenotic, self-emptying process which leaves merely a trace of the self. For different reasons, Taylor and Eliade agree that the self is lost, although the former leaves the self without hope of ever finding a meaningful centre to its existence.

Lacking any transcendent values and meaning for Eliade, history manifests itself as a terror to be encountered by vulnerable beings overawed and overwhelmed by the irrational forces of history. Not only does the spectre of death ominously loom before one within profane time, but a demonic force reigns and decrees heinous crimes, odious cruelty, and absolute absurdity. Human beings are condemned to hopelessness. Because events are out of one's control, one is simply carried along by the flow of events and lost in a maze of suffering. The rapacious nature of history even destroys one's memory. The destruction of memory by history is a theme in some of Eliade's literary works. In 'Youth Without Youth', Matei, the main character, is motivated to commit suicide because of his rapid loss of memory due to arteriosclerosis. After his regeneration, he gains an extraordinary memory that prefigures a future condition of humankind: 'The principal characteristic of the new humanity will be the structure of its psycho-mental life: all that has ever been thought or done by men, expressed orally or in writing, will be recoverable through a certain exercise of concentration.'[6] This assertion about the future of humankind is remarkably similar to Buddhist Yogacara philosophy and its doctrine of storehouse consciousness. In another novella, 'Les Trois Graces', Dr Tâtaru wants to perfect a serum that would produce an anamnesis of the human body of the teleological instinct present in every micro-organism. According to Dr Tâtaru, what Adam and Eve originally lost was youthfulness without ageing or the ability of the body to regenerate itself because their punishment was amnesia. For Eliade, history is something like the following nightmare: You are ready for a good night's rest and feel secure in your comfortable bed, but after falling asleep you dream that you are suddenly run over by a freight train that leaves you in shock and helplessly groping to put the pieces of your mangled body back together, if you could only remember where all the pieces fit on your body. Therefore, even while asleep you are not safe from the runaway freight train of history, and you are forced to acknowledge to yourself that there is no safe place. In the face of this horrible scenario, what amazes Eliade is that some people continue to create: 'They are like that poet who composed his verses seated on a barrel of gunpowder, all the while knowing he could be blown up from one moment to the next, but refusing to let himself be dominated by fear, and who had only one idea in mind: to write in the most authentic and the most perfect way possible.'[7]

From Taylor's perspective, someone like Eliade gains satisfaction from his nostalgic recollections of past events and hopes of future fulfilment. Such satisfaction is illusory because of the intimate connection between history and unhappy consciousness, a continuously discontented victim who lives with deceptive memory and false hope. Caught between an ideal past of origin and a future yet to arrive, the unhappy consciousness is lacerated as it moves from guilt to sin, and tries to negate the self by affirming the other.[8] History ends when erring, a serpentine-like wandering, commences. Without intention, usefulness or certainty, the wanderer follows no particular course of travel toward no designated end. 'Such wandering is erring – erring in which one not only roams, roves, and rambles but also strays, deviates, and errs.'[9] Taylor's model for the faithful wanderer is the biblical figure of Abraham, a lonely nomad and stranger on the earth.[10] Abraham seems to be a curious choice for the erring wanderer because his deep faith always gives him hope, and Taylor claims that there is no hope.

Not all that differently from the picture created by Taylor's a/theology, Eliade asserts that the unsafe, nightmarish, profane world in which we live is a wasteland. Within this irreligious expanse, humans are adrift and not at home in the world, and lack a meaningful centre to their existence. To be separated from the centre of one's existence does not mean for Eliade that one is led astray; it is rather to acknowledge that one finds oneself lost and forgetful. To be lost and forgetful within the wasteland of history is illustrated by the problems of characters in *The Forbidden Forest* that we discussed in previous chapters. In 'Nineteen Roses' Pandele, its leading character, is convinced that the secret of all techniques, physiological and spiritual, is anamnesis as he tries to recall what happened to him on Christmas 1938. And Dominic Matei of 'Youth Without Youth' becomes endowed with a supernatural memory, but he must hide from the Nazis who want to take him into custody and study him. This existential crisis of contemporary life can only have a specifically *religious* solution, because only religion offers the exemplary, transcendental patterns necessary for one to cope with the prodigious problem.

In contrast, there is no religious solution for Taylor because hope died with the demise of God. There is no pure origin in which to take emotional comfort and no perfect end to which to strive because all that remains is a trace. It is difficult to take Taylor seriously when he writes, "This hopelessness, however, does not inevitably lead to despair.'[11] We are condemned to wait, a final losing game and form of damnation, within the ceaseless play of the divine milieu, an acentric totality that is without origin or end. Since this divine milieu is a whole without a centre, those waiting, wandering and playing within it can never find its centre because there was never a centre to be lost, which leaves the wanderer uncertain about his/her origin, present location and future destination.[12] Without direction and location, the serpentine wanderer finds that it is impossible to locate a true centre, which implies even more erring and wandering. The nomad wanders perplexed and delirious through an endless maze of winding and interconnected paths and passages, which ultimately represents an abyss.[13] If for Eliade the self is lost and seeks its true centre, Taylor envisions a trace that mazes through a maze because the self is dead.

From what has been stated, it is easy to understand how one could get lost in Taylor's maze and in the fallen condition of human existence according to Eliade. The possibility of getting lost is also suggested by the danger for Eliade, as discussed in Chapter 2, that the historian of religions could get lost in the plethora of material from different cultures and historical periods. This is a good example of the fact that Eliade's personal quest for a centre of existence and his scholarly work are intimately linked and interdependent. Chapter 2 implied that Eliade is lost in the jungle of *Geisteswissenschaften* (human sciences) and that *Religionswissenschaft* is an elusive and unrealizable ideal. By following Eliade's lead, how does one extricate oneself from the wasteland of history and the discipline of the history of religions?

If the historian of religions, as presented in Chapter 3, is concerned with meaning, if such a scholar encounters a series of messages waiting to be deciphered and comprehended, and if this student of religious phenomena must relive a multitude of existential situations and unravel a number of pre-systematic ontologies, how can that person succeed in the fundamental human situation characterized by fallenness without needing to transform him- or herself into a superhuman being? The multitude of religious phenomena that is encountered by the historian of religions finds its unity within human consciousness, an interior locus of the sacred that forms a structural element of human consciousness. As discussed previously, the unity of the dialectic of the sacred tends to repeat itself indefinitely in a series of archetypes. Thus Eliade, as a part of the fore-structure of his hermeneutics, presupposes a unity of the history of the human mind, which makes it possible, even taking into consideration the desolate human situation, for the historian of religions to understand religious phenomena and behaviour. Since past religious phenomena and events are also given in consciousness, they can become current for us. Thereby, the hermeneutical problems of distance and contemporaneity are bridged. Even though one finds oneself in a certain situation, this is not a completely limiting condition because one can know other situations. Eliade's position seems to suggest that knowing another situation presupposes understanding one's own existential situation. Moreover, there is an existential demand to decipher and to elucidate these crucial situations of oneself and others, which entails placing oneself into the boundary situations – birth, initiation, or death – in order to grasp and understand their condition. To be able to successfully accomplish this type of activity involves widening one's horizons, which results in a deeper knowledge of human nature, enables one to transcend cultural provincialism and to become culturally stimulated. The latter positive result of broadening one's horizons leads to a new, universal humanism.

Eliade's advocacy of a new humanism is connected to his call for a creative hermeneutics which will stimulate philosophical thought, lead to a change in human beings, form a source for new cultural values, and enable one to discover one's place in the world. These benefits are not without risks, because there is the danger of becoming obsessed or trapped by the subject of study and the difficulty of finding the sacred camouflaged within the ordinary. These dangers suggest that a quest for a creative hermeneutics is akin to successfully traversing a wasteland.

While Eliade seeks a creative hermeneutics, Taylor envisions playing and wandering in the divine milieu, which he defines more fully: 'Scripture *is* the divine milieu, and the divine milieu *is* writing.'[14] This divine milieu, as word and writing, is both creative and destructive of all that is and is not. The type of writing conceived by Taylor represents an inversion and subversion of traditional Western theology because a continual dialectic of transgression combined with the divine milieu negates whatever consciousness accepted as real and any divine experience. This negating process purges one's consciousness and experience of the holy in order to make possible a new and radical form of consciousness and experience, which can usher in a new form of God without the former name or image that is already deceased. Taylor explains further that, 'This negation of God appears as the word incarnate in writing.'[15] Taylor gives us a new God that he refers to as a 'God of writing' that represents the embodied word. Yet he informs us that we cannot use the former name or image. Nonetheless, this so-called God of writing is equated with Plato's notion of *pharmakon* (drug, medicine, or poison) *via* Derrida by Taylor, which suggests that this God can heal but can also kill. Moreover, it is difficult to discern how the creative hermeneutics advocated by Eliade could be developed with what Taylor refers to as the divine milieu because its radical relativity seems to preclude any position from which to develop a theory of interpretation.

Taylor's conception of the divine milieu also does not have much in common with the same term in the work of Pierre Teilhard de Chardin. According to the latter, the divine milieu is close to human beings, although it is always withdrawing and drawing creatures along with it toward a common centre, in the form of a divine presence that surrounds and transfixes individuals, even though it eludes one's grasp. Unlike the conception of Taylor, the divine milieu of Teilhard de Chardin gathers apparently contradictory things together in a harmonious way within itself.[16] In sharp contrast to Taylor, the divine milieu for Teilhard de Chardin represents a centre with the power to unite, transfigures all things from within and completes all beings.[17] Taylor claims that the world is empty of God, whereas Teilhard de Chardin wants to emphasize the omnipresence of the divine conceived in terms of Christ. For the latter, the divine milieu is dynamic and grows in individuals and then in the world, representing a 'synthesis of all the elements of the world in Jesus'.[18] There is also nothing liminal about the divine milieu as conceived by Teilhard de Chardin, whereas Taylor envisions a liminal time and space for his marginal nomads to wander in a serpentine fashion.

As we have already noted, Eliade's call for a new humanism is directly connected to dialogue with other cultures. It is Eliade's expectation that hermeneutical dialogue can lead to one being transformed by the truth that emerges from the inter-cultural dialogue. Such a cross-cultural dialogue, as we have noted in Chapter 5, involves understanding the other and oneself because religious dialogue also entails an inner dialogue within oneself. Eliade is convinced that communication is a direct exchange between two or more parties, whereas Taylor is convinced that all communication must be indirect because of the absence of meaning and the play of difference.[19]

In retrospect, if the contemporary human situation is as hopeless, dangerous and meaningless as Eliade and Taylor claim in their assessment of it, can a search for meaning be successful? For Taylor, meaning is impermanent and transitional due to the radical temporal nature of writing. On the one hand, this suggests that meaning can never overcome erring.[20] On the other hand, Eliade's search for a centre of human existence suggests that one might be able to expect to find something that is meaningful. Can the human situation thus be as meaningless as he claims? The answer can only be negative. Eliade's research leads him to believe that every religion possesses a centre, a central conception that informs and shapes the entire religious culture's myths, rituals and beliefs.

From Taylor's perspective, there can be no centre because of the death of God and his acceptance of a radical relativity. Taylor's position suggests that his basic presupposition is that if God is dead, everything else falls. In place of the traditional Western God, Taylor places what he calls the God of writing. Who is this mysterious deity? With the death of God, it is now possible to deify a human being, and Taylor comes close to deifying Hegel or his system, which represents the end of philosophy and theology.[21]

SEEKING THE CENTRE

If the centre is a place where the sacred is located for Eliade, and if the sacred is camouflaged within the world, how can we expect to find the sacred? We have already noted that the sacred is an integral part of human consciousness. But can the sacred be discovered outside human consciousness? Eliade's work suggests an affirmative reply regardless of his bleak assessment of the human situation.

In Chapter 3 we noted that the world reveals itself as language, and the secret language of the world is myth and symbol. Eliade suggests that myth can function as our guide through the wasteland of human existence. How is this possible? Since myth is equivalent to the truth, by knowing the myth, one gains power and ability to learn the secrets of things. Myth, an irruption of the sacred into the world, is an exemplary model for human behaviour and thus informs us how to act in a meaningful way. The creative nature of myth stimulates human initiative and creativity; it helps humans overcome doubts and reassures them. The transformative power of myth is connected to its cathartic function that liberates us from our inhibitions and ignorance. As Chapter 6 demonstrates, myth saves us from desacralization, a form of secularization that eliminates the sacred from the cosmos, and demystification, a denuding of mythology that neutralizes and banalizes the cosmos. Thus myth can liberate by helping us to find our true centre within the fallenness of human existence and the terror of history. The liberating potential of myth is recognized by Pandele, an author by profession, in Eliade's novella 'Nineteen Roses'. Pandele wants to write plays for the theatre with modern themes and extensions into mythology because the basic error of dramatists is that they have attempted to interpret ancient drama, that is, mythology, in the perspective of modern history. Pandele is symbolically reborn in the story, assumes the mythical role of Orpheus, and is liberated from the tyrannical meaninglessness of history. By appearing in Eliade's literary works, such Greek narratives emphasize the cultural significance of myth, reveal the fundamental human condition, and help us to understand the meaning of tragedy, philosophy and our own religion.[22]

Taylor would disagree that myth could ever be liberating or a paradigm for human action. Myths resemble texts because they are constantly interweaving, insubstantial, transitory, and their meaning is in a perpetual state of flux, which makes it impossible to refer to a myth as something stable and static.[23] There is also no such thing as a true origin: we are continually beginning, even if we try to begin for the first time. Taylor writes, 'Beginning, which is never original, marks and remarks the constant disappearance of origin.'[24] Since he thinks that in one sense we can never truly begin and in another way we are always beginning again for the first time, Taylor perceives an interplay between origin and beginning. Moreover, the obverse of beginning is the end, which implies that to lose one is to lose the other. In the final analysis myth fails as nothing more than wounded words, an unmendable tear, that cannot liberate anyone.[25] Eliade can only shed a tear for such a position because it does not begin to do justice to the cultural role of myth.

By living in the myth (for Eliade) one is seized by the sacred, and one leaves profane time and enters a sacred time, a reversible, cyclical, and eternal present. He does not suggest to religious pilgrims that they must manoeuvre themselves carefully through the irrationality and absurdity of history. His solution to the terror of history – the absurd wasteland in which we find ourselves – is very radical: the abolition of time and re-evaluation of Christianity. Similar themes are found in Eliade's literary works. Doctor Tâtaru of the novella 'Les Trois Graces', for instance, believes that in paradise Adam and Eve were periodically rejuvenated by means of neoplasm before the advent of original sin, and thereby abolished time. In the fantastic novella entitled 'Nights at Serampore', the main characters are cast back into the past by means of the occult powers of Suren Bose, a practitioner of Tantra, after interrupting his meditation. The chief characters witness the murder of a man's young wife, which they discover occurred a hundred and fifty years ago. We can abolish time by living in the myth that Eliade creates – the myth of cosmic Christianity. By living in the sacred time embodied in the myth, we become contemporary with the time of origin that recreates our life as we symbolically repeat the cosmogony. As we also noted in Chapter 9, the re-evaluation of Christianity involves a philosophy of freedom that does not exclude God. This freedom engendered by faith enables us to gain autonomy. The soteriological power inherent in myth enables us to find our centre of existence. It is also possible for one to be transformed into a symbol. In a sense, by means of his scholarly and literary works, Eliade transforms himself into a symbol of a pilgrim seeking the centre. Again, this emphasizes the soteriological nature of his work. His comprehension of being lost in the destructive labyrinth of contemporary history motivates Eliade to attempt to reintroduce religious mystery into contemporary life.

Arguing from very different perspectives and along different lines, there are a few remarkable similarities shared by Eliade and Taylor at this point, even though the latter is convinced that it is impossible to find a stable centre. Taylor thinks that with the death of the transcendent, the monotheistic God of the Western religious tradition, a new religious experience of the sacred is possible, which he envisions as coming to completion in modern art. A radically new experience of the sacred is possible in the eternal now embodied in modern art because it overcomes space and time and the sacred 'is totally *present* as total *presence*'.[26] Like Eliade, Taylor thinks that it is possible to abolish time, and that it is necessary to re-evaluate and renew Christian religious experience.

There are also some significant differences between these two thinkers. By returning to the past, both men agree that we paradoxically encounter the future, although for different reasons. But Taylor thinks that this future will never arrive.[27] Since it is impossible for there to be presence without absence for Taylor, a trace of the erasure of presence is the endless post-ponement of the Parousia.[28] What an individual must do is simply wait in a purposeless manner rather like the characters waiting for the arrival of Godot in Samuel Beckett's play.

There are also some important differences with respect to each thinker's understanding of the truth. According to Taylor, truth is relative due to the contextual nature of meaning and the relational nature of being.[29] If relativism is predominant from both epistemological and ontological per-spectives, relativity becomes absolutized and in turn relativizes the absolute in Taylor's work. This negates any possibility for one to appeal to an absolute truth because the only real truth is relativity. Eliade agrees with Taylor that truth can emerge through the reciprocal play of the synchronic and diachronic dimensions of language. Eliade disagrees with Taylor, however, that truth is radically relative because he is convinced that an absolute truth is possible and that it finds its foundation in myth.[30]

BEING AT THE CENTRE

What does it mean to find and be located at the centre for Eliade? To be at the centre means that one can see everything as interconnected; it is to see unity or to have cosmos rather than the chaos typical of historical flux. By having access to cosmic experiences, one becomes open to the cosmos, one shares in its sanctity, and one actively communicates with divine being. When one finds the centre one is at the meeting-point of the levels of the cosmos, one is near heaven, and one can move from one cosmic region to another. This is to live in absolute reality. It is now possible to acknow-ledge, free from the terror of history, that life is meaningful. To have arrived at this meaningful centre is to be transported back to the beginning of time and to have successfully abolished it. This enables one to defend oneself against the rapacious nature of time which becomes devalued. One need not accept oneself as only a historical being because now one lives in a constant present, a moment of true liberation.

To be at the centre entails being close to the sacred, the strong, efficacious and real. It is the end of one's ontological thirst because one is now saturated with being that is equated with the sacred. Since the sacred is equivalent to a power as discussed in Chapter 8, one is not only near the source of power, but one also participates in it and is sustained by it. Eliade would tend to agree with the following statement: The more centred one is, the more one is master of one's world, individual situation, and oneself. To find one's centre of existence suggests being self-related and more interrelated with others. The sacred, power and reality are all embodied in myth, which functions to give us a model to imitate.

In contrast, we have already noted why Taylor thinks that it is impossible to find a centre and certainly not a meaningful one. Since the present is in continual movement and is always, in some sense, absent for Taylor, its constant becoming constitutes an eternal recurrence, a flow of finitude into infinitude and vice versa.[31] By subverting the distinction between time and eternity, Taylor leaves us with ceaseless transition, perpetual relativity, eternal erring and Nietzsche's nightmare of eternal recurrence. Even if one could find a centre in Taylor's erratic play of eternal recurrence, one would still not find anything meaningful because meaning is relative. Dependent upon the dialectic of temporality, meaning is historical, ever-changing, contextual, and indicative of the relativity of truth.[32] If viewed from within the play of differences, meaning is always postponed to some distant future and never becomes present for us. Even though Eliade acknowledges that any experience of the sacred always occurs within an historical and social context, it is not possible for him to imagine human consciousness unconnected to meaning in some way because 'consciousness of a real and meaningful world is intimately linked with the discovery of the sacred.'[33] From Eliade's position, Taylor does not even ask the right question about the meaning of his own existence. The right question concerns the nature of being, which is primary because of its own inherent priority and its intimate connection to the cosmos and meaning.

As previously discussed, the paradigmatic model and centre of existence for contemporary beings that Eliade advocates is cosmic Christianity, a natural religion in tune with the cosmic rhythms. This ancestral religion of eastern European peasants is impregnated by the Christian spirit in which Jesus is not some remote figure. In fact, Jesus sanctifies nature. As a member of cosmic Christianity, one ignores history and becomes married to the cosmos, the bearer of value and meaning. This sanctified cosmos contains metaphysical truths and answers to the mysteries of death and resurrection. As a member of cosmic Christianity, one is free, creative and able to cope with the terror of history because of one's ability periodically to abolish time and regenerate oneself and one's world. Thus cosmic Christianity enables one to transcend time and live in eternity, whereas the divine milieu of Taylor is a liminal time and space for marginal nomads to wander. Rather than repeat the comparison made between Eliade and Taylor in Chapter 4, we will explore further what the latter means by a new form of God, the importance of writing, and the direction that it takes his a/theological enterprise.

Taylor's notion of a new form of God, an embodied word inscribed in writing, that results from cooperation between the transgressive dialectic and divine milieu is a rather odd pretender to divine lordship because it is a thoroughly relative being, without identity, self-presence and sovereignty. Why is this the case? If writing is a never-ending play of differences, it creates a complete relativity of everything. And since writing is a kenotic process, it empties everything of identity and presence. This God of writing is without substantive nature and is not autonomous nor sovereign because everything is co-relative within the flux of a radical relativity. Taylor leaves us with an incarnated word that represents the coincidence of opposites like presence and absence and identity and difference, which can only paradoxically appear by disappearing.[34] Since this is a God that is not a God, because of its appearing and disappearing character, we must assume that Taylor is playing with his reader like an artful magician who makes things appear and disappear.

The death of God, which can be recognized in the incarnated word, possesses primary importance for Taylor because it makes writing possible by the disappearance of the transcendental signified and enables one to inscribe words on an errant margin. Inscribing words joins and separates opposites in a continual process or interplay of identity and difference. In a recent work, Taylor, borrowing a term from Freud, refers to parapraxis, which means a failure, error, or slip, as a way to write beyond the period marking the end of theology, a time that is characterized by a lack of language. This postmodern nature of language does not refer to speech or silence; it indicates rather a failure of words.[35] By using the non-synthetic imagination, parapraxical writing is drawn toward a nothing that cannot be identified with being or nonbeing, uses disjunctive conjunction and vice versa, is non-referential, and non-healing. When words fail, such writing does nothing because it does not intend to mend the tear of difference. By striving to do nothing with words, parapraxis succeeds through its failure.[36] Parapraxical writing is a further development of what Taylor means by erring, which always takes place on a boundary, threshold or margin. By writing in the parapraxical mode, one does not write about the limit, but rather one writes the limit.[37] In this way, the distinction between both inside and outside the text disappears, and we move to the limits of language. From Eliade's perspective, Taylor's a/theology is symptomatic of the desacralization of the world, which is 'due above all to our inability to grasp the mystery of the camouflaging of the sacred in the profane'.[38]

NOSTALGIA FOR THE CENTRE

As discussed in Chapter 4, cosmic Christianity is pervaded by an aura of nostalgia for a paradise characterized by a sanctified cosmos and a place apart from the ravages of history. The sanctification of nature made possible by the presence of Jesus satisfies a nostalgia for the mystery of God. And the nostalgia for the lost unity of the *coincidentia oppositorum* is met by rediscovering our unity with nature. The nostalgia for paradise is an important theme in some of Eliade's literary works. The theme of youth without old age, as we have noted, plays an important role in 'Les Trois Graces'. The regenerated Dominic Matei of 'Youth Without Youth' lives in a mythical time of an eternal youthfulness where death does not reign as absolute or final, which suggests being restored to a paradisaical condition. And the leading character of 'Nineteen Roses' rides into a mythical paradise in the form of a previously destroyed forest at the end of the story.

From Eliade's perspective, this nostalgia for paradise, which he defines as cosmic Christianity, is not some fanciful human wish. The nostalgia for paradise is revealed by the dialectic of the sacred. It represents an ancient archetype hidden within human consciousness. From Eliade's viewpoint, he simply brings it forth into the open. Eliade's discovery and bringing forth of cosmic Christianity as the centre of human existence and the solution to the terror of history is indicative of the fact that he is not merely a scholar of mythology; he is also a mythmaker himself. In other words, he rediscovers the myth of cosmic Christianity in the depths of his own consciousness. Why emphasize such a myth? In short, myth saves human beings from the dangers of history, helps them to find freedom from the wasteland through which they must journey, and enables them to find their centre of existence. By discovering the centre of one's existence, one returns home and rediscovers oneself.[39] To find the centre is akin to completing an initiation rite; it is equivalent to being reborn. In his journal, Eliade confesses that he understands his life as a series of initiatory trials.[40]

Eliade's nostalgia for the beginnings of paradise or something akin to it is not without precedent in modern and postmodern thought. The Romantics of the eighteenth century were convinced that philosophy culminates in a return, a circuitous pilgrimage to a pristine origin, to nature in order to be reintegrated with it and one's own potential. Nietzsche altered the Romantic motif by initially returning to Greek culture, the locus of the beginning of Western culture, and later he discovered the eternal return, an endless repetition of all events that is without beginning, end and middle, that is the paragon of the antimyth. With its emphasis on the present moment, the finite and the individual, eternal recurrence is the antithesis of any faith in infinite progress. Its creed is expressed by the prophet in *Thus Spoke Zarathustra*: 'I beseech you, my brothers, remain faithful to the earth and do not believe those who speak to you of other-worldly hopes.'[41] Zarathustra's espousing of faithfulness to the earth sounds very similar to Eliade's promotion of cosmic Christianity. By returning beyond the Greek culture of the nostalgia of early Nietzsche to the pre-Socratic philosophers, Heidegger nostalgically wishes to recapture the question of Being, which was lost by human beings captive to their anxieties that make them feel uncanny, uncomfortable (*Unheimlichkeit*), and consequently not at home in the world. As Heidegger uses it, the German term *Unheimlichkeit* is the basic kind of Being-in-the-world, although it is covered up in an everyday way.[42] Uncanniness also means not being at home when the nothing and nowhere of *Dasein*'s anxiety finds expression.[43] Since human beings are lost within the world without a sense of Being, Heidegger's purpose is to retrieve the lost sense of Being that he believes can be regained by returning to the pre-Socratic Greek thinkers.

Among those who identify themselves as postmodernist thinkers, one can find a sense of nostalgia in the work of Foucault, if we can take him at his word, when he writes of the return of language that is related to a new form of thought of the future.[44] Inspired by Nietzsche's philosophy that recognized the historical turning-point, Foucault interprets the Nietzschean declaration of the death of God to affirm the end of human beings. The last human and God are engaged in a contest that resembles Nietzsche's nightmare of eternal recurrence. Foucault's vision might be comprehended as a bleak future for humans: 'Thus, the last man is at the same time older and yet younger than the death of God; since he has killed God, it is he himself who must answer for his own finitude; but since it is in the death of God that he speaks, thinks, and exists, his murder itself is doomed to die; new gods, the same gods, are already swelling the future Ocean; man will disappear.'[45] From one perspective, Foucault's futuristic vision – a return of language coinciding with the disappearance of human beings – is an absurdity akin to a nihilistic nostalgia. From another perspective, he envisions the end of a human being formed by the Enlightenment philosophy and culture, and looks forward to the emergence of a postmodern being. In contrast to Foucault's postmodernist vision of the future, nostalgia plays little or no role in Derrida's philosophy or Taylor's a/theology where only *différance* reigns. The only exception for Derrida and Taylor is a kind of nostalgia for writing over speech, whereas Eliade expresses a covert nostalgia for oral tradition.

By following the myth-making lead of Nietzsche or Goethe, Eliade appears to exceed the proper limits of an historian of religions. But as we have seen in the various chapters of this work, he assumes many roles: theologian, philosopher, cross-cultural dialogic participant and novelist. We can best understand his myth-making as a manifestation of his additional prophetic and visionary roles.

NOSTALGIA FOR SYNTHESIS

Eliade views his scholarly work in terms of the history of the mind, which is similar to the philosophical work of Hegel: 'Through that anamnesis the historian of religions is in a way recreating the *phenomenology of the mind*.'[46] In fact, the historian goes beyond Hegel in the comprehensive way in which he/she studies many cultures in order to grasp the total history of the mind. This would be Eliade's grand synthesis. Eliade understands his three-volume *A History of Religious Ideas*, a work that he considers his *magnum opus*, to have autobiographical significance for himself because it enables him to review the total history of the products of the religious mind.[47] It is possible to view Eliade's life and work as an attempted synthesis that he discovers in the unitary world of culture that is ultimately a return to nature. Eliade's encyclopedic approach to his subject, his grand vision, the inclusion of philosophical and theological dimensions to his work, and the synthesis of religious knowledge have given way, at least for a time, to more modest endeavours.

Perceiving a methodological crisis due to uncertainty about the discipline's proper object of study, Kurt Rudolph, for instance, calls for a separation of the history of religions, which is a science (*Wissenschaft*), for him studying the multiplicity of past and present religions, from theology and philosophy. According to Rudolph, the history of religions is a historical and philological discipline. Rudolph does not understand the term philology in a linguistical sense but in a broad sense referring to an investigation of a religious culture.[48] This type of method excludes the use of empathy and intuition found in Eliade's work. His historical method includes the use of a comparative approach in order to grasp his object cross-culturally and to formulate more precise distinctions. Actually, the historian of religions must use a combination of methods by dealing with the psychological and sociological sides of religion.[49] In order to correct the skewed hermeneutic of understanding, Rudolph wants to include a criticism of religious tradi- tions and the history of historical effects.[50] From his methodological emphasis, it is obvious that Rudolph thinks Eliade's approach is ahistorical and too philosophical and theological.

Eliade laments a year before his death in his journal that he did not take the time to reply to his critics.[51] He was too busy with other projects to respond directly to his critics, although the three-volume *A History of Religious Ideas* was a reply to those who criticized him for being ahistorical. After reading an article that appeared in the scholarly journal *Numen* by Ninian Smart that looks beyond the work of Eliade towards the future direction of the history of religions, Eliade laments the eclipse of his contributions to his discipline.[52]

As his life draws to an end, Eliade grieves over work that he does not have time to complete. Yet he accepts an offer from the Macmillan publishing company to be the chief editor of the multi-volume *Encyclopedia of Religion*, even though he is in failing health. He comprehends his accept- ance of this responsibility as a sacrifice with deep meaning in his journal.[53] As he struggles with his poor health to complete his work before his death, he characteristically interprets his sufferings as initiatory ordeals with meaning.[54] Throughout his initiatory trials, Eliade is determined to continue his work regardless of his 'loss of memory, worsening of the myopia, physical fatigue, arthritic pains, and above all the immense difficulty of writing legibly.'[55] In the fourth volume of his journal that ends in 1985, we can see the archetype of the heroic scholar never giving up his hope or determination. If we combine this with the literary and scholarly dedication throughout his life, Eliade reveals himself as a kind of ascetic.

Compared to the Christian monastic tradition, Eliade's pattern of life would not fit into either the eremitic or cenobitic types of asceticism. The former type is too unworldly and fanatic, while the latter is more socially orientated within a context of strict regulation and discipline. If the eremites renounce the world and seek an unworldly style of life apart from social customs and norms, the cenobites renounce themselves and accept various hierarchical and formal means to attain perfection.[56] These two types of Christian ascetics share a mutually negative view of the world, a place without value or transcendence. Since his view of cosmic Christianity enables Eliade to perceive the world as holy, he is an ascetic figure of a third type – a dedicated and even fanatical scholar, who lives in the world and is a part of it. In contrast, the postmodernists that we have discussed practice a nihilistic asceticism by sacrificing the self and assume an anti-humanistic stance.

While discussing the contributions of Pettazzoni to the field of the history of religions to a seminar in 1977, Eliade confessed that the Italian scholar served as a model for him because he tried to study the totality of religion. Thereupon, a student was overwhelmed by the thought of so all-encompassing a discipline, and he emphasized the difficult nature of the history of religions to all the members of the class. Eliade explained in his journal what happened next, 'I could only shrug my shoulders and breathe a sigh, and everyone burst out laughing.'[57] The laughter has died out, but the man's presence, in spite of what postmodernists think, continues in his many works on the history of religions, literary contributions, and the scholarly chair dedicated to him and his accomplishments at the University of Chicago.

Notes

1 INTRODUCTION

1. Mircea Eliade, *Autobiography: Volume 1, 1907–1937, Journey East, Journey West*, trans. Mac Linscott Ricketts (San Francisco: Harper & Row, 1981), p. 41. A more complete biography of the early period of Eliade's life is provided by the massive two-volume work of Mac Linscott Ricketts, *Mircea Eliade: The Romanian Roots, 1907–1945*, 2 vols (Boulder, Colorado: East European Monographs 1988; distributed by Columbia University Press).
2. Eliade, *Autobiography*, p. 94.
3. Ibid., pp. 110–11.
4. Ibid., p. 128.
5. Mircea Eliade, *Autobiography: Volume II, 1937–1960, Exile's Odyssey*, trans. Mac Linscott Ricketts (Chicago and London: University of Chicago Press, 1988), p. 69.
6. Ibid., pp. 63, 66.
7. Ricketts, pp. 892, 901.
8. Ibid., pp. 623, 886, 889, 891.
9. Eliade, *Autobiography II*, p. 13.
10. Ibid., p. 138.
11. Ivan Strenski, *Four Theories of Myth in Twentieth-Century History: Cassirer, Eliade, Lévi-Strauss and Malinowski* (London: Macmillan; Iowa City: University of Iowa Press, 1987), pp. 70–103.
12. Ricketts, pp. 903, 912.
13. Mircea Eliade, *Ordeal by Labyrinth: Conversations with Claude-Henri Rocquet*, trans. Derek Coltman (Chicago, London: University of Chicago Press, 1982), p. 94. In his massive work on the early career of Eliade, Ricketts interprets Eliade's work as a synthesis, an ordering of all the spiritual experiences of a person or a culture in a meaningful way. This synthesis is attempted against the theoretical background of the theory of the three planes of reality, which demonstrates the influence of Nae Ionescu upon Eliade's work. This theory asserted that there were distinct realms of reality with their own life and laws. Thus, religion is to be treated as an autonomous reality and cannot be judged by criteria derived from another plane, which in a practical sense removes religion from criticism originating from another plane (Ricketts, II, pp. 1204–11). Eliade's grand synthesis is not universally accepted. Gregory D. Alles critically states, 'Eliade's obsession with hierophanies combines with his insistence on totality to produce a holism that is premature, if not completely misplaced' (pp. 119–20). Alles also says that totality and meaning are fundamentally incompatible and that hermeneutics cannot study religion in its totality in 'Wach, Eliade, and the Critique from Totality', *Numen*, Vol. XXXV, Fasc. 1 (July 1988): 108–38.
14. Eliade, *Autobiography II*, p. 106.
15. Ibid., p. 149.

16. Ibid., p. 257.
17. Adriana Berger, 'Eliade's Double Approach: A Desire for Unity', *Religious Studies Review*, Vol. 11, no. 1 (January 1985): 9.
18. Lawrence E. Sullivan, review of *A History of Religious Ideas, Vol. 2*, by Mircea Eliade, In *Religious Studies Review* 9 (January 1983): 17–18.
19. Dorthy Libby, review of *Rites and Symbols of Initiation*, by Mircea Eliade, in *American Anthropologist* LXI (1959): 689.
20. William A. Lessa, review of *The Sacred and the Profane*, by Mircea Eliade, In *American Anthropologist* LXI (1959): 1147.
21. Edmund Leach, 'Sermons by a Man on a Ladder', *New York Review of Books* (20 October 1966): 252.
22. Anthony F. C. Wallace, *Religion: An Anthropological View* (New York: Random House, 1966), p. 252.
23. Annemarie de Waal Malefijt, *Religion and Culture: An Introduction to Anthropology of Religion* (New York: Macmillan, 1968), p. 193.
24. John A. Saliba, *'Homo Religiosus' in Mircea Eliade: An Anthropological Evaluation* (Leiden: E. J. Brill, 1976).
25. Antonio Barbosa da Silva, *The Phenomenology of Religion as a Philosophical Problem: An Analysis of the Theoretical Background of the Phenomenology of Religion, in General, and of M. Eliade's Phenomenological Approach, in Particular* (Uppsala: CWK Gleerup, 1982), pp. 121–4.
26. Mac Linscott Ricketts, 'The Nature and Extent of Eliade's "Jungianism",' *Union Seminary Quarterly Review*, Vol. XXV, No. 2 (Winter 1970): 216.
27. Ibid., pp. 216, 223.
28. Jonathan Z. Smith, *Map Is Not Territory: Studies in the History of Religions* (Leiden: E. J. Brill, 1978), p. 259.
29. Idem, *Imagining Religion from Babylon to Jonestown* (Chicago and London: University of Chicago Press, 1982), p. 23.
30. Idem, *Map*, p. 259.
31. Idem, *Imagining*, p. 22.
32. Idem, *To Take Place: Toward Theory in Ritual* (Chicago and London: University of Chicago Press, 1987), p. 14.
33. Ioan Culianu, *Mircea Eliade* (Assisi: Cittadella Editrice, 1977), p. 6.
34. Adrian Marino, *L'herméneutique de Mircea Eliade*, traduit Jean Gouillard (Paris: Gallimard, 1981), p. 87.
35. Ibid., pp. 76–80.
36. Ninian Smart, 'Beyond Eliade: The Future of Theory in Religion', *Numen*, Vol. XXV, Fasc. 2 (August 1978): 182.
37. Marino, p. 158.
38. Ibid., p. 162.
39. Culianu, pp. 55, 24–5.
40. Robert D. Baird, *Category Formation and the History of Religions* (The Hague: Mouton, 1971), p. 152.
41. Ibid., p. 86.
42. Guilford Dudley III, *Religion on Trial: Mircea Eliade and His Critics* (Philadelphia: Temple University Press, 1977), p. 36.
43. da Silva, pp. 109–17.
44. Marino, p. 221.
45. Ibid., p. 235.

46. Dudley, pp. 36, 117.
47. Marino, pp. 127, 132.
48. Don Wiebe, 'A Positive Episteme for the Study of Religion', *Scottish Journal of Religious Studies*, Vol. 6, no. 2 (Autumn 1985): 82–3.
49. Smart, pp. 175–7.
50. Robert F. Brown, 'Eliade on Archaic Religion: Some Old and New Criticisms', *Sciences Religieuses/Studies in Religion*, 10, 4 (1981): 446.
51. Larry E. Shiner, 'Sacred Space, Profane Space, Human Space', *Journal of the American Academy of Religion*, Vol. XL (1972): 425–36.
52. Smith, *To Take Place*, p. 104.
53. Ibid., p. 105.
54. Baird, p. 77.
55. Douglas Allen, *Structure and Creativity in Religion: Hermeneutics in Mircea Eliade's Phenomenology and New Directions* (The Hague: Mouton, 1978), p. 237.
56. Thomas J. J. Altizer, *Mircea Eliade and the Dialectic of the Sacred* (Philadelphia: The Westminster Press, 1963), p. 43.
57. Mircea Eliade, 'Notes for a Dialogue', in *The Theology of Altizer: Critique and Response*, ed. John B. Cobb, Jr (Philadelphia: The Westminster Press, 1970): 236.
58. Valerie Saiving, 'Androcentrism in Religious Studies', *Journal of Religion*, Vol. 56 (April 1976): 177–97.
59. Mircea Eliade, *Rites and Symbols of Initiation*, trans. Willard R. Trask (New York: Harper & Row, 1958), p. 19.
60. Ibid., p. 3.
61. Idem, *The Quest: History and Meaning in Religion* (Chicago and London: University of Chicago Press, 1969), pp. 133–4.
62. Idem, *Rites and Symbols of Initiation*, p. 26.
63. Northrop Frye, 'World Enough Without Time', *Hudson Review*, Vol. 12 (1959): 431.
64. Richard Gombrich, 'Eliade on Buddhism', *Religious Studies*, Vol. 10 (1974): 225–31.
65. Geoffrey Kirk, *Myth: Its Meaning and its Function* (Berkeley: University of California Press, 1970), p. 5.
66. Strenski, p. 70.
67. Mircea Eliade, *Zalmoxis the Vanishing God: Comparative Studies in the Religions and Folklore of Dacia and Eastern Europe*, trans. Williard R. Trask (Chicago: University of Chicago Press, 1972), pp, 33, 48.
68. Charles Tilly, *Big Structures, Large Processes, Huge Comparisons* (New York: Russell Sage Foundation, 1984).

2 RELIGIONSWISSENSCHAFT

1. F. Max Müller, *Introduction to the Science of Religion* (London: Longmans, Green & Co., 1873), p. 7.
2. Ibid., p. 15.
3. F. Max Müller, *Chips from a German Workshop, Vol. 1, Essays on the*

Science of Religion (New York: Charles Scribner & Company, 1869), pp. xix–xx.

4. Cornelis P. Tiele, *Elements of the Science of Religion*, 2 vols (London: William Blackwood & Sons, 1897, 1899), I:18. For an introduction to Tiele's scholarship see Jacques Waardenburg, 'Religion between Reality and Idea', *Numen*, Vol. XIX, Fasc. 2–3 (August–December 1972): 131–6.

5. Tiele, I:18.

6. P. D. Chantepie de la Saussaye, *Manual of the Science of Religion*, trans. Beatrice S. Colyee-Fergusson (London: Longmans, Green & Co., 1891), pp. 3–4. For an introduction to the work of Chantepie de la Saussaye, see Waardenburg, pp. 136–44.

7. Chantepie de la Saussaye, pp. 7–8.

8. See Reinhard Pummer, 'Religionswissenschaft or Religiology?', *Numen*, Vol. XIX, Fasc. 2–3 (August–December 1972): 91–127.

9. Joseph M. Kitagawa, 'The History of Religions (*Religionswissenschaft*) Then and Now', in *The History of Religions: Retrospect and Prospect*, ed. Joseph M. Kitagawa (New York: Macmillan, 1985), p. 131.

10. For a review of more recent literature on the science of religion, see Reinhard Pummer, 'Recent Publications on the Methodology of the Science of Religion', *Numen*, Vol. XXII, Fasc. 3 (December 1975): 161–82. Ursula King deals with methodological debates in the history of religions and phenomenology of religion since the Second World War and considers many figures that I do not cover in this chapter in 'Historical and Phenomenological Approaches to the Study of Religion', In *Contemporary Approaches to the Study of Religion, Volume I: The Humanities*, ed. Frank Whaling, Religion and Reason 27 (Berlin, New York, Amsterdam: Mouton, 1984), pp. 29–163.

11. Hans. H. Penner and Edward A. Yonan, 'Is a Science of Religion Possible?' *Journal of Religion*, Vol. 52, no. 2 (1972): 107–33.

12. Ibid., p. 133.

13. Wiebe, p. 79. It is curious that Wiebe would choose the notion of *episteme* because it is a shortlived notion in Foucault's work and is not a form of knowledge or a type of rationality. For Foucault, *episteme* is the totality of relations that can be discovered for a given period. See Michel Foucault, *The Archaeology of Knowledge and The Discourse on Language*, trans. A. M. Sheridan Smith (New York: Pantheon Books, 1972), p. 191. In an earlier article, Wiebe argues that a science of religion is an attitude and does not and cannot exist: 'Is a Science of Religion Possible?' *Studies in Religion*, Vol. 7, no. 1 (Winter 1978): 5–17.

14. Wiebe, 'A Positive Episteme', p. 82.

15. Ninian Smart, *The Science of Religion and the Sociology of Knowledge* (Princeton: Princeton University Press, 1973), p. 23.

16. See Joachim Wach, *Sociology of Religion* (Chicago and London: University of Chicago Press, 1971), pp. 1–2; Raffaele Pettazzoni, *Essays on the History of Religions* (Leiden: E. J. Brill, 1967), p. 217; C. J. Bleeker, *The Sacred Bridge* (Leiden: E. J. Brill, 1963), p. 3; Friedrich Heiler, *Erscheinungsformen und Wesen der Religion* (Stuttgart: W. Kohlhammer Verlag, 1961), pp. 4–5; Geo Widengren, *Religionsphänomenologie* (Berlin: Walter de Gruyter & Co., 1969), p. 1; Mariasusai Dhavamony, *Phenomenology of Religion*, Documenta Missionalia 7 (Rome: Gregorian University Press, 1973), p. 19.

17.   Mircea Eliade, 'Methodological Remarks on the Study of Religious Symbolism', in *The History of Religions: Essays in Methodology*, eds Mircea Eliade and Joseph M. Kitagawa (Chicago and London: University of Chicago Press, 1959), p. 88; *Myth and Reality*, trans. Willard R. Trask (New York: Harper & Row, 1963), p. 191.
18.   Dudley, pp. 36, 135.
19.   Saliba, p. 105. See also Malefitj, p. 193.
20.   Baird, p. 152.
21.   Dudley, p. 36.
22.   Ibid., p. 36.
23.   Saliba, p. 111.
24.   Ibid., p. 110.
25.   Ibid., p. 111.
26.   Ibid., p. 116.
27.   Leach, pp. 28–31.
28.   Saliba, pp. 116–19.
29.   Dudley, p. 117.
30.   Ibid., p. 118.
31.   Saliba, p. 113.
32.   Karl R. Popper, *The Logic of Scientific Discovery* (London: Hutchinson, 1986; first edn, 1959), pp. 40, 44.
33.   Ibid., p. 42. Thomas S. Kuhn objects to Popper's concept of falsification because its outcome is negative and necessitates the rejection of an established theory in *The Structure of Scientific Revolutions*, International Encyclopedia of United Science, Vol. II, no. 2 (Chicago: University of Chicago Press, 1970, 2nd edn), p. 146. Michael Polanyi makes a distinction between verification of science by experience and validation, a process in which non-scientific systems are tested and accepted with greater personal participation by the individual in *Personal Knowledge: Towards a Post-Critical Philosophy* (London: Routledge & Kegan Paul, 1958; reprint 1983), p. 202.
34.   Popper, p. 47.
35.   Ibid., p. 251.
36.   Karl R. Popper, *Conjectures and Refutations: The Growth of Scientific Knowledge* (London: Routledge & Kegan Paul, 1963; reprint of 4th edn 1985), p. 24; *Objective Knowledge: An Evolutionary Approach* (Oxford: Clarendon Press, 1972; reprint 1986), pp. 77, 79.
37.   Kuhn, p. 109.
38.   Ibid., p. 175. Likewise, Polanyi refers to standards of intellectual satisfaction and beliefs about the nature of things as two examples of forms of the premises of science. He writes, 'Natural science deals with facts borrowed largely from common experience. The methods by which we establish facts in everyday life are therefore logically anterior to the special premises of science, and should be included in a full statement of these premises', p. 161.
39.   Polanyi, p. 134.
40.   Ibid., p. 18. Popper essentially agrees that objective knowledge possesses a conjectural and hypothetical character in *Objective Knowledge*, p. 75.
41.   Polanyi, p. 143.
42.   Popper, *Objective Knowledge*, pp. 9, 111.
43.   Polanyi, p. 138.

44. Kuhn, p. 84.
45. Popper, *Conjectures*, p. 47.
46. Polanyi, p. 163.
47. Popper, *Logic*, p. 28. Popper does argue that Hume reintroduced induction in the guise of a psychological theory in *Conjectures*, p. 46.
48. Popper, *Logic*, pp. 28–29, 34; *Conjectures*, p. 42.
49. Idem, *Conjectures*, p. 28.
50. Ibid., p. 28.
51. Ibid., p. 30.
52. Ibid., p. 28.
53. Kuhn, p. 123.
54. Ibid., p. 191.
55. Popper, *Logic*, p. 278.
56. Ibid., p. 280.
57. Ibid., p. 278.
58. Idem, *Objective Knowledge*, pp. 55, 191–3.
59. Mircea Eliade, *No Souvenirs: Journal, 1957–1969*, trans. Fred H. Johnson, Jr (New York: Harper & Row, 1977), p. 192; hereafter cited as *Journal*.
60. Charles H. Long, 'Human Centers: An Essay on Method in the History of Religions', *Soundings*, 61 (Fall 1978): 408.
61. Eliade, *The Quest*, pp. 60–1.
62. Idem, 'Autobiographical Fragment', in *Imagination and Meaning: The Scholarly and Literary Worlds of Mircea Eliade*, eds Norman J. Girardot and Mac Linscott Ricketts (New York: Seabury Press, 1982), p. 113.
63. Idem, 'Methodological Remarks', p. 88. King asserts that Eliade uses the term science of religion 'to describe a more integral approach to the study of religion which intends to overcome the inherent tension between the history and phenomenology of religion', p. 125.
64. Idem, *Myths, Dreams and Mysteries: The Encounter between Contemporary Faiths and Archaic Realities*, trans. Philip Mairet (New York: Harper & Row, 1967), p. 178.
65. Idem, *Patterns in Comparative Religion*, trans. Rosemary Sheed (Cleveland: The World Publishing Company, 1968), p. 5.
66. Idem, *Journal*, p. 43.
67. Idem, *Myth and Reality*, p. 191.
68. Idem, 'Autobiographical Fragment', pp. 114–15. See also *Ordeal by Labyrinth*, p. 144.
69. Idem, *Symbolism, the Sacred, and the Arts*, ed. Diane Apostolos-Cappandona (New York: Crossroad Publishing Company, 1986), p. 155.
70. Norman J. Girardot, 'Imagining Eliade: A Fondness for Squirrels', in *Imagination and Meaning: The Scholarly and Literary Worlds of Mircea Eliade*, eds Norman J. Girardot and Mac Linscott Ricketts (New York: Seabury, 1982), p. 6.
71. Eliade, 'Methodological Remarks', p. 100.
72. Richard Rorty, *Philosophy and the Mirror of Nature* (Princeton: Princeton University Press, 1979), pp. 346, 353.
73. Idem, 'Method, Social Science, and Social Hope', *Canadian Journal of Philosophy*, Vol. XI, no. 4 (December 1981): 574.
74. Ibid., pp. 570, 580.

75. Charles Taylor, 'Interpretation and the Sciences of Man', *Review of Metaphysics*, Vol. XXV, no. 1 (September 1971), pp. 31, 45. See also his later article, 'Understanding in Human Science', *Review of Metaphysics*, Vol. 34, no. 1 (September 1980): 25–38.
76. Hans-George Gadamer, *Truth and Method*, trans. Garrett Barden and John Cumming (New York: Crossroad Publishing Company, 1982), p. 6.
77. John Y. Fenton sees the need for an economics of religion and the medical study of religion. The latter, for instance, could examine the biochemical changes of the human body during religious experiences, in 'Reductionism in the Study of Religions', *Soundings*, Vol. LIII, No. 1 (Spring 1970), p. 73.

3 THE FORE-STRUCTURE OF HERMENEUTICS

1. Eliade, *The Quest*, p. ii.
2. Smith, *Map*, p. 259. As Geo Widengren indicates, another problem is that terms such as archetype and archetypal are difficult to define and as a result are obscure and uncertain. These terms are also not entities possessing an ontological reality in 'La méthode comparative: entre philologie et phénoménologie', *Numen*, Vol. XVIII, Fasc. 3 (December 1971): 161–72.
3. Smith, *Imagining*, p. 22.
4. Baird, p. 86.
5. Saliba, pp. 110–11.
6. Eliade, *Myths, Dreams and Mysteries*, p. 178.
7. Idem, *Shamanism: Archaic Techniques of Ecstasy*, trans. Willard R. Trask (New York: Pantheon Books, 1964), p. xv.
8. Girardot, p. 4.
9. See Mac Linscott Ricketts, 'Mircea Eliade and the Death of God,' *Religion in Life*, Vol. 36 (Spring 1967); 'In Defense of Eliade', *Journal of Religion*, Vol. 53 (1973): 13–34; David Rasmussen, 'Mircea Eliade: Structural Hermeneutics and Philosophy', *Philosophy Today*, Vol. 12 (1968): 138–46; Douglas Allen, 'Mircea Eliade's Phenomenological Analysis of Religious Experience', *Journal of Religion*, Vol. 52 (1972): 170–86; *Structure and Creativity in Religion*; Robert Luyster, 'The Study of Myth: Two Approaches,' *The Journal of Bible & Religion*, Vol. 34 (1966): 235–43; Marino, *L'herméneutique de Mircea Eliade*.
10. Marino, p. 26. See also his article 'Mircea Eliade's Hermeneutics', in *Imagination and Meaning: The Scholarly and Literary Worlds of Mircea Eliade*, eds Norman J. Girardot and Mac Linscott Ricketts (New York: Seabury Press, 1982), p. 20.
11. See Allen, Rasmussen, Altizer and Marino.
12. See Gadamer, *Truth and Method*. G. Richard Welbon suggests that the methodological presuppositions in Eliade's works can be traced to Rudolf Otto's insights in 'Some Remarks on the Work of Mircea Eliade', *Acta Philosophica*, Vol. 30 (1964): 465–92. Although Welbon is right to a certain extent, I think that following the lead of Gadamer will prove more worthwhile for the overall corpus of Eliade's work. Frank Whaling discusses briefly some of the presuppositions that he finds associated with Eliade's comparative approach in 'Comparative Approaches', in *Contemporary Approaches to the*

Study of Religion, Volume I: The Humanities, ed. by Frank Whaling, Religion and Reason 27 (Berlin, New York, Amsterdam: Mouton, 1984), pp. 165–295.

13. Gadamer, p. 236.
14. Marino, *L'herméneutique*, pp. 105–95.
15. Gadamer, p. 12.
16. Mircea Eliade, *The Sacred and the Profane*, trans. Willard R. Trask (New York: Harcourt, Brace & Company, 1959), p. 97.
17. Idem, *Mephistopheles and the Androgyne: Studies in Religious Myth and Symbol*, trans. J. M. Cohen (New York: Sheed and Ward, 1965).
18. Jacques Derrida, *Of Grammatology*, trans. Gayatri Chakravorty Spivak (Baltimore and London: Johns Hopkins University Press, 1976), p. 65.
19. Ibid., p. 7.
20. Eliade, *Patterns in Comparative Religion*, p. 30.
21. Idem, *Sacred and Profane*, p. 11.
22. Ibid., p. 12. Stephen J. Reno criticizes Eliade's use of hierophanies: 'To put it another way, not only does Eliade not focus upon the exact nature of the structure of the hierophany – which might lead him eventually to some theory of participation or analogy – but he does not undertake to account for the *raison d'être* whereby one takes a progressional view of hierophanies', in 'Eliade's Progressional View of Hierophanies', *Religious Studies*, Vol. 8 (1972), p. 158.
23. Eliade, *Autobiography, Volume II*, pp. 33–4.
24. Idem, *The Quest*, p. 19.
25. Idem, *Patterns in Comparative Religion*, p. xiii.
26. Jacques Derrida, *Writing and Difference*, trans. Alan Bass (Chicago: University of Chicago Press, 1978), p. 132.
27. Gadamer, *Truth and Method*, p. 39.
28. Eliade, *Patterns in Comparative Religion*, p. 26.
29. Ibid., p. 13.
30. Idem, *The Quest*, p. 133.
31. Idem, *Ordeal by Labyrinth*, pp. 153–4; *Journal*, p. 313.
32. Idem, *A History of Religious Ideas, Vol. I: From the Stone Age to the Eleusinian Mysteries*, trans. Willard R. Trask (Chicago: University of Chicago Press, 1978), p. xvi.
33. Idem, *Patterns in Comparative Religion*, p. 463.
34. Ibid., p. 465.
35. Ibid., p. 30.
36. Idem, *Shamanism*, p. xvii.
37. Jacques Derrida, *Speech and Phenomena and Other Essays on Husserl's Theory of Signs*, trans. David B. Allison (Evanston: Northwestern University Press, 1973), p. 120.
38. Ibid., pp. 130, 134.
39. Ibid., p. 134.
40. Eliade, *Ordeal by Labyrinth*, p. 121.
41. Idem, *Journal*, p. 154.
42. Jacques Derrida, *Positions*, trans. Alan Bass (Chicago: University of Chicago Press, 1981), p. 27.
43. Ibid., p. 81.
44. Gadamer, p. 269.

45. Mircea Eliade, *Images and Symbols: Studies in Religious Symbolism*, trans. Philip Mairet (New York: Sheed and Ward, 1961), pp. 32–3.
46. Derrida, *Positions*, p. 56.
47. Idem, *Dissemination*, trans. Barbara Johnson (Chicago: University of Chicago Press, 1981), p. 168.
48. Eliade, *Images and Symbols*, p. 34.
49. Derrida, *Writing and Difference*, p. 292.
50. Gadamer, p. 269.
51. Ibid., p. 271.
52. Ibid., p. 273.
53. Mircea Eliade, *The Forge and the Crucible*, trans. Stephen Corrin (New York: Harper & Row, 1971), p. 143.
54. Gadamer, p. 271. Gadamer thinks that hermeneutics both bridges the distance between individuals and reveals the foreignness of the other person in *Philosophical Hermeneutics*, trans. and ed. David E. Linge (Berkeley: University of California Press, 1977), p. 100.
55. Eliade, *The Quest*, p. 3.
56. Gadamer, *Truth and Method*, p. 271.
57. Eliade, *The Quest*, p. 7.
58. Idem, *Shamanism*, p. xiv.
59. Smart, 'Beyond Eliade', pp. 176–7.
60. Baird, p. 77.
61. Eliade, *The Quest*, p. 58.
62. Ibid., pp. 61–6. Marino interprets Eliade's creative hermeneutics as militant because it is distinctly orientated towards actions capable of changing spiritual states, attitudes of the mind and points of view commonly admitted in *L'herméneutique*, p. 285.
63. Idem, *Ordeal by Labyrinth*, p. 129. Gadamer agrees that by understanding a text we come to understand ourselves, in *Philosophical Hermeneutics*, p. 57.
64. Matei Calinescu, 'Imagination and Meaning: Aesthetic Attitudes and Ideas in Mircea Eliade's Thought', *Journal of Religion*, Vol. 57 (January 1977), p. 15.
65. Eliade, *Ordeal by Labyrinth*, p. 120.
66. Rasmussen, p. 143.
67. Eliade, *Patterns in Comparative Religion*, p. 30.
68. Idem, 'Methodological Remarks on the Study of Religious Symbolism', p. 97.
69. Idem, *Shamanism*, p. xv.
70. Idem, *Journal*, p. 298. Due to his emphasis on structure, William G. Doty calls Eliade a structuralist or, at least, a protostructuralist in *Mythography: The Study of Myths and Rituals* (Alabama: University of Alabama Press, 1986), p. 197. Doty's characterization of Eliade's method tends to be misleading because he is, as Norman J. Girardot wittily states, 'the binary opposite of Lévi-Strauss.' Girardot comes to this conclusion because Eliade 'affirms the phenomenological principle that there is a necessary continuity between experience and reality,' p. 4.
71. Derrida, *Positions*, p. 27.
72. Eliade, *Journal*, p. 162.
73. Idem, *Patterns in Comparative Religion*, p. 5.
74. Idem, *Journal*, p. 55.

75. Fenton, pp. 68, 63.
76. Eliade, *Ordeal by Labyrinth*, p. 153.
77. Derrida, *Dissemination*, p. 268.
78. Allen, *Structure and Creativity*, p. 147.
79. Eliade, *Shamanism*, p. xvii.
80. Allen, *Structure and Creativity*, p. 176.
81. Ibid., p. 204.
82. Gadamer, *Truth and Method*, p. 277.
83. Wilfred Cantwell Smith, *Towards a World Theology* (Philadelphia: Westminster Press, 1981), p. 97.
84. Eliade, *Journal*, p. 289.
85. Marino, *L' herméneutique*, p. 321.
86. Stanley Rosen, *Hermeneutics as Politics* (New York, Oxford: Oxford University Press, 1987), p. 73.
87. Ibid., p. 141.

4 THEOLOGY OF NOSTALGIA

1. Eliade, *Journal*, p. 74.
2. Ibid., p. 83.
3. David Tracy, *The Analogical Imagination: Christian Theology and the Culture of Pluralism* (New York: Crossroad Publishing Company, 1986), p. 205.
4. Mark C. Taylor, *Erring: A Postmodern A/theology* (Chicago and London: University of Chicago Press, 1984), p. 6.
5. Eliade, *Myths, Dreams and Mysteries*, p. 18; *The Sacred and the Profane*, p. 210.
6. Idem, *Myths, Dreams and Mysteries*, p. 18.
7. Idem, *Ordeal by Labyrinth*, pp. 148–9.
8. Idem, *Journal*, p. 186.
9. Ibid., p. 67.
10. Idem, *Mephistopheles and the Androgyne*, p. 122.
11. Taylor, p. 6.
12. Eliade, *Symbolism, the Sacred, and the Arts*, p. 83.
13. Idem, *Journal*, p. 156.
14. Taylor, p. 33.
15. Ibid., p. 30.
16. Ibid., p. 20.
17. Eliade, *Myths, Dreams and Mysteries*, p. 154.
18. Ibid., p. 37.
19. Idem, *The Myth of the Eternal Return*, trans. Willard R. Trask (New York: Pantheon Books, 1954), p. 151.
20. Ibid., p. 161.
21. Taylor, p. 68.
22. Ibid., p. 72.
23. Eliade, *The Sacred and the Profane*, p. 203.
24. Ibid., p. 204.
25. Ibid., p. 167.
26. Ibid., pp. 169–72.

27. Idem, *Myths, Dreams and Mysteries*, p. 119.
28. Idem, *The Myth of the Eternal Return*, pp. 85–6.
29. Ibid., p. 17; *The Sacred and the Profane*, p. 37.
30. Kenneth Hamilton, '*Homo Religiosus* and Historical Faith', *The Journal of Bible and Religion* 33 (1965): 220.
31. Eliade, *Ordeal by Labyrinth*, p. 89.
32. Idem, *Patterns in Comparative Religion*, pp. 291, 381.
33. Idem, *Ordeal by Labyrinth*, p. 95.
34. Ibid., p. 100.
35. Ibid., p. 100.
36. Idem, *Autobiography*, p. 189.
37. Taylor, p. 135.
38. Ibid., p. 48.
39. Ibid., p. 49.
40. Ibid., p. 51.
41. Eliade, *Journal*, p. 80; *Autobiography*, p. 224.
42. Thomas J. J. Altizer, 'Mircea Eliade and the Death of God', *Cross Currents* 29/3 (1979): 262.
43. Mac Linscott Ricketts, 'Mircea Eliade and the Death of God', pp. 40–52.
44. Eliade, *Myth and Reality*, p. 98.
45. Ibid., p. 95.
46. Ibid., p. 95; *Autobiography*, p. 74.
47. Idem, *The Sacred and the Profane*, p. 126.
48. Idem, *Patterns in Comparative Religion*, p. 99.
49. Idem, *The Quest*, p. 87.
50. Taylor, p. 30.
51. Ibid., p. 23.
52. Ibid., p. 32.
53. Eliade, *Journal*, p. 282.
54. Ibid., pp. 297–8.
55. Idem, *Ordeal by Labyrinth*, p. 167.
56. Idem, *Journal*, p. 54.
57. Ibid., p. 267.
58. Idem, *Mephistopheles and the Androgyne*, p. 82.
59. Ibid., p. 122.
60. Taylor, p. 107.
61. Eliade, *The Myth of the Eternal Return*, p. 162.
62. Idem, *Journal*, p. 110.
63. Taylor, p. 135.
64. Ibid., p. 137.
65. Ibid., pp. 139–41.
66. Eliade, *Myth and Reality*, p. 171.
67. Idem, *Zalmoxis*, p. 251.
68. Idem, *Myth and Reality*, pp. 172–3.
69. Ibid., p. 173.
70. Idem, *Ordeal by Labyrinth*, pp. 56–7, 116; *Journal*, pp. 93, 206.
71. Idem, *Journal*, p. 261.
72. Idem, *Symbolism, the Sacred, and the Arts*, p. 92.
73. Saliba, pp. 99–141.

74. Taylor, p. 113.
75. Ibid., pp. 115, 118.
76. Ibid., p. 156.
77. Ibid., pp. 116, 119.
78. Eliade, *Patterns in Comparative Religion*, p. 434.
79. Ibid., p. 383.
80. Idem, *Autobiography*, p. 16.
81. Ibid., p. 16.
82. Idem, *Images and Symbols*, p. 35.
83. Ibid., p. 35.
84. Richard A. Ray, 'Is Eliade's Metapsychoanalysis an End Run Around Bultmann's Demythologization?', in *Myth and the Crisis of Historical Consciousness*, eds Lew W. Gibbs and W. Taylor Stevenson (Missoula, Montana: Scholars Press, 1975), p. 66.
85. Taylor, p. 158.
86. Ibid., p. 160.
87. Ibid., pp. 160–1.
88. Ibid., p. 161.
89. Ibid., p. 168.
90. Ibid., pp. 155–6.
91. Ibid., p. 11.
92. Ibid., p. 13.
93. Ibid., p. 104.
94. Ibid., p. 119.
95. Derrida, *Dissemination*, pp. 268, 304.

5 DIALOGUE AND THE OTHER

1. Gordon D. Kaufman, 'The Historicity of Religions and the Importance of Religious Dialogue', *Buddhist–Christian Studies*, Vol. 4 (1984): 14.
2. Hans Küng, Josef van Ess, Heinrich von Stietencron and Heinz Bechert, *Christianity and the World Religions: Paths of Dialogue with Islam, Hinduism, and Buddhism*, trans. Peter Heinegg (Garden City, New York: Doubleday, 1986), p. xviii.
3. Wilfred Cantwell Smith, *Towards a World Theology*, p. 193.
4. Jürgen Moltmann, *The Church in the Power of the Spirit*, trans. Margaret Kohn (New York: Harper & Row, 1977), p. 159.
5. Raimundo Panikkar, *The Intrareligious Dialogue* (New York: Paulist Press, 1978), p. xxvii.
6. Ninian Smart, *The Science of Religion and the Sociology of Knowledge*, p. 12.
7. Donald K. Swearer, *Dialogue: The Key to Understanding Other Religions* (Philadelphia: Westminster Press, 1977), p. 41.
8. Hans Waldenfels, *Absolute Nothingness: Foundations for a Buddhist–Christian Dialogue*, trans. J. W. Heisig (New York: Paulist Press, 1980), p. 121.
9. Winston L. King, 'Buddhist–Christian Dialogue Reconsidered', *Buddhist–Christian Studies*, Vol. 2 (1982): 10.
10. Paul Tillich, *Christianity and the Encounter of the World Religions* (New York: Columbia University Press, 1963), p. 62. For a critical discussion of Tillich's

contribution to cross-cultural dialogue, see Carl Olson, 'Tillich's Dialogue with Buddhism', *Buddhist–Christian Studies*, Vol. 7 (1987): 183–95.

11. John B. Cobb, Jr, *Beyond Dialogue: Toward a Mutual Transformation of Christianity and Buddhism* (Philadelphia: Fortress Press, 1982), p. viii.
12. Ibid., p. 47.
13. Raimundo Panikkar, *Myth, Faith and Hermeneutics: Cross-Cultural Studies* (New York: Paulist Press, 1979), p. 243.
14. Ibid., p. 346.
15. Idem, *Intrareligious Dialogue*, p. 9.
16. Ibid., p. 50.
17. Ibid., p. 40.
18. Carl Raschke, 'Religious Pluralism and Truth: From Theology to a Hermeneutical Dialogy', *Journal of the American Academy of Religion*, Vol. L, No. 1 (March 1982): 39.
19. Ibid., p. 42.
20. Ibid., p. 44.
21. George A. Lindbeck, *The Nature of Doctrine: Religion and Theology in a Postliberal Age* (Philadelphia: Westminster Press, 1984), pp. 55–6.
22. Karl Rahner, *Theological Investigations Vol. V*, trans. Karl H. Kruger (London: Darton, Longman & Todd, 1966), pp. 121, 131–2.
23. Wolfhart Pannenberg, 'Toward a Theology of the History of Religions', in *Basic Questions in Theology Vol. II*, trans. George H. Kelm (Philadelphia: Fortress Press, 1971), p. 115.
24. Raimundo Panikkar, *The Unknown Christ of Hinduism* (London: Darton, Longman & Todd, 1964), pp. 6, 17, 54, 58.
25. Lindbeck, p. 61.
26. Paul Clasper, *Easter Paths and the Christian Way* (Maryknoll, New York: Orbis Books, 1980), p. 103.
27. King, p. 11.
28. See Küng and other scholars.
29. John Hick, *God Has Many Names* (Philadelphia: Westminster Press, 1980), p. 91.
30. Eliade, *Ordeal by Labyrinth*, p. 107.
31. Idem, *Journal*, p. 179.
32. Idem, *Myths, Dreams and Mysteries*, p. 8.
33. Ibid., p. 9–10. *Mephistopheles and the Androgyne*, p. 13.
34. Idem, *Myth, Dreams and Mysteries*, p. 12.
35. Ibid., pp. 11–12.
36. Ibid., p. 8; *Mephistopheles and the Androgyne*, p. 11.
37. Idem, *Mephistopheles and the Androgyne*, p. 12.
38. Jürgen Habermas, *The Theory of Communicative Action, Volume 2: Lifeworld and System: A Critique of Functionalist Reason*, trans. Thomas McCarthy (Boston: Beacon Press, 1987), p. 119.
39. Ibid., p. 126.
40. Julia Kristeva, *Desire in Language: A Semiotic Approach to Literature and Art*, trans. Thomas Gora, Alice Jardine, and Leon S. Roudiez (New York: Columbia University Press, 1980), p. 66.
41. Ibid., p. 66.
42. Idem, *Polylogue* (Paris: Éditions du Seuil, 1977), pp. 78, 96.

43. Idem, *Desire*, p. 74.
44. Idem, *Revolution in Poetic Language*, trans. Margaret Waller (New York: Columbia University Press, 1984), p. 48.
45. Ibid., p. 47.
46. Habermas, *Theory 2*, p. 62.
47. Ibid., p. 64.
48. Ibid., p. 13.
49. Eliade, *Ordeal by Labyrinth*, p. 121.
50. Kristeva, *Polylogue*, p. 71.
51. Idem, *Revolution*, p. 172.
52. Ibid., pp. 28, 182.
53. Idem, *Polylogue*, p. 79.
54. Idem, *Revolution*, p. 215.
55. Idem, *Polylogue*, p. 97.
56. Eliade, *Ordeal by Labyrinth*, p. 137.
57. Idem, *The Quest*, p. 19.
58. Allen, p. 115.
59. Eliade, *Patterns in Comparative Religion*, p. 30.
60. Allen, p. 127.
61. Julia Kristeva, *Powers of Horror: An Essay on Abjection*, trans. Leon S. Roudiez (New York: Columbia University Press, 1982), p. 138.
62. Idem, *Desire*, p. 78.
63. Ibid., p. 79.
64. Rasmussen, p. 143.
65. Jürgen Habermas, *The Theory of Communicative Action, Volume 1: Reason and the Rationalization of Society*, trans. Thomas McCarthy (Boston: Beacon Press, 1884), p. 287; Vol. 2, p. 120.
66. Idem, *Theory, Vol. 1*, p. 38.
67. Ibid., p. 287.
68. Eliade, *A History of Religious Ideas, Vol I*, p. xvi.
69. Idem, *Images and Symbols*, pp. 32–3.
70. Idem, *The Quest*, p. 3.
71. John S. Dunne, *The Way of All the Earth: Experiments in Truth and Religion* (Notre Dame: University of Notre Dame Press, 1972), p. 53.
72. Ibid., p. 151.
73. Ibid., p. 198.
74. Habermas, *Theory, Vol. 1*, p. 278.
75. Kristeva, *Polylogue*, pp. 92–3.
76. Eliade, *Myths, Dreams and Mysteries*, p. 106.
77. Idem, *Mephistopheles and the Androgyne*, pp. 75–6.
78. Idem, *Ordeal by Labyrinth*, p. 131.
79. Ibid., p. 146.
80. Habermas, *Theory, Vol. 2*, p. 132.
81. Ibid., p. 149.
82. Kristeva, *Polylogue*, p. 99.
83. Eliade, *Myths, Dreams and Mysteries*, p. 233.
84. Paul Ricoeur, *Interpretation Theory: Discourse and the Surplus of Meaning* (Fort Worth, Texas: Texas Christian University Press, 1976), p. 17.
85. Kristeva, *Polylogue*, p. 99.

86. Idem, *Powers*, p. 208.
87. Ibid., p. 128.
88. Jürgen Habermas, *Der philosophische Diskurs der Moderne. Zwölf Vorlesungen* (Frankfurt am Main: Suhrkamp Verlag, 1985), p. 197.
89. Ibid., pp. 213–14.
90. Eliade, *Ordeal by Labyrinth*, p. 121.
91. Gadamer, *Philosophical Hermeneutics*, p. 67.
92. Panikkar, *Intrareligious Dialogue*, p. 50.
93. Wilfred Cantwell Smith, p. 6.
94. Raschke, p. 41.
95. See Baird, p. 152; Dudley, 'Mircea Eliade as the "Anti-Historian" of Religions,' pp. 345–59.

6 SACRED LANGUAGE AND SOTERIOLOGY

1. Julia Kristeva, *Language – The Unknown: An Initiation into Linguistics*, trans. Anne M. Menke (New York: Columbia University Press, 1989).
2. Voltaire, *The Complete Works of Voltaire*, 59, Second Edition, ed. J. H. Brumfitt (Toronto: University of Toronto Press, 1969), p. 105.
3. David Hume, *The Natural History of Religion*, in *The Philosophical Works*, *Vol. IV* (Boston: Little, Brown and Company, 1854), p. 428.
4. Ibid., pp. 478–9.
5. Giambattista Vico, *The New Science*, 3rd edn, trans. Thomas Goddard Bergin and Max Harold Fisch (New York: Cornell University Press, 1968), pp. 81, 221.
6. Ernst Cassirer, *The Philosophy of Symbolic Forms*, 2 vols, trans. Ralph Mannheim (New Haven: Yale University Press, 1953–7), I:3.
7. Friedrich Schlegel, *Dialogue on Poetry and Literary Aphorisms*, trans. Ernst Behler and Roman Struc (University Park and London: Pennsylvania State University Press, 1968), p. 82.
8. Ibid., p. 86.
9. Friedrich W. J. von Schelling, *Einleitung Philosophie der Mythologie* in *Werke*, 6 vols, ed. Manfred Schröten (München: E. H. Beck Berlagsbuchhandlung, 1943–56), VI: 396.
10. Ibid., p. 208.
11. Ibid., p. 126.
12. Ibid., p. 209.
13. Ibid., p. 218.
14. David Friedrich Strauss, *A New Life of Jesus*, trans. Marian Evans (London: Williams & Norgate, 1865), p. 206.
15. Ibid., p. 209.
16. Friedrich Nietzsche, *The Birth of Tragedy*, trans. Wm A. Haussmann, in *The Complete Works of Friedrich Nietzsche*, 18 vols, ed. Oscar Levy (New York: Russell & Russell, Inc., 1964), I: 174.
17. Ibid., p. 84.
18. Max Müller, *Comparative Mythology* (London: G. Routledge, 1909; reprint Arno Press, 1977), p. 178.

19. Sigmund Freud, *The Future of an Illusion*, trans. James Strachey (New York: W. W. Norton & Company, 1961), p. 30.

20. C. G. Jung and C. Kerényi, *Essays on a Science of Mythology*, trans. R. F. C. Hull, Bollingen Series XXII (Princeton: Princeton University Press, 1973), p. 72.

21. Clyde Kluckhohn, 'Myths and Rituals: A General Theory', in *Reader in Comparative Religion: An Anthropological Approach*, eds William A. Lessa and Evon Z. Vogt (New York: Harper & Row, 1972): 93–105. This essay appeared earlier in the *Harvard Theological Review*, Vol. XXXV (January 1942): 45–79.

22. Bronislaw Malinowski, *Magic, Science and Religion and Other Essays* (Garden City, New York: Doubleday & Company, Anchor Books, 1954), p. 101.

23. Claude Lévi-Strauss, *Structural Anthropology*, trans. Claire Jacobson and Brooke Grundfest Schoepf (New York: Basic Books, 1963), p. 229.

24. Van der Leeuw, II: 413.

25. Pettazzoni, p. 26.

26. Julia Kristeva, 'From Symbol to Sign', trans. Seán Hand in *The Kristeva Reader*, ed. Toril Moi (New York: Columbia University Press, 1986), p. 65.

27. Ibid., p. 65.

28. Ibid., p. 65.

29. Eliade, *Images and Symbols*, p. 12.

30. Idem, *Mephistopheles and the Androgyne*, p. 95.

31. Ibid., p. 201. Karl Jaspers agrees with Eliade that symbols, or what the former calls ciphers because they suggest speech rather than the inseparability of symbol and what it symbolizes, open one to Being and infuse one with Being in *Truth and Symbol*, trans. Jean T. Wilde, William Kluback and William Kimmel from *Von der Wahrheit* (New York: Twayne, 1959), p. 38.

32. Derrida, *Of Grammatology*, p. 145.

33. Eliade, *Mephistopheles and the Androgyne*, p. 205. According to Paul Ricoeur, symbolic signs are opaque, representing the depth dimension of a symbol in *The Symbolism of Evil*, trans. Emerson Buchanan (New York: Harper and Row, 1967), pp. 10–11. According to Karl Jaspers a cipher, a secret language of appearances that is not identical with appearances, is infinite and no thought is adequate to it in *Philosophical Faith and Revelation*, trans. E. B. Ashton (New York: Harper & Row, 1962), p. 102. For Jaspers, a symbol is not something that can be verified as valid because its truth is linked with *Existenz*, a non-determined self that forms the potential ground for freedom for thought and action in *Philosophical Faith and Revelation*, p. 92.

34. Eliade, *Mephistopheles and the Androgyne*, p. 203.

35. Ibid., p. 203.

36. Idem, *Patterns in Comparative Religion*, p. 453.

37. Derrida, *Of Grammatology*, pp. 70–1.

38. Eliade, *Mephistopheles and the Androgyne*, p. 208.

39. Ibid., p. 210.

40. Ibid., p. 201.

41. Kristeva, 'From Symbol to Sign', p. 70.

42. Eliade, *The Sacred and the Profane*, p. 27.

43. Kristeva, 'From Symbol to Sign', p. 70.

44. Ibid., p. 71.
45. Ibid., p. 72.
46. Jacques Derrida, *The Postcard: From Socrates to Freud and Beyond*, trans. Alan Bass (Chicago and London: University of Chicago Press, 1987), p. 9.
47. Eliade, *Myth and Reality*, p. 141.
48. Doty, p. 13.
49. Derrida, *Of Grammatology*, p. 139.
50. Eliade, *The Sacred and the Profane*, p. 95.
51. Idem, *Myth and Reality*, p. 11.
52. Derrida, *Of Grammatology*, p. 74.
53. Ibid., p. 61.
54. Eric Gould, *Mythical Intentions in Modern Literature* (Princeton: Princeton University Press, 1981), pp. 42–3.
55. Eliade, *Myth and Reality*, p. 202.
56. Gould, p. 45.
57. Derrida, *Of Grammatology*, p. 314.
58. Ibid., p. 144.
59. Gould, pp. 178–9.
60. Ibid., p. 185.
61. Eliade, *The Sacred and the Profane*, p. 97.
62. Gould, p. 189.
63. Derrida, *Dessemination*, p. 139.
64. Gould, pp. 63, 66.
65. Mircea Eliade, 'The Prestige of the Cosmogonic Myth', *The Divinity School News*, Vol. XXVI, no. 1 (February 1959): 3. There are scholars who do not share Eliade's opinion regarding the primary significance of the creation myth. To cite just one contrary opinion from Jewish religious history, Howard Eilberg-Schwartz writes, 'Eliade overstates the importance of cosmogony by seeking to understand all rituals and religious conceptions as a rearticulation of a creation myth.' (p. 358) Eilberg-Schwartz shows that the purity/impurity dichotomy in the Jewish Mishnah's theory finds no parallel and hence no justification in the priestly cosmogony, although the Mishnah equates the human capacity to classify with the divine work of creation. This means that human activity and thought can serve as a criterion for classifying things into different categories and possesses the power to change basic properties of objects (p. 372), in 'Creation and Classification in Judaism: From Priestly to Rabbinic Conceptions', *History of Religions*, Vol. 26, no. 4 (May 1987). In contrast to Eilberg-Schwartz's criticism of Eliade, Lawrence E. Sullivan argues, 'Here Eliade claims neither that all cultures possess cosmogonic myths, nor that cosmogonies are given first place of priority in those cultures which possess them.' Review of *A History of Religious Ideas, Vol. 2: From Gautama Buddha to the Triumph of Christianity*, by Mircea Eliade, in *Religious Studies Review*, Vol. 9, no. 1 (January 1983): 16.
66. Eliade, *Myth and Reality*, p. 15.
67. Jacques Derrida, *Glas*, trans. John P. Leavey, Jr and Richard Rand (Lincoln and London: University of Nebraska Press, 1986), pp. 169–170.
68. Eliade, *Myth and Reality*, p. 18.
69. Derrida, *Of Grammatology*, p. 61.
70. Eliade, *Ordeal by Labyrinth*, p. 166.

71. Strenski, p. 75.
72. Derrida, *Of Grammatology*, p. 37.
73. Eliade, *Journal*, pp, 71, 95.
74. Ibid., p. 144.
75. Idem, *The Quest*, p. 126. Leszek Kolakowski also tries to trace myth in non-mythical areas of experience and thought, and thinks that metaphysical questions and beliefs are an extension of the mythical core of a culture in *The Presence of Myth*, trans. Adam Czerniawski (Chicago and London: University of Chicago Press, 1989).
76. Ibid., p. 126; *Symbolism, the Sacred, and the Arts*, p. 82.
77. Idem, *Myths, Dreams and Mysteries*, p. 27.
78. Idem, *Myth and Reality*, p. 141.
79. Idem, *Journal*, p. 310.
80. Ibid., p. 288.
81. For an informative discussion, see Matei Calinescu, '"The Function of the Unreal": Reflections on Mircea Eliade's Short Fiction', in *Imagination and Meaning: The Scholarly and Literary Worlds of Mircea Eliade*, ed. Norman J. Girardot and Mac Linscott Ricketts (New York: Seabury Press, 1982), pp. 138–61.
82. Eliade, *The Quest*, p. iii.
83. Idem, *Journal*, p. 296.
84. Derrida, *Of Grammatology*, p. 57.
85. Idem, *Dissemination*, p. 137.
86. Kristeva, *Revolution in Poetic Language*, pp. 43, 74.
87. Ibid., p. 80.
88. Ibid., p. 79.
89. Idem, *Powers of Horror*, p. 206.
90. Derrida, *Speech and Phenomena*, p. 140.
91. Doty, p. 55.
92. Strenski, p. 107.
93. Derrida, *Dissemination*, p. 63.
94. Gadamer, *Truth and Method*, p. 93, 97.
95. Paul Ricoeur, *The Symbolism of Evil*, trans. Emerson Buchanan (New York: Harper & Row, 1967), p. 237.
96. Gadamer, *Truth and Method*, p. 105.

7 ONTOLOGY AND THE SACRED

1. Mircea Eliade, 'A Detail from Parsifal (from *Insula lui Euthanasius*)', in *Imagination and Meaning: The Scholarly and Literary Worlds of Mircea Eliade*, eds Norman J. Girardot and Mac Linscott Ricketts (New York: Seabury Press, 1982), p. 194.
2. Martin Heidegger, *An Introduction to Metaphysics*, trans. Ralph Manheim (New Haven and London: Yale University Press, 1959), p. 1.
3. Eliade, *Myths, Dreams and Mysteries*, p. 17.
4. Idem, *Journal*, p. 179.
5. Idem, *The Sacred and the Profane*, pp. 20–2.
6. Derrida, *Speech and Phenomena*, p. 158.

7.   Idem, *Spurs*, trans. Barbara Harlow (Chicago and London: University of Chicago Press, 1979), pp. 103–5.
8.   Eliade, *The Sacred and the Profane*, p. 23.
9.   Derrida, *Speech and Phenomena*, p. 86.
10. Eliade, *The Sacred and the Profane*, p. 64.
11. Ibid., p. 94.
12. Derrida, *Writing and Difference*, p. 279.
13. Friedrich Nietzsche, *The Birth of Tragedy*, trans. Wm A. Haussmann, in *The Complete Works of Friedrich Nietzsche, Vol. 1*, ed. Oscar Levy (New York: Russell & Russell, 1964), pp. 22–7.
14. Eliade, *The Sacred and the Profane*, p. 117.
15. Ibid., p. 167.
16. Ibid., p. 165.
17. Ibid., p. 166.
18. Idem, *Myth and Reality*, p. 92.
19. Derrida, *Speech and Phenomena*, p. 154.
20. Eliade, *The Myth of the Eternal Return*, p. 34.
21. Ibid., p. 34.
22. Derrida, *Writing and Difference*, p. 260.
23. Ibid., p. 141.
24. Ibid., p. 126.
25. Eliade, *Rites and Symbols of Initiation*, p. xi.
26. Derrida, *Speech and Phenomena*, p. 153.
27. Ibid., p. 134.
28. Ibid., p. 156.
29. Idem, *Of Grammatology*, p. 167.
30. E. E. Evans-Pritchard, *Theories of Primitive Religion* (Oxford: Oxford University Press, 1965), p. 65.
31. Ibid., p. 65.
32. Robin Horton, 'The Kalabari World-view: An Outline and Interpretation', *Africa*, 32 (1962): 197–219.
33. Alfonso Ortiz, *The Tewa World: Space, Time, Being, and Becoming in a Pueblo Society* (Chicago and London: University of Chicago Press, 1969), pp. 9, 17.
34. Sam D. Gill, *Native American Religions: An Introduction* (Belmont, California: Wadsworth Publishing Company, 1982), p. 34.
35. Godfrey Lienhardt, *Divinity and Experience: The Religion of the Dinka* (Oxford: Oxford University Press, 1961), p. 159.
36. Christopher Vecsey, 'American Indian Environmental Religions,' in *American Indian Environments: Ecological Issues in Native American History*, ed. Christopher Vecsey and Robert W. Venables (Syracuse, New York: Syracuse University Press, 1980), p. 31.
37. Ake Hultkrantz, *Belief and Worship in Native North America*, ed. Christopher Vecsey (Syracuse, New York: Syracuse University Press, 1981), p. 122.
38. A. Irving Hallowell, 'Ojibwa Ontology, Behavior, and World View', in *Teachings from the American Earth: Indian Religion and Philosophy*, ed. Dennis Tedlock and Barbara Tedlock (New York: Liveright, 1975), pp. 141–78.

39. Lienhardt, p. 27.
40. Ibid., p. 117.
41. Eliade, *Symbolism, the Sacred, and the Arts*, p. 3.
42. Idem, *Myth and Reality*, p. 206.
43. Idem, *Symbolism, the Sacred, and the Arts*, p. 12.
44. Ibid., p. 13.
45. Jacques Derrida, *Glas*, trans. John P. Leavey, Jr and Richard Rand (Lincoln and London: University of Nebraska Press, 1986), p. 9.
46. Ibid., p. 9.
47. Eliade, *The Sacred and the Profane*, p. 130.
48. Ibid., p. 131.
49. Idem, *Myths, Dreams and Mysteries*, p. 15.
50. Derrida, *Glas*, p. 8.
51. Martin Heidegger, *Holzwege* (Frankfurt: Vittorio Klostermann, 1963), p. 286.
52. Eliade, *Myths, Dreams and Mysteries*, p. 16.
53. Idem, *Journal*, p. 290.
54. Idem, *Myths, Dreams and Mysteries*, p. 16.
55. Ake Hultkrantz, *Native Religions of North America* (San Francisco: Harper & Row, 1987), p. 62.
56. Ibid., p. 42.
57. Gill, p. 36.
58. Ortiz, p. 121.
59. Gill, p. 61.
60. Ibid., p. 81.
61. Victor Turner, *The Forest of Symbols: Aspects of Ndembu Ritual* (Ithaca, New York: Cornell University Press, 1967), p. 43.
62. E. E. Evans-Pritchard, *Nuer Religion* (Oxford: Oxford University Press, 1956), p. 141.
63. Benjamin C. Ray, *African Religions: Symbols, Ritual, and Community* (Englewood Cliffs, New Jersey: Prentice-Hall, 1976), p. 24.
64. Ortiz, p. 84.
65. Arnold van Gennap, *The Rites of Passage*, trans. Monika B. Vizedom and Gabrielle C. Caffee (Chicago: University of Chicago Press, 1968).
66. Eliade, *Rites and Symbols of Initiation*, p. x.
67. Ibid., p. xii.
68. Malefijt, p. 193.
69. Eliade, *Shamanism*, pp. 33–144.
70. Idem, *Yoga: Immortality and Freedom*, 2nd edn, trans. Willard R. Trask, Bollingen Series LVI (Princeton: Princeton University Press, 1969), p. 4.
71. Ibid., p. 98.
72. Idem, *Mephistopheles and the Androgyne*, p. 77.
73. Derrida, *Of Grammatology*, p. 292.
74. Ortiz, pp. 41–2.
75. Evans-Pritchard, *Nuer*, p. 255.
76. Turner, *The Forest of Symbols*, pp. 93–110.
77. Ibid., p. 255.
78. Dominique Zahan, *The Religion, Spirituality, and Thought of Traditional Africa* (Chicago and London: University of Chicago Press, 1979), p. 60.

79. James R. Walker, *Lakota Belief and Ritual*, ed. Raymond J. De Mallie and Elaine A. Jahner (Lincoln and London: University of Nebraska Press, 1980), p. 182.
80. Joseph Epes Brown (ed.), *The Sacred Pipe* (New York: Penguin Books, 1979), p. 71.
81. Derrida, *of Grammatology*, p. 143.
82. Ibid., p. 184.
83. Ibid., p. 69.
84. Idem, *Glas*, p. 136.
85. John S. Mbiti, *African Religions and Philosophy* (Garden City, New York: Doubleday, 1970), p. 203.
86. Gill, p. 110.
87. Derrida, *Writing and Difference*, p. 145.

8 THE PHENOMENON OF POWER

1. Ake Hultkrantz, *The Religions of the American Indians*, trans. Monica Setterwall (Berkeley: University of California Press, 1980), p. 14.
2. Wing-tsit Chan, trans. *The Way of Lao Tzu (Tao-te-ching)* (Indianapolis: Bobbs-Merrill, 1963), 14. See Ellen Marie Chen, 'Nothingness and the Mother Principle in Early Chinese Taoism', *International Philosophical Quarterly*, Vol. IX, no. 3 (September 1969): 391–405.
3. Chan, 1. See Ellen Marie Chen, 'The Origin and Development of Being (*Yu*) from Non-Being (*Wu*) in the *Tao Te Ching*', *International Philosophical Quarterly*, Vol. XIII, No. 3 (September 1973): 403–17.
4. Chan, 51.
5. Ibid., 65.
6. Walter O. Kaelber, 'Tapas, Birth, and Spiritual Rebirth in the Veda', *History of Religions*, Vol. 15, no. 4 (May 1976), p. 343.
7. J. Gonda, *Die Religionen Indiens I: Veda und älterer Hinduismus* (Stuttgart: W. Kohlhammer, 1960), pp. 184–5.
8. Eliade, *The Sacred and the Profane*, p. 12; *Myths, Dreams and Mysteries*, p. 130.
9. Idem, *Patterns in Comparative Religion*, p. 216.
10. Idem, *Myths, Dreams and Mysteries*, p. 125.
11. Ibid., p. 128.
12. Idem, *Patterns in Comparative Religion*, p. 227.
13. Idem, *The Forge and the Crucible*, p. 27.
14. Idem, *Myths, Dreams and Mysteries*, p. 125.
15. Idem, *Patterns in Comparative Religion*, p. 437.
16. Idem, *Myths, Dreams and Mysteries*, p. 124, 126.
17. Idem, *Patterns in Comparative Religion*, p. 24.
18. Ibid., p. 30.
19. Ibid., pp. 14–15.
20. Ibid., p. 18.
21. G. van der Leeuw, *Religion in Essence and Manifestation*, 2 vols (New York: Harper & Row, 1963; reprint, Gloucester, MA: Peter Smith, 1967), I: 42.

22. Ibid., I: 44.
23. Ibid., I: 28.
24. Ibid., I: 35.
25. Ibid., I: 286–7.
26. Ibid., I: 28. *Der Mensch und die Religion* (Basel: Verlag Haus zum Falken, 1941), pp. 40, 102.
27. Ibid., I: 28.
28. Ibid., I: 48.
29. Ibid., I: 26.
30. Ibid., I: 49.
31. Ibid., I: 52.
32. Michel Foucault, *The History of Sexuality, Volume I: An Introduction*, trans. Robert Hurley (New York: Vintage/Random House, 1980), p. 45.
33. Van der Leeuw, *Religion in Essence and Manifestation*, I: 147.
34. Ibid., I: 148.
35. Ibid., I: 157.
36. Ibid., I: 30.
37. Foucault, pp. 92–3. See also his *Power/Knowledge: Selected Interviews and Other Writings 1972–1977*, ed. Colin Gordon and trans. Colin Gordon, Leo Marshall, John Mepham and Kate Soper (New York: Pantheon Books, 1980), p. 89.
38. Idem, *Power/Knowledge*, p. 98.
39. Ibid., p. 99.
40. Idem, 'The Subject and Power', in *Michel Foucault: Beyond Structuralism and Hermeneutics*, 2nd edn, ed. Hubert L. Dreyfus and Paul Rabinow (University of Chicago Press, 1983), p. 219.
41. Ibid., p. 220.
42. Van der Leeuw, *Religion in Essence and Manifestation*, I: 191.
43. Eliade, *The Sacred and the Profane*, p. 17.
44. Foucault, *Power/Knowledge*, p. 188.
45. Ibid., pp. 57–8.
46. Eliade, *The Sacred and the Profane*, pp. 20–3.
47. Ibid., p. 52.
48. Idem, *Patterns in Comparative Religion*, p. 367.
49. Ibid., p. 368.
50. Foucault, *The History of Sexuality*, p. 83.
51. Van der Leeuw, *Religion in Essence and Manifestation*, I: 47.
52. Ibid., II: 393.
53. Foucault, *Power/Knowledge*, p. 141.
54. Eliade, *The Sacred and the Profane*, p. 68.
55. Ibid., pp. 80–2.
56. Idem, *Patterns in Comparative Religion*, p. 394.
57. Ibid., p. 393.
58. Van der Leeuw, *Religion in Essence and Manifestation*, II: 385. Van der Leeuw also suggests that genuine power is not far removed from impotency in *Der Mensch und Die Religion*, p. 78.
59. Ibid., II: 390.
60. Eliade, *The Sacred and the Profane*, p. 64.

61. Foucault, *Power/Knowledge*, p. 142.
62. Idem, *The History of Sexuality*, pp. 94–5.
63. Van der Leeuw, *Religion in Essence and Manifestation*, II: 340.
64. Ibid., II: 356–7.
65. Ibid., I: 165.
66. Ibid., I: 198.
67. Ibid., I: 195, 201.
68. Ibid., II: 378.
69. Eliade, *Patterns in Comparative Religion*, p. 448.
70. Ibid., pp. 38–9, 58.
71. Ibid., p. 59.
72. Ibid., pp. 182–3.
73. Idem, *A History of Ideas, Vol, I*, p. 267.
74. Idem, *Myth and Reality*, p. 6.
75. Ibid., pp. 18, 15, 142.
76. Ibid., p. 90.
77. Foucault, *Power/Knowledge*, p. 52.
78. Eliade, *Myth and Reality*, p. 36. See also Eliade's article 'The prestige of the Cosmogonic Myth', pp. 1–12.
79. Michel Foucault, *Discipline and Punish: The Birth of the Prison*, trans. Alan Sheridan (New York: Pantheon Books, 1977), p. 194.
80. Idem, *The History of Sexuality*, p. 105.
81. Idem, *Power/Knowledge*, p. 119.
82. Van der Leeuw, *Religion in Essence and Manifestation*, I: 40.
83. Ibid., II: 403–5.
84. Ibid., II: 413.
85. Ibid., II: 435–6.
86. Ibid., II: 546.
87. Ibid., II: 551.
88. Ibid., II: 679.
89. Eliade, *Shamanism*, p. 481.
90. Ibid., p. 474.
91. Idem, *Forge and the Crucible*, p. 81.
92. Idem, *Shamanism*, p. 85.
93. Ibid., pp. 19, 94, 104.
94. Ibid., p. 107.
95. Ibid., p. 98.
96. Idem, *Yoga: Immortality and Freedom*, p. 96.
97. Ibid., p. 335.
98. Idem, *Australian Religions: An Introduction* (Ithaca and London: Cornell University Press, 1973), p. 129.
99. Ibid., pp. 130–57.
100. Van der Leeuw, *Religion in Essence and Manifestation*, I: 43.
101. Ibid., II: 120–3.
102. Ibid., I: 141–4.
103. Ibid., I: 75.
104. Foucault, *Discipline and Punish*, p. 201.
105. Ibid., p. 223.
106. Idem, *Power/Knowledge*, p. 98.

9 TIME AND NOSTALGIA

1. Shirley Jackson Case, *The Christian Philosophy of History* (Chicago: University of Chicago Press, 1943), p. 17.
2. Rudolf Bultmann, *History and Eschatology: The Presence of Eternity* (New York: Harper & Row Publishers, 1957), p. 21.
3. Eliade, *The Myth of the Eternal Return*, p. 104.
4. Karl Löwith, *Meaning in History* (Chicago: University of Chicago Press, 1964), p. 182.
5. E. C. Rust, *The Christian Understanding of History* (London: Lutterworth Press, 1947), p. 158.
6. Bultmann, p. 40.
7. Eliade, *Autobiography I*, pp. 4–5.
8. Bultmann, p. 59. Reinhold Niebuhr writes, 'Augustine was the first to fully develop the implications of the Biblical view of time and history.' In *Faith and History* (New York: Charles Scribner's Sons, 1949), p. 65.
9. Augustine, *The Confessions,* Nicene and Post-Nicene Fathers Vol. I, ed. Philip Schaff (Michigan: Wm B. Eerdman, 1965), 11.15.18.
10. Ibid., 11.15.18.
11. Ibid., 11.16.21.
12. Ibid., 11.27.36.
13. Ibid., 11.24.31.
14. Ibid., 11.28.23.
15. Ibid., 11.20.26.
16. Ibid., 11.30.40.
17. Quoted from the work of Martin Heidegger, *Being and Time*, trans. John Robinson and John Macquarrie (New York: Harper & Row, 1962), p. 485.
18. Martin Buber, *Between Man and Man*, trans. Ronald Gregor Smith (New York: Macmillan, 1966), p. 141.
19. Eliade, *The Myth of the Eternal Return*, p. 89.
20. Idem, *The Sacred and the Profane*, pp. 68–9.
21. Idem, *The Myth of the Eternal Return*, p. 89.
22. Idem, *The Sacred and the Profane*, p. 73.
23. Idem, *The Myth of the Eternal Return*, p. 155. Seymour Cain points to a basic ambivalence in Eliade's attitude toward history and his emphasis on the transhistorical in 'Mircea Eliade: Attitudes Toward History', *Religious Studies Review*, Vol. 6, no. 1 (January 1980): 13–16.
24. Idem, *The Sacred and the Profane*, p. 80.
25. Ibid., p. 82.
26. Idem, *The Myth of the Eternal Return*, pp. 14, 154.
27. Ibid., p. 142.
28. Ibid., pp. 85–6.
29. Idem, *The Forbidden Forest*, trans. Mac Linscott Ricketts and Mary Park Stevenson (Notre Dame, London: University of Notre Dame Press, 1978), p. 313.
30. Ibid., p. 314.
31. Michel Foucault, *The Order of Things: An Archaeology of the Human Sciences*, trans. Alan Sheridan Smith (New York: Random House, 1973), p. 9.
32. Ibid., p. 9.

33. Ibid., pp. 159–60, 170–71.
34. Idem, *The History of Sexuality, Volume I*, pp. 1–13.
35. Idem, *Discipline and Punish*, p. 26.
36. Idem, *The History of Sexuality, Volume I*, pp. 5–6.
37. Idem, 'Nietzsche, Genealogy, History', in *Language, Counter-Memory, Practice: Selected Essays and Interviews*, ed. Donald F. Bouchard and trans. Donald F. Bouchard and Sherry Simon (Ithaca, New York: Cornell University Press, 1977), p. 153.
38. Ibid., pp. 152–7.
39. Ibid., p. 150.
40. Ibid., p. 140.
41. Ibid., p. 151.
42. Idem, 'Nietzsche, Freud, Marx,' In *Nietzsche*, Proceeding of the Seventh International Philosophical Colloquium of the Cahiers de Royaumont, 4–8 July 1964 (Paris: Editions de Minuit, 1967), p. 189.
43. Augustine, *City of God*, Nicene and Post-Nicene Fathers Vol. II, ed. Philip Schaff (Michigan: Wm B. Eerdman, 1956), 15.5.
44. Ibid., 14.28.
45. Löwith, p. 169.
46. Augustine, *City of God*, 15.1.
47. Ibid., 15.5.
48. Löwith, p. 169.
49. G. W. F. Hegel, *The Philosophy of History*, trans. J. Sibree (New York: Dover Publications, 1956), p. 19.
50. Ibid., p. 20.
51. Ibid., p. 21.
52. Ibid., p. 33.
53. Foucault, *Power/Knowledge*, p. 114.
54. Ibid., p. 15.
55. Idem, *Madness and Civilization: A History of Insanity in the Age of Reason*, trans. Richard Howard (New York: Random House, 1973), p. 40.
56. Allan Megill, *Prophets of Extremity: Nietzsche, Heidegger, Foucault, Derrida* (Berkeley: University of California Press, 1985), pp. 234, 243; Larry Shiner interprets Foucault's method as 'an anti-method in the sense that it seeks to free us from the illusion that an apolitical method is possible', (p. 386) in 'Reading Foucault: Anti-Method and the Genealogy of Power–Knowledge', *History and Theory*, 21 (1982); Mark Poster calls Foucault the anti-historical historian in 'Foucault and History', *Social Research*, 49 (1982): 116–42.
57. See Rosen, *Hermeneutics as Politics*, who is more categorically certain about the political nature of all hermeneutics than I am inclined to believe because I would like to think that a neutral hermeneutics is possible and desirable.
58. Eliade, *Ordeal by Labyrinth*, p. 121.
59. Ibid., p. 126.
60. Idem, *The Forbidden Forest*, p. 304.
61. Ibid., p. 418.
62. Ibid., p. 509.
63. Ibid., p. 171. Edward J. Cronin compares Eliade's attitude toward history with two of James Joyce's characters in his novel *Ulysses*: Leopold Bloom,

a representative of Eliade's archaic individual, and Stephen Dedalus, an example of the modern person in 'Eliade, Joyce, and the "Nightmare of History"', *Journal of the American Academy of Religion*, Vol. L, no. 3 (September 1982): 435–48.

64. Eliade, *The Myth of the Eternal Return*, p. 156.
65. Idem, *Zalmoxis*, p. 255.
66. Idem, *A History of Religious Ideas, Vol. I*, p. 55. *The Forge and the Crucible*, pp. 173–4.
67. Idem, *Shamanism*, p. 103.
68. Idem, *Myths, Dreams and Mysteries*, p. 36.
69. Idem, *The Myth of the Eternal Return*, p. 160.
70. Ibid., p. 160.
71. Ibid., pp. 160–1.
72. Ibid., p. 162.
73. According to the critical perspective of Maurice Friedman, Eliade understands linear or historical time from the apocalyptic standpoint and not from the prophetic. On the one hand, history is overcome in the future by the former. On the other hand, the prophetic approach to history promises a consummation of creation. The prophet is concerned with the experienced moment and its possibility in 'The Human Way: A Dialogical Approach to Religion and Human Experience', *Journal of the American Academy of Religion*, Vol. LI, no. 1 (March 1983): 67–77.
74. Augustine, *Confessions*, 11.5.
75. Ibid., p. 11.13.
76. Idem, *City of God*, 12.20.
77. Hegel, p. 54.
78. Ibid., p. 19.
79. Ibid., p. 63.
80. Ibid., p. 72.
81. Hubert L. Dreyfus and Paul Rabinow, *Michel Foucault: Beyond Structuralism and Hermeneutics*, 2nd edn, (Chicago: University of Chicago Press, 1983), p. 87.
82. Foucault, *The Order of Things*, p. 120.
83. Eliade, *Zalmoxis*, p. 227.
84. George Uscatescu, 'Time and Destiny in the Novels of Mircea Eliade', in *Myths and Symbols: Studies in Honor of Mircea Eliade*, eds Joseph M. Kitagawa and Charles H. Long (Chicago and London: University of Chicago Press, 1969), p. 404.
85. Eliade, *Zalmoxis*, p. 254.
86. Idem, *The Forbidden Forest*, pp. 237–8.
87. Ibid., p. 69.
88. Virgil Ierunca quotes from Eliade's *Journal* in 'The Literary Work of Mircea Eliade', in *Myths and Symbols: Studies in Honor of Mircea Eliade*, eds Joseph M. Kitagawa and Charles H. Long (Chicago and London: University of Chicago Press, 1969), p. 357.
89. G. L. Keyes argues that Augustine expresses an explicit philosophy of history in *Christian Faith and the Interpretation of History* (Lincoln: University of Nebraska Press, 1966), p. 193. On the other hand, Karl Löwith argues that the history of the world possesses no intrinsic interest or meaning for Augustine.

Löwith contends that what Augustine attempts is a dogmatic-historical interpretation of Christianity (p. 166). Alan Richardson agrees with Löwith in
History Sacred and Profane (Philadelphia: Westminster Press, 1964), p. 56.
90.   Hegel, p. 49.
91.   Foucault, *The Order of Things*, p. 205; 'Nietzsche, Genealogy, History,'
      p. 161.
92.   Idem, 'Nietzsche, Genealogy, History,' p. 160.
93.   Idem, *The Birth of the Clinic: An Archaeology of Medical Perception*, trans.
      A. M. Sheridan Smith (New York: Vintage/Random House, 1975), p. xix.
94.   Edith Wyschogrod, *Spirit in Ashes: Hegel, Heidegger and Man-Made Mass
      Death* (New Haven and London: Yale University Press, 1985).

10   SEEKING THE CENTRE

1.   Gill, pp. 83–4.
2.   Taylor, *Erring*, p. 158.
3.   Idem, *Tears* (Albany: State University of New York Press, 1990), p. 203.
4.   Mircea Eliade, *Journal III, 1970–1978*, trans. Teresa Lavender Fagan
      (Chicago and London: University of Chicago Press, 1989), p. 19.
5.   Taylor, *Erring*, p. 135.
6.   Mircea Eliade, *Youth Without Youth and Other Novellas*, ed. Matei Calinescu
      and trans. Mac Linscott Ricketts (Columbus: Ohio State University, 1988),
      p. 98.
7.   Idem, *Journal III*, p. 310.
8.   Taylor, *Erring*, p. 152.
9.   Ibid., p. 150.
10.   Idem, *Deconstructing Theology*, American Academy of Religion Studies in
      Religion 28 (New York: Crossroad Publishing Company and Scholars Press,
      1982), p. 5.
11.   Idem, *Erring*, p. 155.
12.   Ibid., p. 156.
13.   Ibid., p. 168.
14.   Ibid., p. 116.
15.   Ibid., p. 116.
16.   Pierre Teilhard de Chardin, *The Divine Milieu: An Essay on The Interior Life*
      (New York, Evanston, and London: Harper & Row, 1960), p. 90.
17.   Ibid., pp. 93, 95.
18.   Ibid., p. 110. Teilhard de Chardin also conceives of a unity in the universe in
      The Phenomenon of Man (New York and Evanston: Harper & Row, 1965),
      pp. 41–2.
19.   Ibid., pp. 99–100, 174.
20.   Ibid., p. 175.
21.   Ibid., pp. 54, 98.
22.   Eliade, *Journal III*, pp. 3, 31.
23.   Taylor, *Erring*, p. 179.
24.   Ibid., p. 97.
25.   Idem, *Tear*, p. 223.

26. Ibid., p. 3.
27. Ibid., p. 5.
28. Ibid., p. 84.
29. Idem, *Deconstructing Theology*, pp. 48, 57.
30. Eliade, *Ordeal by Labyrinth*, p. 156.
31. Taylor, *Erring*, p. 114.
32. Idem, *Deconstructing Theology*, pp. 49–52.
33. Eliade, *Ordeal by Labyrinth*, p. 153.
34. Taylor, *Erring*, pp. 118–19.
35. Idem, *Tear*, p. 223.
36. Ibid., p. 225.
37. Ibid., p. 224.
38. Eliade, *Journal III*, p. 235.
39. Ibid., p. 231.
40. Ibid., p. 277.
41. Friedrich Nietzsche, *The Portable Nietzsche*, trans. Walter Kaufman (Baltimore: Penguin Books, 1959), p. 125.
42. Martin Heidegger, *Sein und Zeit* (Tubingen: Max Niemeyer Verlag, 1972), pp. 276–7.
43. Ibid., p. 188.
44. Foucault, *The Order of Things*, pp. 384–6.
45. Ibid., p. 385.
46. Eliade, *Ordeal by Labyrinth*, p. 121.
47. Idem, *Journal III*, p. 279.
48. Kurt Rudolph, *Historical Fundamentals and the Study of Religions* (New York and London: Macmillan, 1985), p. 28.
49. Ibid., p. 52.
50. Ibid., pp. 68–9.
51. Mircea Eliade, *Journal IV 1979–1985*, trans. Mac Linscott Ricketts (Chicago, London: University of Chicago Press, 1990), p. 143.
52. Ibid., p. 85.
53. Ibid., p. 43.
54. Ibid., p. 68.
55. Ibid., p. 108.
56. Geoffrey Galt Harpham, *The Ascetic Imperative in Culture and Criticism* (Chicago and London: University of Chicago Press, 1987), p. 29.
57. Eliade, *Journal III*, p. 288.

Bibliography

Allen, Douglas, 'Mircea Eliade's Phenomenological Analysis of Religious Experience', *Journal of Religion* 52 (1972): 170–86.

_____, 'Phenomenological Method and the Dialectic of the Sacred', in *Imagination and Meaning: The Scholarly and Literary Worlds of Mircea Eliade*, eds Norman J. Girardot and Mac Linscott Ricketts (New York: Seabury Press, 1982, pp. 70–81).

_____, *Structure and Creativity in Religion: Hermeneutics in Mircea Eliade's Phenomenology and New Directions* (The Hague: Mouton, 1978).

Gregory D. Alles, 'Wach, Eliade, and the Critique from Totality', *Numen*, Vol. XXXV, Fasc. 1 (July 1988): 108–38.

Altizer, Thomas J. J., 'Mircea Eliade and the Death of God', *Cross Currents*, Vol. XXIX, no. 3 (Fall 1979): 257–68.

_____, *Mircea Eliade and the Dialectic of the Sacred* (Philadelphia: The Westminster Press, 1963).

_____, 'Mircea Eliade and the Recovery of the Sacred', *The Christian Scholar* 45 (1962): 267–89.

Augustine, *City of God and Christian Doctrine*, in Nicene and Post Nicene Fathers, Vol. II, ed. Philip Schaff (Michigan: Wm B. Eerdman, 1956).

_____, *The Confessions*, in Nicene and Post Nicene Fathers, vol. I, ed. Philip Schaff (Michigan: Wm B. Eerdman, 1956).

Baird, Robert D., *Category Formation and the History of Religions* (The Hague: Mouton, 1971).

Berger, Adriana, 'Eliade's Double Approach: A Desire for Unity', *Religious Studies Review*, Vol. 11, no. 1 (January 1985): 9–12.

Bleeker, C. J., *The Sacred Bridge* (Leiden: E. J. Brill, 1963).

Brown, Joseph Epes (ed.), *The Sacred Pipe* (New York: Penguin Books, 1979).

Brown, Robert F., 'Eliade on Archaic Religion: Some Old and New Criticisms', *Sciences Religieuses/Studies in Religion*, 10, 4 (1981): 429–49.

Buber, Martin, *Betweeen Man and Man*, trans. Ronald Gregor Smith (New York: Macmillan, 1966).

Bultmann, Rudolf, *History and Eschatology: The Presence of Eternity* (New York: Harper & Row, 1957).

Cain, Seymour, 'Mircea Eliade: Attitudes toward History', *Religious Studies Review*, Vol. 6, no. 1 (January 1980): 13–16.

Calinescu, Matei, 'Imagination and Meaning: Aesthetic Attitudes and Ideas in Mircea Eliade's Thought', *Journal of Religion*, Vol. 57 (January 1977): 1–15.

_____, '"The Function of the Unreal": Reflections on Mircea Eliade's Short Fiction', in *Imagination and Meaning: The Scholarly and Literary Worlds of Mircea Eliade*, eds Norman J. Girardot and Mac Linscott Ricketts (New York: Seabury Press, 1982), pp. 138–161.

Case, Shirley Jackson, *The Christian Philosophy of History* (Chicago: University of Chicago Press, 1943).

Cassirer, Ernst, *The Philosophy of Symbolic Forms*, 2 vols, trans. Ralph Mannheim (New Haven: Yale University Press, 1953–57).

Chan, Wing-tsit, trans. *The Way of Lao Tzu (Tao-te Ching)* (Indianapolis: Bobbs-Merrill, 1963).

Chen, Ellen Marie, 'Nothingness and the Mother Principle in Early Chinese Taoism', *International Philosophical Quarterly*, Vol. IX, no. 3 (September 1969): 391–405.

_____, 'The Origin and Development of Being (*Yu*) from Non-Being (*Wu*) in the *Tao Te Ching*', *International Philosophical Quarterly*, Vol. XIII, no. 3 (September 1973): 403–17.

Clasper, Paul, *Eastern Paths and the Christian Way* (Maryknoll, New York: Orbis Books, 1980).

Cobb, Jr, John B., *Beyond Dialogue: Toward a Mutual Transformation of Christianity and Buddhism* (Philadelphia: Fortress Press, 1982).

Cronin, Edward J., 'Eliade, Joyce, and the "Nightmare of History"', *Journal of the American Academy of Religion*, Vol. L, no. 3 (September 1982): 435–48.

Culianu, Ioan, *Mircea Eliade* (Assisi: Cittadella Editrice, 1977).

Derrida, Jacques, *Dissemination*, trans. Barbara Johnson (Chicago: University of Chicago Press, 1981).

_____, *Glas*, trans. John P. Leavey, Jr and Richard Rand (Lincoln and London: University of Nebraska, 1986).

_____, *Margins of Philosophy*, trans. Alan Bass (Chicago: University of Chicago Press, 1986).

_____, *Of Grammatology*, trans. Gayatri Chakravorty Spivak (Baltimore and London: Johns Hopkins University Press, 1976).

_____, *Positions*, trans. Alan Bass (Chicago: University of Chicago Press, 1981).

_____, *The Postcard: From Socrates to Freud and Beyond*, trans. Alan Bass (Chicago and London: University of Chicago Press, 1987).

_____, *Speech and Phenomena And Other Essays on Husserl's Theory of Signs*, trans. David B. Allison (Evanston: Northwestern University Press, 1973).

_____, *Spurs*, trans. Barbara Harlow (Chicago and London: University of Chicago Press, 1979).

_____, *Writing and Difference*, trans. Alan Bass (Chicago: University of Chicago Press, 1978).

Dhavamony, Mariasusai, *Phenomenology of Religion*, Documenta Missionalia 7 (Rome: Gregorian University Press, 1973).

Doty, William G., *Mythography: The Study of Myths and Rituals* (Alabama: University of Alabama Press, 1986).

Dreyfus, Hubert L. and Rabinow, Paul, *Michel Foucault: Beyond Structuralism and Hermeneutics*, 2nd edn (Chicago: University of Chicago Press, 1983).

Dudley III, Guilford, 'Mircea Eliade as the "Anti-Historian" of Religions,' *Journal of the American Academy of Religion*, Vol. XLIX, no. 2 (June 1976): 345–59.

_____, *Religion on Trial: Mircea Eliade and His Critics* (Philadelphia: Temple University Press, 1977).

Dunne, John S., *The Way of All the Earth: Experiments in Truth and Religion* (Notre Dame: University of Notre Dame Press, 1978).

Eilberg-Schwartz, Howard, 'Creation and Classification in Judaism: From Priestly to Rabbinic Conceptions', *History of Religions*, Vol. 26, no. 4 (May 1987): 357–81.

Eliade, Mircea, *Australian Religions: An Introduction* (Ithaca and London: Cornell University Press, 1973).

_____, 'Autobiographical Fragment', in *Imagination and Meaning: The Scholarly and Literary Worlds of Mircea Eliade*, eds Norman J. Girardot and Mac Linscott Ricketts (New York: Seabury Press, 1982), pp. 113–27.

_____, *Autobiography, Volume I: 1907–1937, Journey East, Journey West*, trans. Mac Linscott Ricketts (San Francisco: Harper & Row, 1981).

_____, *Autobiography, Volume II: 1937–1960, Exile's Odyssey*, trans. Mac Linscott Ricketts (Chicago and London: University of Chicago Press, 1988).

_____, 'Cosmical Homology and Yoga', *Journal of the Indian Society of Oriental Arts*, Vol. 5 (1937): 188–203.

_____, 'A Detail from Parsifal (from *Insula lui Euthanasius*)', in *Imagination and Meaning: The Scholarly and Literary Worlds of Mircea Eliade*, eds Norman J. Girardot and Mac Linscott Ricketts (New York: Seabury Press, 1982), pp. 191–5.

_____, *The Forbidden Forest*, trans. Mac Linscott Ricketts and Mary Park Stevenson (Notre Dame and London: University of Notre Dame Press, 1978).

_____, *The Forge and the Crucible*, trans. Stephen Corrin (New York: Harper & Row, 1971).

_____, *A History of Religious Ideas, Vol. I: From the Stone Age to the Eleusinian Mysteries*, trans. Willard R. Trask (Chicago: University of Chicago Press, 1978).

_____, *A History of Religious Ideas, Vol. 2: From Gautama Buddha to the Triumph of Christianity*, trans. Willard R. Trask (Chicago and London: University of Chicago Press, 1982).

_____, *A History of Religious Ideas, Vol. 3: From Muhammad to the Age of Reforms*, trans. Alf Hiltebeitel and Diane Apostolos-Cappadona (Chicago and London: University of Chicago Press, 1985).

_____, *Image and Symbols: Studies in Religious Symbolism*, trans. Philip Mairet (New York: Sheed & Ward, 1961).

_____, *Journal III: 1970–1978*, trans. Teresa Lavender Fagan (Chicago and London: University of Chicago Press, 1989).

_____, *Journal IV: 1979–1985*, trans. Mac Linscott Ricketts (Chicago and London: University of Chicago Press, 1990).

_____, *Mephistopheles and the Androgyne: Studies in Religious Myth and Symbol*, trans. J. M. Cohen (New York: Sheed and Ward, 1965).

_____, 'Methodological Remarks on the Study of Religious Symbolism', in *The History of Religions: Essays in Methodology*, eds Mircea Eliade and Joseph M. Kitagawa (Chicago and London: University of Chicago Press, 1959), pp. 86–107.

_____, *Myth and Reality*, trans. Willard R. Trask (New York: Harper & Row, 1963).

_____, *The Myth of the Eternal Return*, trans. Willard R. Trask (New York: Pantheon Books, 1954).

_____, *Myths, Dreams and Mysteries: The Encounter between Contemporary Faiths and Archaic Realities*, trans. Philip Mairet (New York: Harper & Row, 1967).

_____, *No Souvenirs, Journal: 1957–1969*, trans. Fred H. Johnson, Jr (New York: Harper & Row, 1977).

_____, 'Notes for a Dialogue', in *The Theology of Altizer: Critique and Response*, ed. John B. Cobb, Jr (Philadelphia: Westminster Press, 1970), pp. 234–41.

_____, *The Old Man and the Bureaucrats*, trans. Mary Park Stevenson (Notre Dame and London: University of Notre Dame Press, 1979).

_____, *Ordeal by Labyrinth: Conversations with Claude-Henri Rocquet*, trans. Derek Coltman (Chicago and London: University of Chicago Press, 1982).

_____, *Patterns in Comparative Religion*, trans. Rosemary Sheed (Cleveland: The World Publishing Company, 1968).

_____, 'The Prestige of the Cosmogonic Myth', *The Divinity School News*, Vol. XXVI, no. 1 (February 1959): 1–12.

_____, *The Quest: History and Meaning in Religion* (Chicago and London: University of Chicago Press, 1969).

_____, *Rites and Symbols of Initiation: The Mysteries of Birth and Rebirth*, trans. Willard R. Trask (New York: Harper & Row, 1958).

_____, *The Sacred and the Profane*, trans. Willard R. Trask (New York: Harcourt, Brace & Company, 1959).

_____, *Shamanism: Archaic Techniques of Ecstasy*, trans. Willard R. Trask, Bollingen Series LXXVI (New York: Pantheon Books, 1964).

_____, *Symbolism, the Sacred and the Arts*, ed. Diane Apostolos-Cappadona (New York: Crossroad Publishing Company, 1986).

_____, *Two Tales of the Occult*, trans. William Ames Coates (New York: Herder and Herder, 1970).

_____, *Tales of the Sacred and the Supernatural* (Philadelphia: Westminster Press, 1981).

_____, *Yoga: Immortality and Freedom*, 2nd edn, trans. Willard R. Trask, Bollingen Series LVI (Princeton: Princeton University Press, 1969).

_____, *Youth Without Youth and Other Novellas*, ed. Matei Calinescu and trans. Mac Linscott Ricketts (Columbus: Ohio State University Press, 1988).

_____, *Zalmoxis the Vanishing God: Comparative Studies in the Religions and Folklore of Dacia and Eastern Europe*, trans. Willard R. Trask (Chicago: University of Chicago Press, 1972).

Evans-Pritchard, E. E., *Nuer Religion* (Oxford: Oxford University Press, 1956).

_____, *Theories of Primitive Religion* (Oxford: Oxford University Press, 1965).

Fenton, John Y., 'Reductionism in the Study of Religions', *Soundings*, Vol. LIII, no. 1 (Spring 1970): 61–76.

Foucault, Michel, *The Archaeology of Knowledge and The Discourse on Language*, trans. A. M. Sheridan Smith (New York: Pantheon Books, 1972).

_____, *The Birth of the Clinic: An Archaeology of Medical Perception*, trans. A. M. Sheridan Smith (New York: Vintage/Random House, 1975).

_____, *Discipline and Punishment: The Birth of the Prison*, trans. Alan Sheridan (New York: Pantheon Books, 1977).

_____, *The History of Sexuality, Volume I: An Introduction*, trans. Robert Hurley (New York: Vintage/Random House, 1980).

_____, *Madness and Civilization: A History of Insanity in the Age of Reason*, trans. Richard Howard (New York: Random House, 1973).

_____, 'Nietzsche, Freud, Marx', in *Nietzsche*, Proceedings of the Seventh International Philosophical Colloquium of the Cahiers de Royaumont, 4–8 July 1964 (Paris: Editions de Minuit, 1967), pp. 183–200.

_____, 'Nietzsche, Genealogy, History', in *Language, Counter-Memory, Practice: Selected Essays and Interviews*, ed. Donald F. Bouchard and trans. Donald F. Bouchard and Sherry Simon (Ithaca, New York: Cornell University Press, 1977), pp. 137–164.

_____, *The Order of Things: An Archaeology of the Human Sciences*, trans. Alan Sheridan Smith (New York: Random House, 1973).

_____, *Power/Knowledge: Selected Interviews and Other Writings 1972–1977*, ed. Colin Gordon and trans. Colin Gordon, Leo Marshall, John Mepham, Kate Soper (New York: Pantheon Books, 1980).

_____, 'The Subject and Power', in *Michel Foucault: Beyond Structuralism and Hermeneutics*, ed. Hubert L. Dreyfus and Paul Rabinow, 2nd edn (Chicago: University of Chicago Press, 1983).

_____, *The History of Sexuality*, Vol. 2: *The Use of Pleasure*, trans. Robert Hurley (New York: Vintage Books, 1986).

Freud, Sigmund, *The Future of an Illusion*, trans. James Strachey (New York: W. W. Norton & Company, 1961).

Friedman, Maurice, 'The Human Way: A Dialogical Approach to Religion and Human Experience', *Journal of the American Academy of Religion*, Vol. LI, no. 1 (March 1983): 67–77.

Frye, Northrop, 'World Enough Without Time', *Hudson Review*, Vol. 12 (1959): 423–31.

Gadamer, Hans-Georg, *Philosophical Hermeneutics*, trans. and ed. David E. Linge (Berkeley: University of California Press, 1977).

_____, *Truth and Method*, trans. Garrett Barden and John Cumming (New York: Crossroad Publishing Company, 1982).

Gennap, Arnold van, *The Rites of Passage*, trans. Monika B. Vizedom and Gabrielle C. Caffee (Chicago: University of Chicago Press, 1969).

Gill, Sam D., *Native American Religions: An Introduction* (Belmont, California: Wadsworth Publishing Company, 1982).

Girardot, Norman J., 'Imagining Eliade: A Fondness for Squirrels', in *Imagination and Meaning: The Scholarly and Literary Worlds of Mircea Eliade*, eds Norman J. Girardot and Mac Linscott Ricketts (New York: Seabury Press, 1982), pp. 1–16.

Gombrich, Richard, 'Eliade on Buddhism', *Religious Studies* 10 (1974): 225–31.

Gonda, J., *Die Religionen Indiens I: Veda und älterer Hinduismus* (Stuttgart: W. Kohlhammer, 1960).

Gould, Eric, *Mythical Intentions in Modern Literature* (Princeton: Princeton University Press, 1981).

Habermas, Jürgen, *Der philosophische Diskurs der Moderne, Zwölf Vorlesungen* (Frankfurt am Main: Suhrkamp Verlag, 1985).

_____, *The Theory of Communicative Action, Volume 1: Reason and the Rationalization of Society*, trans. Thomas McCarthy (Boston: Beacon Press, 1984).

_____, *The Theory of Communicative Action, Volume 2: Lifeworld and System: A Critique of Functionalist Reason*, trans. Thomas McCarthy (Boston: Beacon Press, 1987).

Hallowell, A. Irving, 'Ojibwa Ontology, Behavior, and World View', in *Teachings from the American Earth: Indian Religion and Philosophy*, eds Dennis Tedlock and Barbara Tedlock (New York: Liveright, 1975).

Hamilton, Kenneth, '*Homo Religiosus* and Historical Faith', *The Journal of Bible and Religion* 33 (1965): 213–22.

Harpham, Geoffrey Galt, *The Ascetic Imperative in Culture and Criticism* (Chicago and London: University of Chicago Press, 1987).

Hegel, G. W. F., *The Philosophy of History*, trans. J. Sibree (New York: Dover Publications, 1956).

Heidegger, Martin, *An Introduction to Metaphysics*, trans. Ralph Mannheim (New Haven and London: Yale University Press, 1959).

_____, *Being and Time*, trans. John Robinson and John Macquarrie (New York: Harper & Row, 1962).

_____, *Holzwege* (Frankfurt: Vittorio Klostermann, 1963).

_____, *Sein und Zeit* (Tübingen: Max Niemeyer Verlag, 1972).

Heiler, Friedrich, *Erscheinungsformen und Wesen der Religion* (Stuttgart: W. Kohlhammer Verlag, 1961).

Hick, John, *God Has Many Names* (Philadelphia: Westminster Press, 1980).

Horton, Robin, 'The Kalabari World-view: An Outline and Interpretation', *Africa* 32 (1962): 197–219.

Hultkrantz, Ake, 'An Ideological Dichotomy: Myths and Folk Beliefs Among the Shoshoni Indians of Wyoming', *History of Religions*, Vol. 11, no. 4 (May 1972): 339–53.

_____, *Belief and Worship in Native North America*, ed. Christopher Vecsey (Syracuse: Syracuse University Press, 1981).

_____, *Native Religions of North America* (San Francisco: Harper & Row, 1987).

_____, *The Religions of the American Indians*, trans. Monica Setterwall (Berkeley: University of California Press, 1980).

Hume, David, *The Natural History of Religion*, in *The Philosophical Works* Vol. IV (Boston: Little, Brown and Company, 1854).

Ierunca, Virgil, 'The Literary Work of Mircea Eliade', in *Myths and Symbols: Studies in Honor of Mircea Eliade*, eds Joseph M. Kitagawa and Charles H. Long (Chicago and London: University of Chicago Press, 1969), pp. 343–63.

Jaspers, Karl, *Philosophical Faith and Revelation*, trans. E. B. Ashton (New York: Harper & Row, 1962).

_____, *Philosophy*, Vol. 3, trans. E. B. Ashton (Chicago and London: University of Chicago Press, 1971).

_____, *Truth and Symbol* (from *Von der Wahrheit*), trans. Jean T. Wilde, William Kluback and William Kimmel (New York: Twayne Publishers, 1959).

Jung, C. G. and Kerényi, C., *Essays on a Science of Mythology*, trans. R. F. C. Hull, Bollingen Series XXII (Princeton: Princeton University Press, 1973).

Kaelber, Walter O., 'Tapas, Birth, and Spiritual Rebirth in the Veda', *History of Religions*, Vol. 15, no. 4 (May 1976): 343–86.

Kaufman, Gordon D., 'The Historicity of Religions and the Importance of Religious Dialogue', *Buddhist–Christian Studies*, Vol. 4 (1984): 5–15.

Keyes, G. L., *Christian Faith and the Interpretation of History* (Lincoln: University of Nebraska Press, 1966).

King, Ursula, 'Historical and Phenomenological Approaches to the Study of Religion', in *Contemporary Approaches to the Study of Religion, Volume I: The Humanities*, ed. Frank Whaling, Religion and Reason 27 (Berlin, New York, Amsterdam: Mouton, 1984), pp. 29–163.

King, Winston L., 'Buddhist–Christian Dialogue Reconsidered', *Buddhist–Christian Studies*, Vol. 2 (1982): 5–11.

Kirk, Geoffrey, *Myth: Its Meaning and Its Function* (Berkeley: University of California Press, 1970).

Kitagawa, Joseph M., 'The History of Religions (*Religionswissenschaft*) Then and Now', in *The History of Religions: Retrospect and Prospect*, ed. Joseph M. Kitagawa (New York: Macmillan, 1985).

Kluckhohn, Clyde, 'Myths and Rituals: A General Theory', in *Reader in Comparative Religion: An Anthropological Approach*, eds William A. Lessa and Evon Z. Vogt (New York: Harper & Row, 1972), pp. 93–105.

Kolakowski, Leszek, *The Presence of Myth*, trans. Adam Czerniawski (Chicago and London: University of Chicago Press, 1989).

Kristeva, Julia, *Desire in Language: A Semiotic Approach to Literature and Art*, trans. Thomas Gora, Alice Jardine, and Leon S. Roudiez (New York: Columbia University Press, 1980).

———, 'From Symbol to Sign', trans. Seán Hand, in *The Kristeva Reader*, ed. Toril Moi (New York: Columbia University Press, 1986), pp. 62–73.

———, *Language – The Unknown: An Initiation into Linguistics*, trans. Anne M. Menke (New York: Columbia University Press, 1989).

———, *Polylogue* (Paris: Éditions du Seuil, 1977).

———, *Powers of Horror: An Essay on Abjection*, trans. Leon S. Roudiez (New York: Columbia University Press, 1982).

———, *Revolution in Poetic Language*, trans. Margaret Waller (New York: Columbia University Press, 1984).

Kuhn, Thomas S., *The Structure of Scientific Revolutions*, 2nd edn, *International Encyclopedia of Unified Science Vol. II*, No. 2 (Chicago: University of Chicago Press, 1970).

Küng, Hans; van Ess, Josef; von Stietencron, Heinrich; and Bechert, Heinz, *Christianity and the World Religions: Paths of Dialogue with Islam, Hinduism and Buddhism*, trans. Peter Heinegg (Garden City, NY: Doubleday, 1986).

Leach, Edmund, 'Sermons by a Man on a Ladder', *New York Review of Books* (20 October 1966): 28–31.

van der Leeuw, Gerardus, *Der Mensch und die Religion* (Basel: Verlag Haus zum Falken, 1941).

———, *Religion in Essence and Manifestation* 2 vols (New York: Harper & Row, 1963; reprint, Gloucester, Massachusetts: Peter Smith, 1967).

Lévi-Strauss, Claude, *The Naked Man: Introduction to a Science of Mythology* 4, trans. John and Doreen Weightman (New York: Harper & Row, 1981).

———, *Structural Anthropology*, trans. Claire Jacobson and Brooke Grundfest Schoepf (New York: Basic Books, 1963).

Lienhardt, Godfrey, *Divinity and Experience: The Religion of the Dinka* (Oxford: Oxford University Press, 1961).

Lindbeck, George A., *The Nature of Doctrine: Religion and Theology in a Postliberal Age* (Philadelphia: Westminster Press, 1984).

Long, Charles H., 'Human Centers: An Essay on Method in the History of Religions', *Soundings* 61 (Fall 1978): 400–14.

Löwith, Karl, *Meaning in History* (Chicago: University of Chicago Press, 1964).

Luyster, Robert, 'The Study of Myth: Two Approaches', *The Journal of Bible & Religion* 34 (1966): 235–43.

———, 'Mircea Eliade's Hermeneutics', in *Imagination and Meaning: The Scholarly and Literary Worlds of Mircea Eliade*, eds Norman J. Girardot and Mac Linscott Ricketts (New York: Seabury Press, 1982), pp. 19–69.

Malefijt, Annemarie de Waal, *Religion and Culture: An Introduction to Anthropology of Religion* (New York: Macmillan, 1968).

Malinowski, Bronislaw, *Magic, Science and Religion and Other Essays* (Garden City, NY: Doubleday, Anchor, 1954).

Marino, Adrian, *L'herméneutique de Mircea Eliade*, traduit Jean Gouillard (Paris: Gallimard, 1981).

Mbiti, John S., *African Religions and Philosophy* (Garden City, NY: Doubleday, 1970).

Megill, Allan, *Prophets of Extremity: Nietzsche, Heidegger, Foucault, Derrida* (Berkeley: University of California Press, 1985).

Moltmann, Jürgen, *The Church in the Power of the Spirit*, trans. Margaret Kohl (New York: Harper & Row, 1977).

Müller, Max, *Comparative Mythology* (London: G. Routledge, 1909; reprint New York: Arno Press, 1977).

_____, *Introduction to the Science of Religion* (London: Longmans, Green & Company, 1873).

Niebuhr, Reinhold, *Faith and History* (New York: Charles Scribner's Sons, 1949).

Nietzsche, Friedrich, *The Birth of Tragedy*, trans. Wm A. Haussmann, in *The Complete Works of Friedrich Nietzsche*, 18 vols, ed. Oscar Levy, Vol. 1 (New York: Russell & Russell, 1964).

_____, *The Portable Nietzsche*, trans. Walter Kaufmann (Baltimore: Penguin Books, 1959).

Olson, Carl, 'Tillich's Dialogue with Buddhism', *Buddhist–Christian Studies*, Vol. 7 (1987): 183–95.

Ortiz, Alfonso, *The Tewa World: Space, Time, Being and Becoming in a Pueblo Society* (Chicago and London: University of Chicago Press, 1969).

Panikkar, Raimundo, *The Intrareligious Dialogue* (New York: Paulist Press, 1978).

_____, *Myth, Faith and Hermeneutics: Cross-Cultural Studies* (New York: Paulist Press, 1979).

_____, *The Unknown Christ of Hinduism* (London: Darton, Longman & Todd, 1964).

Pannenberg, Wolfhart, 'Toward a Theology of the History of Religions', trans. George H. Kehm, in *Basic Questions in Theology*, Vol. II (Philadelphia: Fortress Press, 1971), pp. 65–118.

Penner, Hans H. and Yonan, Edward A., 'Is a Science of Religion Possible?', *Journal of Religion* 52, 2 (1972): 107–33.

Pettazzoni, Raffaele, *Essays on the History of Religions*, trans. H. J. Rose (Leiden: E. J. Brill, 1954).

Polanyi, Michael, *Personal Knowledge: Towards a Post-Critical Philosophy* (London: Routledge & Kegan Paul, 1958; reprint 1983).

Popper, Karl R., *Conjectures and Refutations: The Growth of Scientific Knowledge* (London: Routledge & Kegan Paul, 1963; reprint 4th edn, 1985).

_____, *The Logic of Scientific Discovery* (London: Hutchinson, 1959; reprint 1986).

_____, *Objective Knowledge: An Evolutionary Approach* (Oxford: Clarendon Press, 1972; reprint 1986).

Poster, Mark, 'Foucault and History', *Social Research* 49 (1982): 116–42.

Pummer, Reinhard, 'Recent Publications on the Methodology of the Science of Religion', *Numen*, Vol. XXII, Fasc. 3 (December 1975): 161–82.

_____, 'Religionswissenschaft or Religiology?', *Numen*, Vol. XIX, Fasc. 2–3 (August and December 1972): 91–127.

Rahner, Karl, *Theological Investigations*, Vol. V, trans. Karl H. Kruger (London: Darton, Longman & Todd, 1966).

Raschke, Carl A., 'Religious Pluralism and Truth: From Theology to a Hermeneutical Dialogy', *Journal of the American Academy of Religion*, Vol. L, no. 1 (March 1982): 35–48.

Rasmussen, David, 'Mircea Eliade: Structural Hermeneutics and Philosophy', *Philosophy Today*, Vol. 12 (1968): 138–46.

Ray, Benjamin C., *African Religions: Symbol, Ritual, Community* (Englewood Cliffs, NJ: Prentice-Hall, 1976).

Ray, Richard A., 'Is Eliade's Metapsychoanalysis an End Run Around Bultman's Demythologization?', in *Myth and the Crisis of Historical Consciousness*, eds Lew W. Gibbs and W. Taylor Stevenson (Missoula, Montana: Scholars Press, 1975), pp. 57–74.

Reno, Stephen J., 'Eliade's Progressional View of Hierophanies', *Religious Studies* 8 (1972): 153–60.

Richardson, Alan, *History Sacred and Profane* (Philadelphia: Westminster Press, 1964).

Ricketts, Mac Linscott, 'In Defense of Eliade', *Journal of Religion* 53 (1973): 13–34.

_____, *Mircea Eliade: The Romanian Roots, 1907–1945* (Boulder: East European Monographs; and New York: distributed by Columbia University Press, 1988).

_____, 'Mircea Eliade and the Death of God', *Religion in Life* Vol. 36, Spring 1967: 40–52.

_____, 'The Nature and Extent of Eliade's "Jungianism"', *Union Seminary Quarterly Review*, Vol. XXV, no. 2 (Winter 1970): 211–34.

Ricoeur, Paul, *Interpretation Theory: Discourse and the Surplus of Meaning* (Fort Worth, Texas: Texas Christian University Press, 1976).

_____, *The Symbolism of Evil*, trans. Emerson Buchanan (New York: Harper & Row, 1967).

Rorty, Richard, 'Method, Social Science, and Social Hope', *Canadian Journal of Philosophy*, Vol. XI, no. 4 (December 1981): 569–88.

_____, *Philosophy and the Mirror of Nature* (Princeton: Princeton University Press, 1979).

Rosen, Stanley, *Hermeneutics as Politics* (New York and Oxford: Oxford University Press, 1987).

Rudolph, Kurt, *Historical Fundamentals and the Study of Religions* (New York and London: Macmillan, 1985).

Rust, E. C., *The Christian Understanding of History* (London: Lutterworth Press, 1947).

Saiving, Valerie, 'Androcentrism in Religious Studies', *Journal of Religion*, Vol. 56 (April 1976): 177–97.

Saliba, John A., *'Homo Religiosus' in Mircea Eliade: An Anthropological Evaluation* (Leiden: E. J. Brill, 1976).

Schlegel, Friedrich, *Dialogue on Poetry and Literary Aphorisms*, trans. Ernst Behler and Roman Struc (University Park and London: Pennsylvania State University Press, 1968).

von Schelling, Friedrich W. J., *Einleitung Philosophie der Mythologie*, Vol. 6, in *Werke*, ed. Manfred Schröten, 6 vols (Müchen: E. H. Beck Berlagsbuchhandlung 1943–1956).

Shiner, Larry, 'Reading Foucault: Anti-Method and the Genealogy of Power–Knowledge', *History and Theory* 21 (1982): 382–98.

_____, 'Sacred Space, Profane Space, Human Space', *Journal of the American Academy of Religion*, Vol. XL (1972): 425–36.

Silva, Antonio Barbosa da, *The Phenomenology of Religion as a Philosophical Problem: An Analysis of the Theoretical Background of the Phenomenology of Religion, in General, and of M. Eliade's Phenomenological Approach, in Particular* (Uppsala: C. W. K. Gleerup, 1982).

Smart, Ninian, 'Beyond Eliade: The Future of Theory in Religion', *Numen*, Vol. XXV, Fasc. 2 (August 1978): 171–83.

_____, *The Science of Religion and the Sociology of Knowledge* (Princeton: Princeton University Press, 1973).

Smith, Jonathan Z., *Imagining Religion from Babylon to Jonestown* (Chicago and London: University of Chicago Press, 1982).

_____, *Map Is Not Territory: Studies in the History of Religions* (Leiden: E. J. Brill, 1978).

_____, *To Take Place: Toward Theory in Ritual* (Chicago and London: University of Chicago Press, 1987).

Smith, Wilfred Cantwell, *Towards a World Theology: Faith and the Comparative History of Religion* (Philadelphia: Westminster Press, 1981).

Strauss, David Friedrich, *A New Life of Jesus*, trans. Marian Evans (London: Williams & Norgate, 1865).

Strenski, Ivan, *Four Theories of Myth in Twentieth-Century History: Cassirer, Eliade, Lévi-Strauss and Malinowski* (London: Macmillan; Iowa City: University of Iowa Press, 1987).

Sullivan, Lawrence E., Review of *A History of Religious Ideas*, Vol. 2 by Mircea Eliade, in *Religious Studies Review* 9 (January 1983): 13–22.

Swearer, Donald K., *Dialogue: The Key to Understanding Other Religions* (Philadelphia: Westminster Press, 1977).

Taylor, Charles, 'Interpretation and the Sciences of Man', *Review of Metaphysics*, Vol. XXV, no. 1 (September 1971): 3–51.

_____, 'Understanding in Human Science', *Review of Metaphysics*, Vol. 34, no. 1 (September 1980): 25–38.

Taylor, Mark C., *Deconstructing Theology*, American Academy of Religion Studies in Religion 28 (New York: Crossroad Publishing Company & Scholars Press, 1982).

_____, *Erring: A Postmodern A/theology* (Chicago and London: University of Chicago Press, 1984).

_____, *Tears* (Albany: State University of New York Press, 1990).

Teilhard de Chardin, Pierre, *The Divine Milieu* (New York, Evanston and London: Harper & Row, 1960).

_____, *The Phenomenon of Man* (New York and Evanston: Harper & Row, 1965).

Tiele, Cornelis P., *Elements of the Science of Religion*, 2 vols (London: William Blackwood & Sons, 1897, 1899).

Tillich, Paul, *Christianity and the Encounter of the World Religions* (New York and London: Columbia University Press, 1963).

Tilly, Charles, *Big Structures, Large Processes, Huge Comparisons* (New York: Russell Sage Foundation, 1984).

Tracy, David, *The Analogical Imagination: Christian Theology and the Culture of Pluralism* (New York: Crossroad Publishing Company, 1986).

Turner, Victor, *The Forest of Symbols: Aspects of Ndembu Ritual* (Ithaca, New York: Cornell University Press, 1967).

Uscatescu, George, 'Time and Destiny in the Novels of Mircea Eliade', in *Myths and Symbols: Studies in Honor of Mircea Eliade*, eds Joseph M. Kitagawa and Charles H. Long (Chicago and London: University of Chicago Press, 1969), pp. 397–406.

Vecsey, Christopher, 'American Indian Environmental Religions', in *American Indian Environments: Ecological Issues in Native American History*, eds

Christopher Vecsey and Robert W. Venables (Syracuse, New York: Syracuse University Press, pp. 1–37).

_____, *Imagine Ourselves Richly: Mythic Narratives of North American Indians* (New York: Crossroad Publishing Company, 1988).

Vico, Giambattista, *The New Science of Giambattista Vico*, 3rd edn, trans. Thomas Goddard Bergin and Max Harold Fisch (New York: Cornell University Press, 1968).

Voltaire, *The Complete Works of Voltaire*, 59, 2nd edn, ed. J. H. Brumfitt (Toronto: University of Toronto Press, 1969).

Waardenburg, Jacques, 'Religion between Reality and Idea', *Numen*, Vol. XIX, Fasc. 2–3 (August and December 1972): 128–203.

Wach, Joachim, *Sociology of Religion* (Chicago and London: University of Chicago Press, 1971).

Waldenfels, Hans, *Absolute Nothingness: Foundations for a Buddhist–Christian Dialogue*, trans. J. W. Heisig (New York: Paulist Press, 1980).

Walker, James R., *Lakota Belief and Ritual*, eds Rayond J. de Maillie and Elaine A. Jahner (Lincoln and London: University of Nebraska Press, 1980).

Wallace, Anthony F. C., *Religion: An Anthropological View* (New York: Random House, 1966).

Welbon, G. Richard, 'Some Remarks on the Work of Mircea Eliade', *Acta Philosophica* 30 (1964): 465–92.

Whaling, Frank, 'Comparative Approaches', in *Contemporary Approaches to the Study of Religion, Volume I: The Humanities*, ed. Frank Whaling (Berlin, New York, Amsterdam: Mouton, 1984), pp. 165–295.

Widengren, Geo, 'La Methode Comparative: Entre Philologie et Phénoménologie', *Numen*, Vol. XVIII, Fasc. 3 (December 1971): 161–72.

_____, *Religionsphänomenologie* (Berlin: Walter de Gruyter & Company, 1969).

Wiebe, Don, 'A Positive Episteme for the Study of Religion', *Scottish Journal of Religious Studies*, Vol. 6, no. 2 (Autumn 1985): 78–95.

_____, 'Is a Science of Religion Possible?', *Studies in Religion*, Vol. 7, no. 1 (Winter 1978): 5–17.

Wyschogrod, Edith, *Spirit in Ashes: Hegel, Heidegger and Man-Made Mass Death* (New Haven and London: Yale University Press, 1985).

Zahan, Dominique, *The Religion, Spirituality, and Thought of Traditional Africa* (Chicago and London: University of Chicago Press, 1979).

Index

216

Index